Vad summer

Roy S Bab

THE UNFORGETTABLE SEASON

By the Same Author

George Alfred Lawrence and the Victorian Sensation Novel
Rossetti and the Pre-Raphaelite Brotherhood
That Ne'er Shall Meet Again: Rossetti, Millais, Hunt
The Young Whistler

THE
UNFORGETTABLE
SEASON

G. H. Fleming

Foreword by
Lawrence Ritter

HOLT, RINEHART and WINSTON
New York

Published by Holt, Rinehart and Winston,
383 Madison Avenue, New York, New York 10017.

Published simultaneously in Canada by
Holt, Rinehart and Winston of Canada, Limited.

Library of Congress Cataloging in Publication Data

Fleming, Gordon H 1920–
The unforgettable season.

Includes index.
1. National League of Professional Baseball Clubs—
History—Addresses, essays, lectures. 2. New York
(City). Baseball club (National League, Giants)—
History—Addresses, essays, lectures. I. Title.
GV875.A3F55   796.357′64′0973   80-18299
ISBN 0-03-056221-X

First Edition

Designer: Constance T. Doyle

Printed in the United States of America

10 9 8 7 6 5 4 3 2 1

To Muggsy and Big Six,
To The Iron Man and Turkey Mike,
To The Chief and Laughing Larry,
To Pancho and Pep,
To The Rajah and Irish Emil,
To Highpockets and The Fordham Flash,
To King Carl and Prince Hal,
To Fat Freddy and Master Melvin,
To Frisco Lefty and Memphis Bill,
To Leo the Lip and Eddie the Brat,
To The Barber and The Kid Who Said, "Say Hey!"

and to every other New York Baseball Giant
this book is gratefully dedicated.

Foreword

If the expression "Truth is stranger than fiction" did not originate in 1908, it should have. Because not even the most imaginative of story-tellers could have dreamed up what actually happened that memorable year as the Pittsburgh Pirates, New York Giants, and Chicago Cubs schemed and clawed their way in quest of the elusive National League pennant. More than seven decades have passed since that extraordinary season, but the years quickly melt away as we fall under the spell of G. H. Fleming's masterful reconstruction of one of baseball's most sus-penseful pennant races; and before we realize it, the day-to-day tides of battle become as immediate and dramatic as a late-breaking news flash.

The changing fortunes of war, favoring first one team and then an-other, build up a tension that is compounded even further by a marvelous cast of characters. Baseball in those days, like America at large, had more than its share of idiosyncratic personalities, many of them reflecting the regional and individual differences that still characterized the nation at the turn of the century. Today, ball players are named Willie, Jim, and Tom, just like everyone else. But not then: Dummy Taylor, Iron Man Joe McGinnity, Turkey Mike Donlin, and Three-Finger Brown were *sui generis*. Not to mention McGraw and Matty of the Giants, the great Honus Wagner of the Pirates, and the Cubs' fabled Tinker, Evers, and Chance—names that have become legendary with the passage of time. All of these, and more, come to life once again in the pages that follow.

Luther (Dummy) Taylor, for example, was a deaf mute from Olathe, Kansas, whose pitching skills helped the New York Giants win over 100 games in the early years of the century. Despite his handicap he was an integral member of the team, off the field as well as on, because Manager John McGraw insisted that all the Giants become proficient in the deaf-and-dumb alphabet. McGraw often gave his on-the-field signals that way, spelling out S-T-E-A-L on his fingers so plainly that anyone who knew the system could read his instructions. When Taylor retired from the game, he joined the faculty of a school for the deaf in Kansas.

(Iron Man) Joe McGinnity, another of McGraw's pitchers, came from Rock Island, Illinois. Winner of close to 250 games during his ten-year big-league career—seven times winning at least 20 games and twice more than 30—McGinnity became famous by pitching both halves of doubleheaders, a feat he accomplished on five different occasions in the major leagues. Three times he won both games. The 1908 season was his last in the major leagues, but he continued to pitch for many more years in the minors. In 1925, at the age of 54, he notched 6 wins and 6 losses with Dubuque in the Mississippi Valley League. That year McGinnity, who was also the team's manager and part owner, said: "I have to pitch because it's the best way I know to protect my investment."

Another of McGraw's favorites was Turkey Mike Donlin, one of the hardest hitters and most popular players of his day. He hit .351 in 1903 and .356 in 1905. But Mike's heart was not in baseball. A fine singer and raconteur, the life of the party, Mike was not overly devoted to abstemious habits. He married stage star Mabel Hite in 1906, and thereafter played only one more full season (in 1908, when he hit .334). Increasingly Donlin turned to vaudeville, where he and Mabel were tremendous box-office attractions, and wound up spending most of the rest of his life making movies in Hollywood.

For their part, the Chicago Cubs countered with Mordecai Peter Centennial (Three-Finger) Brown—his parents threw in the extra middle name because he was born in 1876. A farm boy from Indiana, Brown joined the Cubs in 1904 and won 20 or more games every season from 1906 through 1911. As a youngster he had an accident with some farm equipment, which necessitated the amputation of most of the index finger on his right hand (his throwing hand). The same accident also rendered the little finger of that hand useless. Nevertheless, his pitching hardly suffered; indeed, he always claimed the injury gave his sinker ball that extra something no one else could duplicate. In crucial Cubs-Giants games it was invariably Three-Finger Brown vs. Christy Mathewson on the mound—and 13 out of 24 times the decision went to Brown!

Even so, it was generally acknowledged that the greatest pitcher of his generation was Christy Mathewson. To a large extent it was Matty, more than anyone, who changed the public image of baseball and elevated it into the mainstream of American life. Until the turn of the century, professional baseball was looked upon as a rowdy sport, played mainly by roughnecks. Few women attended games, and even many fathers would think twice before taking their sons to a professional game. Matty helped change all that. Handsome, well educated, reserved, he was the very embodiment of the all-American boy, and his entrance into the sport gave it a big push toward respectability and middle-class acceptance. Born in Pennsylvania, the son of well-to-do parents, he played football in addition to baseball at Bucknell—where he also found time to join the glee club and the literary society. Later, he gained fame as checkers champion of half a dozen states. Indeed, his passion for checkers was so great that some suspected it ranked above baseball in his priorities. All of which would have been irrelevant had he not also been the best pitcher of his time, perhaps of all time. In 1903, '04, and '05 he won 30, 33, and 31 games, respectively, and then went on to his most remarkable season, in 1908. It is doubtful if any baseball player has ever been cited so often as a model of deportment to errant offspring by fathers and mothers the length and breadth of the land.

The Cubs also had shortstop Joe Tinker, second baseman Johnny Evers, and manager–first baseman Frank Chance (the Peerless Leader), whom newspaper columnist Franklin P. Adams, a rabid Giant fan, immortalized with his lament over their double-play skills:

> These are the saddest of possible words—
> Tinker to Evers to Chance.
> Trio of Bear Cubs and fleeter than birds—
> Tinker to Evers to Chance.

Frank Chance had become manager of the Chicago Cubs in 1905, when he was but 27 years of age. He had been attending Washington College in California in 1898, planning to become a doctor, when an opportunity arose to try out with the Cubs. He made the club as a second-string catcher—never having played a day in the minors—and became a star when he was shifted to first base several years later. His intelligence and leadership qualities were so obvious that it was no surprise when he was appointed playing manager after having been a regular for only two years.

So far as the population of Pittsburgh was concerned, however, there was only one star in the firmament and his name was Wagner. Close to 6 feet tall, a solid 200 pounds, bowlegged as a pair of parentheses, Honus

Wagner's ability was exceeded only by his modesty. He hit .300 or better for 17 consecutive seasons, led the National League in batting 8 times, and stole over 700 bases during his career. He remains the greatest short-stop who ever lived and possibly the greatest baseball player of all time (rivaled only by Babe Ruth and Ty Cobb).

And last, but far from least: 19-year-old rookie Fred Merkle. Because the Giants' regular first baseman, veteran Fred Tenney, developed a bad back, the inexperienced Merkle replaced him in the starting lineup for a crucial late-season game. As fate would have it, Fred Merkle inadvertently played a larger role in the pennant race—at least in the eyes of the press—than any of the more established stars.

In those days, long before radio and television, the daily press played a distinctive role in disseminating baseball results to an eagerly awaiting public. The day's scores were published, almost inning by inning, in special late afternoon and early evening editions, and a newspaper's reporters became as identified with particular teams as radio and television play-by-play announcers are with teams today. By virtue of their unique status and long tenure, many of the reporters—like some broadcasters today—had no hesitation about expressing their opinions on topics only remotely connected to the game they were supposed to be covering. Indeed, racism and anti-Semitism turn up in the sports pages of the era in ways that would now be considered shocking. It is sobering to realize that prejudice and bigotry were evidently as American as apple pie back in those idyllic "good old days" of yesteryear.

G. H. Fleming's skillful reconstruction of the 1908 season brings that exciting pennant race alive as though it were taking place today. In the process, it also provides a jarring glimpse of an America that was not quite as tranquil and serene as nostalgia would generally have us believe.

—Lawrence Ritter

Acknowledgments

While I worked on this book, numerous people assisted me. I received valuable suggestions and answers to questions from Betty Cook, Stanley Coveleski, Ashbel Green, Carl Hubbell, George (Highpockets) Kelly, the late Richard (Rube) Marquard, Eddie Mulligan, Larry Ritter, Wilfred (Rosy) Ryan, Arthur Schott, and Horace Stoneham. At the National League headquarters, in New York, I was hospitably received by Katy Feeney and her colleagues, who directed me to useful material in the league files. At the Newspaper Division of the New York Public Library I was helped by members of the staff. From the Pittsburgh Baseball Club I was given two excellent glossy photographs of Honus Wagner and Fred Clarke. At my home base of operations, the New Orleans branch of Louisiana State University, I was helped in various ways by Elizabeth Ashin, Jody Blake, Rayza Caballero, Evelyn Chandler, Anna Lloyd, Raeburn Miller, Jean Montero, Gregory Spano, and Nita Walsh. After completing the first draft, which was too long for publication, I was excellently advised by Jeffrey C. Smith on how to reduce it to manageable proportions. To all of these persons I extend thanks.

Preface

On Sunday, November 10, 1907, the sporting section of New York's most widely circulated morning newspaper, the *American*, startled readers with this banner headline: BRESNAHAN TO SUCCEED M'GRAW AS MANAGER OF THE NEW YORK GIANTS. John T. Brush, the Indianapolis textiles tycoon who had owned the Giants since November 11, 1902, was reportedly ready to sack his manager, John J. McGraw, in favor of his catcher, Roger Bresnahan. This was New York's most electrifying baseball news since July 1902, when this same John McGraw, already famous at the age of 29 after a decade with the legendary Baltimore Orioles, became the Giants' manager. Buried in the National League cellar, from which they had not strayed far in seven years, the Giants were a local embarrassment, almost a national joke. McGraw had had scant opportunity to elevate the 1902 team, but in 1903, with 67 victories by the greatest of pitching pairs, Christy Mathewson and (Iron Man) Joe McGinnity, the Giants rose to second place, just 6½ games behind Pittsburgh. And in 1904, finishing 13 games ahead of second-place Chicago, they won the pennant. In two and a half years McGraw had raised his team from the basement to the penthouse. The 1904 season ended, however, on a sour note. Even though the Boston Red Sox had won the initial interleague championship in 1903, John Brush refused to recognize what he regarded as the upstart American League, and so there was no World Series in 1904. But never again would a club owner be able to act thus peremptorily, and after the Giants had repeated as champions in 1905 they defeated Connie Mack's Philadelphia Athletics in the World Series four games to one, with Mathewson pitching his probably never-to-be-equaled three shut-outs.

The Giants now ruled the sporting world, and in 1906 no one doubted that they would win a third straight pennant. No one, that is, but Frank Chance's Chicago Cubs, who finished the season 20 games ahead of New York. In 1907, McGraw's Giants suffered a total collapse, finishing

25½ games behind Chicago and also trailing Pittsburgh and Philadelphia. Fourth place would have been a pleasure palace for the old Giants, but it was intolerable for John T. Brush, especially since his manager often seemed more interested in horse races than ball games. And so, it was rumored, McGraw might soon be left free to follow the horses.

But McGraw was not discharged, and partly because of his continuing control of the Giants no one who took even a remote interest in baseball then would ever forget the National League season of 1908. "The game," McGraw wrote prophetically not long before his death, "will never know another battle like that of 1908."

Viewed from the perspective of McGraw's Giants, that battle, which a later *Spalding's National League Guide* called "unparalleled in baseball's history," is the subject of this book. Hardly anyone alive remembers that distant season, but in the following pages we can vicariously relive those memorable days. The narrative, however, is not mine. The story will be told by those who saw and heard all that happened. I have read every relevant issue of New York's twelve daily newspapers of 1908, as well as the Brooklyn *Eagle*, three daily papers from Philadelphia, two from Boston, two from Pittsburgh, three from Chicago, two from St. Louis, and one from Cincinnati, along with the two baseball weeklies, *The Sporting News* and *Sporting Life*, and I have selected, edited, and reproduced the most vivid, provocative writings on the activities—inside and beyond the field of combat—of players, managers, owners, umpires, spectators, and ordinary citizens. Through the eyes and ears of those who were there, we shall thus restore this vanished culture, and, day by day, in all its significant details, we shall again experience the excitement of that unforgettable season.

Play ball!

—G. H. Fleming

THE PLAYERS

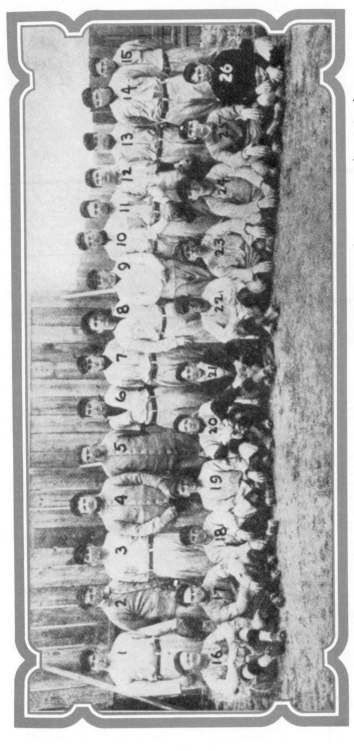

THE 1908 NEW YORK GIANTS: 1, Bresnahan; 2, Tenney; 3, Seymour; 4, Mathewson; 5, Devlin; 6, Snodgrass; 7, Wiltse; 8, Brain; 9, McGraw, Mgr.; 10, Merkle; 11, McGinnity; 12, Needham; 13, McCormick; 14, Crandall; 15, Doyle; 16, Taylor; 17, Donlin; 18, Herzog; 19, Barry; 20, Ames; 21, Bridwell; 22, Marquardt; 23, Wilson; 24, Durham; 25, Beecher; 26, DeVore.

Pictorial News Co. Photo., courtesy New York Public Library.

John J. McGraw, manager of the Giants
(below, coaching at third base). *Photoworld.*

Christy Mathewson, the great "Matty."

Roger Bresnahan. *Culver Pictures, Inc.*

"Iron Man" Joe McGinnity. *Photoworld.*

Mike Donlin and his wife, the actress Mabel Hite. *Library of Congress.*

Fred Merkle. *Culver Pictures.*

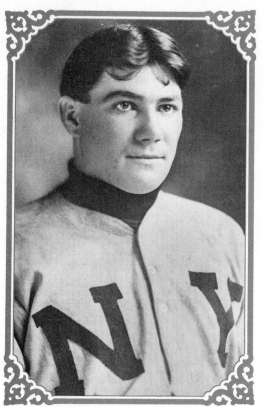

Larry Doyle. *The Bettmann Archive.*

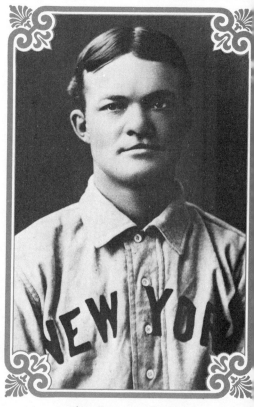

Luther "Dummy" Taylor.
Library of Congress, Baine Collection.

Honus Wagner, "The Flying Dutchman." *The Bettmann Archive.*

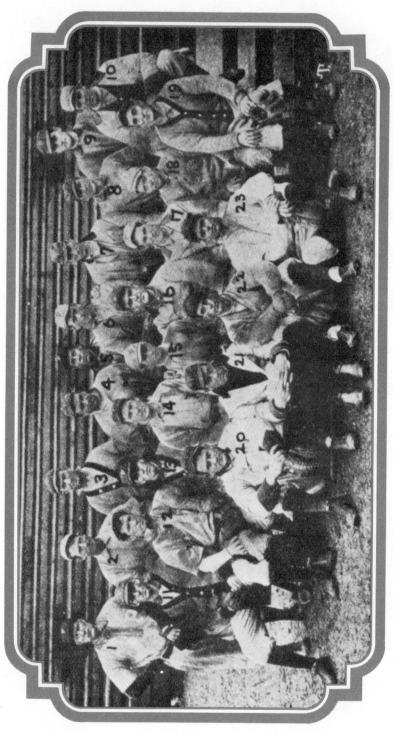

THE 1908 PITTSBURGH PIRATES: 1, Shannon; 2, Clarke, Mgr.; 3, Wilson; 4, Phelps; 5, Brandon; 6, Moeller; 7, Leever; 8, O'Connor; 9, Camnitz; 10, Leifield; 11, Thomas; 12, Kane; 13, Vail; 14, Phillippe; 15, Leach; 16, Abbaticchio; 17, Maddox; 18, Starr; 19, Wagner; 20, Gill; 21, Willis; 22, Storke; 23, Gibson. *Pictorial News Co. Photo., courtesy New York Public Library.*

THE 1908 CHICAGO CUBS: 1, Zimmerman; 2, Reulbach; 3, Fraser; 4, Pfeister; 5, Durbin; 6, Steinfeldt; 7, Lundgren; 8, Campbell; 9, Moran; 10, Overall; 11, Brown; 12, Howard; 13, Kling; 14, Evers; 15, Chance, Capt.; 16, Tinker; 17, Slagle; 18, Sheckard; 19, Schulte; 20, Hofman. *Courtesy New York Public Library.*

The great infield double-play combination of the Chicago Cubs: "Tinker to Evers to Chance." *Culver Pictures.*

"Three-Finger" Mordecai Brown. *Photoworld.*

Frank Chance, the "Peerless Leader"
of the Chicago Cubs. *Culver Pictures.*

THE UNFORGETTABLE SEASON

———◇ SUNDAY, NOVEMBER 10, 1907 ◇———

"Johnny McGraw will not be manager of the Giants next season. He is too fond of the race track, and doesn't seem to want to give it up. He will at best have to make a choice quickly."

A man prominent in baseball circles and personal acquaintance of President {John T.} Brush, of the Giants, made this statement yesterday.

Roger Bresnahan, the Giants' famous catcher, was named as possible successor.

President Brush and Secretary {Fred} Knowles are dissatisfied with McGraw's conduct and the consequent wreck of the Giants, he said, and have decided that a change is necessary.

McGraw's contract has not more than a year to run, so it will be possible to remove him without involving too great a financial sacrifice.

The utter failure of the Giants last season to make anything like a good showing is supposed to have wiped out the last of President Brush's patience. McGraw had a wonderful array of ball players, all the material necessary for a great team {but} the play of the Giants became listless and their teamwork fell away to almost nothing {they finished in fourth place}. There were frequent rumors of internal disturbances and quarrels, and McGraw was often seen at the track during the Summer meetings.

Neither President Brush nor Secretary Knowles could be located last night, but it is probable that no official announcement will come until the change is put into effect.   —New York *American*

———◇ MONDAY, NOVEMBER 11 ◇———

Whenever John J. McGraw has been asked why the Giants made such a poor showing last season, he said that the umpires would not let him get out on the coaching lines and "pump ginger" into his players. This really is a weak excuse, for McGraw could have stayed on the coaching lines as long as he wanted to if he would only restrict himself, but Mac usually got into a row with the umpires and was ordered off the grounds.

—New York *Evening Journal*

◇ WEDNESDAY, NOVEMBER 13 ◇

President John T. Brush has by this time been asked point blank a dozen times whether McGraw is to go, and in no case has he availed himself of the simple denial.

There are just two possible explanations of the attitude that President Brush has taken. The club may be seizing this opportunity to get a little off-season advertising, but this can be thrown out. Undenied statements that a manager as well known as McGraw is to be hurried out of his job so he can have more time to devote to the races is not healthy advertising for any club.

The only other explanation is that McGraw is to be let out, and that the time for the official announcement is not yet. Impartially reviewing McGraw's record as a manager in the last two years, there will not be a great deal of surprise when the announcement comes.

The shopworn references to the glory of the world's champions and the injustice of fans who want pennants all the time have lost their punch. Fans don't want pennants all the time, but they want good, sincere baseball and a team that is "up there." Finishing fourth in a league as poorly balanced as the National cost the ex-world's champions many a friend.   —New York *American*

◇ THURSDAY, NOVEMBER 14 ◇

John McGraw of the Giants has quit the race track.

The leader of the local National League team has not been seen at the Aqueduct course since the announcement that his devotion to horse racing had put his job in jeopardy.

McGraw also failed to turn up at his usual haunts on Broadway yesterday, and as the men at the head of the club maintained silence on the subject, the McGraw mystery is as deep as ever.

—George Sands, New York *American*

After all the recent hysterics about John J. McGraw being released as manager of the Giants, the fact that he is still the manager and will continue to be so as long as he wants the job should go a great way toward calming the hysterical ones.

McGraw will be manager of the Giants next year and {New York catcher} Roger Bresnahan will not.

Roger possibly has managerial aspirations, but he is altogether too hotheaded to be given full authority to dictate to a team of players who know as much if not more about baseball than he does.

McGraw is a born leader of ball players, and there is not a Giant or any other player who has ever played under him who did not appreciate the value of his leadership and the results he obtained by his thorough knowledge of the game.

—Sam Crane, New York *Evening Journal*

——◇ **TUESDAY, NOVEMBER 19** ◇——

Big, awkward, conscientious, good-natured {Pirate shortstop} Hans Wagner, steady and strong in his years of baseball lore, this year established a new record for long batting success on the diamond, this being the fifth year that he has held the National League title. He won the batting championship with a mark of .350 and the base-running honors with 61 stolen bases.

No one ever saw anything graceful or picturesque about Wagner on the diamond. His movements have been likened to the gambols of a caracoling elephant. He is ungainly and so bowlegged that when he runs his limbs seem to be moving in a circle after the fashion of a propeller. But he can run like the wind. When he starts after a grounder every outlying portion of his anatomy apparently has ideas of its own about the proper line of direction to be taken. His position at the bat is less awkward and the muscular swing of his great arms and shoulders is strong enough to drive the ball farther than most batters who hit from their toe spikes up.

There is no question that Wagner is the greatest all-round ball player of this or probably any other season. —New York *American*

———◇ **SATURDAY, NOVEMBER 20** ◇———

Mike Donlin will be the field captain of the New York Giants, Secretary Fred Knowles informed the baseball public yesterday. Knowles and McGraw decided to give Mike a little responsibility, for it would be, in their opinion, a good thing for him to have to maintain the dignity necessary to the character of field captain.

Mike will have to watch everything carefully that takes place during a contest, as it will be up to him to do the official talking. Knowles and McGraw feel that the honor of the position will cause Mike to quit his kidding ways and make him an example to the rest of the team in deportment. —New York *American*

Nobody knows what Frank Chance draws as manager of the Cubs, but President {C. Webb} Murphy has stated for publication that he gets more money than any other player ever did. His salary as a player is large, for he is one of the stars of the game. Added to that is his salary as manager of the club, and besides this are the dividends he receives for the 100 shares of stock he holds in the club, presented to him by Charles P. Taft when the club was originally purchased from James A. Hart.

—*Sporting Life*

———◇ **TUESDAY, NOVEMBER 26** ◇———

CHICAGO, Nov. 26—Mike Donlin is again a Giant.

Last night the great outfielder and batsman, who was formerly the star player of the New York National club, signed a contract for another season with the Giants. Secretary Fred Knowles, who has been here for several days, concluded arrangements with Donlin, who has promised to be good and redeem himself in the eyes of the New York fans.

Secretary Knowles has been in communication with the swell hitter

{ 5 }

for some time. Knowles came out here ostensibly to see the Carlisle-Chicago football game last Saturday, but in reality he was after Donlin. Donlin wanted a wartime salary and he finally got it on condition that he keep in trim throughout the season of 1908, refrain from all intoxicants and make the Spring training trip to Texas with the team. {The term *wartime* refers to conditions that had prevailed a few years earlier when the National League would not recognize the status of the newly formed American League, and the two leagues competed with each other for the services of players.}   —New York *Evening Journal*

——◇ **MONDAY, DECEMBER 9** ◇——

Beginning tomorrow and for nearly the balance of the week magnates of the National League will be in session at the Waldorf-Astoria, where they will do some baseball legislating, but possibly more posing around the round tables in the big cafe.

It was President Harry Pulliam's pet idea for the magnates to break away from Broadway and hold forth at the more exclusive Fifth Avenue hostelry. {Opened in 1893, the Waldorf-Astoria was then located on Fifth Avenue between 33rd and 34th streets. Earlier meetings of the National League had been held at a comparatively modest hotel on Broadway.}

There does not appear to be any desire on the part of the magnates to change the present playing rules. The general feeling is that it is better to leave well enough alone. The past season was one of the most successful financially in the history of the organization, and every club made money.

Possibly that is why the Waldorf-Astoria was selected as the place of meeting.   —Sam Crane, New York *Evening Journal*

——◇ **TUESDAY, DECEMBER 10** ◇——

PITTSBURGH, Dec. 9—Hans Wagner, the Pirates' veteran shortstop, will not be in the game next year if he takes his doctor's advice.

"Big Honus" went to see his doctor yesterday. They had a powwow over the big fellow's rheumatic shoulder, and the man of medicine gave his verdict—quit baseball.

Wagner is almost crippled with the rheumatism, which has settled in his right arm and shoulder.

"I'm comfortably fixed financially," he said, "and I'm ready to quit. My old friend, the M.D., settled it for me yesterday. I am out of professional baseball for good." —New York *American*

———◇ **WEDNESDAY, DECEMBER 11** ◇———

Owners of the National League baseball clubs who may have come to New York to trade players made little progress yesterday. Rumors were thicker than drops of vapor in a Southern cloud, but there was little to give encouragement to the reports.

Much of the business transacted yesterday was purely routine. Mr. Pulliam recommended that the sale of liquids in bottles be prohibited at all baseball grounds and that no intoxicants be sold in grandstands. He also went on record against mutually arranged seven-inning games where doubleheaders are to be played. He would also make it compulsory that postponed games be played on stipulated dates in the future, taking from the home club the right to announce a date satisfactory to itself. Under that provision whenever a game is postponed the future date of its playing will be immediately known. —New York *Herald*

President C. Webb Murphy, of the Chicago club, does not do anything by halves. He is the whole Swiss cheese at this meeting—holes and all. He came here like a conquering hero and really he is the whole show. Charley showed this in a most appealing way by buying two rounds of drinks before the Waldorf-Astoria bar.

—Sam Crane, New York *Evening Journal*

———◇ **SATURDAY, DECEMBER 14** ◇———

The Board of Directors voted to advance Harry Pulliam's salary by $2,000. The president of the league, with that advance, will receive not far from $10,000 a year. —New York *Herald*

By one of the biggest deals in the history of National League baseball, Manager McGraw last night succeeded in materially strengthening the New York club for next season.

After a long conference between McGraw and Joe Kelley, Boston's new manager, it was announced that {Dan} McGann, {Bill} Dahlen, {George} Browne, {Frank} Bowerman and {Cecil} Ferguson had been traded to Boston for {Fred} Tenney {the former manager}, {Al} Bridwell and {Tom} Needham.

The Giants' infield will be greatly strengthened by the addition of Tenney at first and Bridwell at short. The two working with {Arthur} Devlin and {Larry} Doyle will form a fast combination which should prove a winner. Needham will be valuable as an assistant to Roger Bresnahan behind the bat.

For a long time McGraw has contemplated the separation of Bresnahan and Bowerman. Ever since the world's championship series of 1905, when Bresnahan caught every game, there has been friction between the two receivers.

Charley Murphy, president of the Chicago club, was not backward in saying he hoped McGraw could pull off a deal with Boston that would strengthen the Giants, for he felt it essential to the prosperity of the league that New York have a first-class team in the next pennant race.

—Sam Crane, New York *Evening Journal*

——◇ MONDAY, DECEMBER 16 ◇——

Still "The Talk of New York" is the big deal pulled off by John McGraw. The acquisition of Tenney is regarded not only locally, but everywhere else, as an excellent thing for the McGraw combination. Harry Pulliam characterizes the eight-player swap as one in which both clubs got the better of it, while Ned Hanlon {manager of four National League teams, 1889–1907} said McGraw had made a ten-strike in landing Tenney.

"Fred is one of the hardest men in the country to pitch to and makes the man in the box put them over for him. He can sacrifice beautifully and also can change tactics on a second's notice and carry through the hit-and-run play. Tenney is certainly a nice Christmas present for the Giants."

In Pulliam's estimation New York got a live asset in Al Bridwell, Harry C. thinking that McGraw will correct the youngster's indeterminate style at the plate and make a first-class hitter of him. Baseball sharps agree that Bridwell is a beautiful fielder, who is fast on his feet and knows intuitively what to do with the ball.

Few players stay so long in one city as Tenney stayed in Boston. Fred went there in 1894 from Brown University {a member of the class of 1894, Tenney was the first college graduate to achieve baseball stardom}, and has been a Beaneater ever since, save for about two weeks during his first season, when he was sent to the Springfield farm, where he acted as backstop for John Dwight Chesbro {famed spitball pitcher who competed for Pittsburgh, 1899–1902, and then for the New York Yankees}. {Frank} Selee, managing Boston then, liked Fred's style, and a left-handed receiver was no novelty, as Jack Clements was backstopping for Philadelphia. The new Giant caught and played in the outfield in his first season with Boston, and was windpaddist {catcher} and suburbanite {outfielder} during the following two campaigns. In 1897 Fred became a first baseman.

In thirteen full years in the National League, Tenney has played in 1,598 games, and his grand batting average is .308. As a fielder Tenney for the last seven seasons has topped all National League first-sackers in the number of assists.

Bridwell is a juvenile. He was with Atlanta in 1903, Columbus in 1904, Cincinnati in 1905 and Boston in 1906 and 1907. Bridwell's National League batting average is .230. —New York *Press*

———◇ **WEDNESDAY, DECEMBER 18** ◇———

With nearly all of the Giant pitchers greatness is a memory, not a reality. Three years ago {Christy} Mathewson, {Joe "Iron Man"} McGinnity, {George} Wiltse and {Luther "Dummy"} Taylor won games almost before they went into the box. They were believed and believed themselves to be invincible. But that is no more.

In 1906, after his great year of the championship, Mathewson began to slip. "Antitoxin for the nasal diphtheria," said the wise ones. "It'll die out and he'll be all right next season."

Next season found Mathewson even easier to solve. He no longer inspired fear. Teams that formerly threw away their bats when he stepped into the box slammed his favorite slants all over the lot. Mathewson is by no means a "dead one," but no stretch of the imagination would place him as the best twirler in the league. And he is kingpin of the staff.

Of the others, McGinnity and Taylor seem pretty nearly past the days of big league usefulness. And that is no shame to either. Both have done noble work at the Polo Grounds for years, but their performances last season could hardly be rated first class.

Wiltse is plainly a second-class man now. {Leon "Red"} Ames would be a great pitcher if he had any knowledge of the direction likely to be taken by the ball after he lets go. This wildness has been a chronic weakness with "Red" for so long that it is idle to hope he will get over it.

The Giants' pitching staff is now very much second class, and unless it is refitted there will be no National League ribbon at the Polo Grounds next Fall. —New York *American*

————◇ **THURSDAY, DECEMBER 19** ◇————

Did Joe Kelley hand McGraw a lemon? Tenney, a back number; Bridwell, a poor hitter; and Needham, a minor league catcher, handed over for Bowerman, Dahlen, McGann, Browne, and Ferguson. If that isn't sure enough quince, I will admit that McGraw has more brains than all the judges in America. While Tenney is still a good player and is greatly the superior of McGann, it's no cinch that Tenney will help the Giants. But cutting Tenney and McGann out of it, it's a joke to think Needham can fill one of Bowerman's shoes, while Bridwell, at shortstop, will look like an amateur in the absence of the heady Dahlen, even though Dahlen has gone back. Ferguson doesn't count. Browne, outside of Beaumont and Kelley, is a better man than any of the Boston outfielders last year.
—Joe Vila, *The Sporting News*

————◇ **SUNDAY, DECEMBER 22** ◇————

Practically completed are all arrangements for the Spring training trip of the Giants, who will get into condition at Marlin Springs, Tex.

This will be the Giants' first trial of Texas as a training place. Manager John McGraw likes the climate of California, but says that the journey to and from the Pacific coast is too long. Texas suits the Little Napoleon as a training camp, and he thinks he has picked the most available place in Marlin Springs, about forty miles from Dallas.

Since 1902 the Giants have taken training trips, visiting Savannah in 1903 and 1904, Birmingham in 1905, Memphis in 1906 and Los Angeles last Spring. Previously the Giants trained at the Polo Grounds, in Lakewood and in Jacksonville, having a record now of training in seven states—California, Tennessee, Alabama, Georgia, Florida, New Jersey and New York. Texas will be the eighth.   —New York *Press*

──◇ MONDAY, DECEMBER 23 ◇──

While Fred Tenney at present seems assured of holding down first base for the Giants next season, he will have to play up to a high mark to hold the place, for he has a young, ambitious rival in Fred Merkle, the Toledo High School boy. In fact, the struggle of the youngster to supplant the veteran will be an interesting feature of Spring practice, and the battle will probably be waged throughout the year.

In Merkle, Tenney has a rival that would worry any veteran. Although but nineteen years of age, he has already shown major league caliber. He played with the Giants at the tail end of last season, and the way he whipped the ball over to Dahlen and Doyle aroused the enthusiasm of local fans. Merkle is also strong at the bat. The youngster is six feet in height and is splendidly proportioned. Best of all, he has plenty of nerve and a cool head.   —New York *American*

──◇ WEDNESDAY, DECEMBER 25 ◇──

PITTSBURGH, Dec. 24—It will not be a merry Christmas for Hans Wagner, the big shortstop of the Pirates, nor will it be a merry Christmas for the person who sent out the fact than Hans is suffering from rheumatism, if Wagner gets his hands on him. Wagner feels bad enough with his occasional twinges of rheumatism in his right shoulder, "but," he sobbed this evening, "it isn't half as bad as to have every old woman and every quack in the country hounding the life out of you."

Since the public came to know that Wagner has rheumatism, every mail and every express wagon brought him hundreds of remedies, and this evening all the medicines were sent to West Penn Hospital, whose superintendent was told to do what he pleased with them.

—New York *American*

WASHINGTON, Dec. 25—John Heydler, secretary and treasurer of the National League, in this city spending the holidays, has no hesitation in saying that he disapproves of any changes in the rules which have for an object increased batting.

"I cannot believe," said Heydler, "that there is any necessity for changes at this time. The cry that the public wants more batting is not borne out by existing conditions. If the rules were not satisfactory the attendance would certainly prove it, and attendance is improving every year.

"I am in favor of the rules remaining as they are. Why break up a winning combination? If it is essential to have more batting, there is a way of doing it without changing the rules. Have the manufacturers of the ball increase the amount of rubber in it, and the batting can easily be increased. A ball can be made so lively that a batting average of .500 will be commonplace."   —New York *Evening Journal*

——◇ THURSDAY, DECEMBER 26 ◇——

It costs more to run a major league baseball team than a fair-sized racing stable. Frank J. Farrell, owner of the Yankees, can vouch for it. Farrell enjoys the unique distinction of being one of the most prominent men in two big professional sports. He is a power in baseball, and every racing man knows of his turf operations.

On the two sports he spends at a conservative estimate $138,000 a year, and of this close to $98,000 is spent on the team that is managed by Clark Griffith. The cost of running his ball team is about as follows: salaries of 25 players, $40,000; traveling expenses, $11,000; hotel bills,

$6,375; Spring training trip, $5,000; incidentals, clerks and attendants, $15,000, making a total of $97,375.   —New York *American*

────◇ **MONDAY, DECEMBER 30** ◇────

Among wishes for the new year by John McGraw, Christopher Mathewson, and followers of the New York Giants will be that in 1908 the Giants will be more successful against Mordecai Brown of the Cubs than in the past, and particularly will there be a wish that the Polo Grounds combination will be able to beat the Three-Fingered Wonder when he is opposed by the Bucknell boy. {Known as "Three-Finger" Brown, the Cub pitching star gained his nickname from a youthful accident when his right hand became caught in a piece of farm machinery and he lost most of his forefinger as well as the use of his little finger. This mishap enabled Brown to give a peculiar, frequently puzzling twist to his curve ball.} The Miner {Brown had been a coal miner} and the Collegian {for three years Mathewson had played baseball and football at Bucknell University} have hooked up eleven times since they have been big league rivals, and Matty has gone down before the man with missing digits seven times.

—New York *Press*

────◇ **TUESDAY, JANUARY 7, 1908** ◇────

McGraw will leave for the coast in a few days. He received the signed contract of McGinnity yesterday and said that he was having no trouble over contracts with the veterans.

"It is the new men that think they are getting the worst of it," said McGraw. "We send them a contract for $1,200 or $1,500, and they think they are worth a great deal more. They are worth more when they are good, and after they have proved that to our satisfaction we always give them considerably more than the contract calls for.

"These young fellows are unable to understand the position of the club. If we signed them for $2,000 or more, and failed to find a place for them on the team, it would be very difficult to dispose of them to minor league clubs at such a high figure."   —New York *American*

Joe McGinnity will be a Giant next year, and the good old "Iron Man" will again endeavor to twirl the horsehide in a way that will put the Giants in the running. {Contrary to popular belief, McGinnity did not gain his nickname because during a single month, August of 1903, he pitched and won three doubleheaders. The name derived from his employment, prior to entering professional baseball, in an iron foundry.}

Manager McGraw received a letter from McGinnity yesterday, in which the redoubtable "Iron Man" wrote that the terms offered him were eminently satisfactory, and he was greatly pleased to be back with the Giants.

McGraw said yesterday, "McGinnity's letter showed the right spirit. He is one of the best Spring pitchers any club ever had, simply because his control is so perfect. He never showed up with a lame arm, and he has been one of the most willing workers I ever had."

—Sam Crane, New York *Evening Journal*

———◇ **THURSDAY, JANUARY 9** ◇———

McGraw left yesterday for Los Angeles, where he will have the chance to watch the horses run at Arcadia for at least a month before he goes to Marlin Springs. McGraw has evidently decided that further deals for players are unnecessary. —New York *Sun*

Secretary Knowles received a letter from a Massachusetts genius who claims to have invented a pitching machine that can do everything a star twirler can and a great deal more.

"These fellows will never learn," said Knowles, "that a perfect pitching machine is of no use, for it would lack the very human weaknesses that it is necessary for a batsman to learn and anticipate. One of these inventions has turned up every season for several years just before Spring practice. They have been tried and found wanting. I am sorry for the men who waste their time inventing them."

—New York *Evening Journal*

──◇ **THURSDAY, JANUARY 16** ◇──

McGraw will stand pat. He should have made a big effort to strengthen his pitching, in addition to securing a competent second baseman, but he ignored all suggestions in this respect and said he was satisfied with the Giants as they are. It's a little early for predictions, but I'll take a chance with the prophecy that Chicago, Pittsburgh, Philadelphia, Brooklyn, and Boston will finish ahead of the Giants this year.

—Joe Vila, *The Sporting News*

──◇ **SATURDAY, JANUARY 18** ◇──

New York baseball "fans" {short for "fanatics"} missed one treat last Fall, a chance to see Merkle play first base. He joined the Giants in the West, and when the team returned to this city, the season was over. He remained with the players and went through Pennsylvania with them on their barnstorming trip. Every player who returned to New York for the Winter was loud in his praise of this Toledo boy. What surprised the old fellows in regard to Merkle was the boy's wonderful speed. McGraw says he is the fastest man to touch runners and to touch the base he ever saw. He made two plays in Chicago so quickly that {Charles} Rigler, the umpire, lost both of them, and after they were explained to him admitted he had decided wrong.   —New York *Evening Telegram*

──◇ **FRIDAY, JANUARY 31** ◇──

The identity of the umpire who won the championship for putting players out of games has just been made public. Charles Rigler, Pulliam's new fighting "ump" from Massillon, Ohio, was the boss banisher of the year, for he evicted 37 men. He was the only man on the staff who had trouble with all eight clubs. Billy Klem is entitled to a crown for favoritism, for he scored 14 put-outs against the Giants. Altogether 111 men were ejected.

Men indefinitely suspended were Al Bridwell of the {Boston} Doves, now a Giant, Frank Chance of the Cubs and Manager John McCloskey of the Cardinals. Brid and Jawn J. {John McGraw} got back after seven-day layoffs while it took Pulliam eight days to investigate the pop-bottle incident in which Chance figured. {In Brooklyn, Frank Chance threw back into the bleachers a bottle that had been hurled at him.}

John McGraw stood No. 1 on the list of players chased, being told to skiddoo seven times. Other Giants ejected were Dahlen, 4 times; {Sammy} Strang, 4; McGann, 3; Bresnahan, 2; {Danny} Shay, 2; Mathewson, 1; McGinnity, 1; Devlin, 1.　　　　　　　　　　　　—New York *Press*

——◇ SATURDAY, FEBRUARY 1 ◇——

The first gun of the baseball season was fired today with the departure of Groundkeeper John Murphy, of the Polo Grounds, for Marlin Springs. Murphy sailed on the *Nueces* for Galveston, Texas.

Murphy had the Giants' bat bag with him, filled with enough "Louisville sluggers" to break all back fences in the National League, scraped and sliced to a finish. Before McGraw left for Los Angeles he went down to the cellars of A. G. Spalding & Brothers and selected six dozen bats that spell base hits. When he selected the bats, he said, "It is the bats that tell the story and make ball players. Pitchers may be all right, but give me the bat I want—the one that feels good to me—and I will make the other fellows extend their grounds."

—Sam Crane, New York *Evening Journal*

——◇ WEDNESDAY, FEBRUARY 5 ◇——

Unless there is a change for the better, Frank Chance, manager and first baseman of the Chicago Cubs, may not be able to play ball again. Chance, in California, is suffering from neuritis in the left foot, which began to develop last year from a bruise. The best specialists on the coast are trying to avert an operation by using every possible treatment, but it seems as if Chance would have to submit to the knife to be entirely cured.

—New York *Sun*

——◇ THURSDAY, FEBRUARY 6 ◇——

Bridwell, the Giants' new shortstop, can't hit an airship with a shotgun charge.   —Joe Vila, *The Sporting News*

——◇ SATURDAY, FEBRUARY 8 ◇——

The advocates of Sunday baseball playing still believe they will be able to play games on the first day of the week during the coming season in Greater New York, particularly in Brooklyn. {Sunday baseball was prohibited in New York as well as Boston, Philadelphia, and Pittsburgh.} The Baseball Managers' Protective Association has taken the matter in hand, and the first steps to be taken will be to amend the bill which now lies with an Assembly committee in the Legislature {so that} games may be played between 3:30 and 6:30.   —*Sporting Life*

——◇ MONDAY, FEBRUARY 10 ◇——

The origin of the "spit ball," used by nearly all the star pitchers nowadays, has been a matter of endless discussion. Billy Hart, a veteran boxman {whose career ended in 1901}, has just thrown some interesting light on the subject: "I notice they claim Chesbro and {Elmer} Stricklett were the first to discover the 'spit ball.' Well, back in 1896, when I was pitching for St. Louis, I met Catcher Bowerman, who was with Baltimore that year. Calling me aside in St. Louis one day, he took the ball and requested me to get back of the catcher and watch his curves. I did so and was surprised to see how the ball acted as it neared the catcher. I asked Bowerman what made the ball act so. He explained that he simply spit on the ball, held onto it with his thumb at the seam and let it go. The odd part of it was that there was no speed to the ball that Bowerman pitched, whereas today they claim that the 'spit ball' can only be delivered with speed. I mastered it after a while, but found that it injured my arm, as it brought into play muscles not generally used. I advise any pitcher with good speed and curves to let the 'spit ball' severely alone. It will ruin an arm of steel in due time."   —New York *Sun*

———◇ WEDNESDAY, FEBRUARY 12 ◇———

Four young Giants sailed today on the Morgan liner *Creole* for New Orleans, from where the party will go by rail to Marlin Springs, Texas. At the pier a horde of baseball fans wanted to see the youngsters. John O'Brien, the big outfielder, got many a handshake. Indeed, he said that if he could stay here another day the hand shaking would almost put his arm in condition.

W. J. {Bill} Malarkey, a new pitcher, took well with the crowd, and John McKinney, the "Rusie of Oyster Bay," had to break away and hide in his stateroom. {Charley} Herzog, the young infielder, was labeled O.K. by the crowd. {A legendary Giant pitcher of the 1890s, Amos Rusie won more than 30 games in each of four seasons, and gained 233 victories in eight years.} —J. J. Karpf, New York *Evening Mail*

This is the Summer of "Larry" Doyle's prosperity or discontent. Doyle played so streakily last year that it was almost out of the question to get any fixed line on his ability. One day he would be a dead wall which nothing could pass, and the next he wabbled on every hit that came to him, like a boxcar on a coal railroad. Some days he could hit the ball on both sides of the seams, and on other days he missed all sides.

Some baseball men are confident that it is merely a question of time when Doyle will establish himself as a sterling, dependable player. If they have failed to read the signs right they are willing to be sentenced to eat five dozen hard boiled eggs and eighteen caviar sandwiches as punishment. —New York *Evening Telegram*

———◇ FRIDAY, FEBRUARY 14 ◇———

With the Giants, off the coast of Florida, Feb. 14. Everything is lovely on the steamship *Creole*, except for a little seasickness. The young fellows early this morning looked over the rail, and when no one was looking batted a few out to the fish. The war correspondents {Sid Mercer and Sam Crane, the two baseball writers who would cover the Giants' spring training} are helping things along wonderfully. They are doing so good that the fish come right up to thank them.

—Sid Mercer, New York *Globe*

Bresnahan will chaperone a second bunch of Giants to Marlin from St. Louis next Tuesday. It was McGraw's plan to keep the old-timers away till early March, but he has changed his plan. He considers it necessary to have a good catcher with him, one that can coach the young pitchers, and he is using excellent judgment. When coaching young pitchers it is absolutely necessary to have a veteran catcher to steady them.

—New York *Evening Mail*

————◇ **SATURDAY, FEBRUARY 15** ◇————

Unless Manager McGraw is mistaken in his estimate, the Giants will have a grand shortstop in Albert H. Bridwell. Bridwell always has been rated as a clever fielder, but fans belittled his abilities because he did not knock down fences when he swung at the ball. At that, Bridwell last year hit eleven points better than the man he succeeds—Dahlen—having a stick credit of .218. McGraw thinks Bridwell will be a .275 whaler with the Giants, and considers the former Bostonian one of the most promising players in the business. —New York *Press*

————◇ **MONDAY, FEBRUARY 17** ◇————

Baseball magnates will take a step in the right direction if they put in effect the suggestion of Clark Griffith and Frank Chance to prohibit a pitcher to soil a new ball. The custom of a pitcher getting down on his knees and rubbing a new ball in the grass has long been an irritation to patrons. The practice causes delays and should be stopped.

The pitcher rubs the ball in the grass to wear off the gloss, which enables him to get a better grip on the sphere.

—New York *Evening Mail*

Roger Bresnahan said he would certainly use his big shinguards again, but he denied any intention of using headgear. He said he had been hit in his time and wasn't in the least afraid of being hit again. {In 1907 Bresnahan had been the first, and only, catcher to wear shinguards.}

—New York *American*

◇ THURSDAY, FEBRUARY 20 ◇

{Because only two baseball writers, Sam Crane and Sid Mercer, were with the Giants in Marlin Springs, virtually all spring training reports will come from the pages of the *Evening Journal* and the *Globe*.}

MARLIN SPRINGS, Tex., Feb. 20—After being on the road a few hours over a week, the four Giant recruits, McKinney, Malarkey, O'Brien, and Herzog, with Trainers Richards and {John} Leggett and party consisting of nine persons in all, arrived yesterday afternoon. They were enthusiastically greeted by Groundkeeper John Murphy.

"By gum, Sam," Murphy said, "McGraw has picked out a great place for training. Wait till you see the grounds. They are as level as a billiard table, a bit sandy and a skin diamond {a hard, dirt diamond with little grass}, but as smooth as a floor. It's luck they sent me down ahead, for the grounds had been given up to steers, stray pigs and horses, so I had my work laid out to fix things right."

The boys are quartered at the Arlington Hotel, a swell hostelry in appearance. I know the rooms are all right, and Murphy tells me the "feed" is O.K. too; and Murphy knows something besides corned beef and cabbage.

The players will have the benefit, and it is a great one, of the bath house run with the hotel. The water used in the baths comes from the same hot springs used for drinking, and Murphy says the baths and drinking combined will make new men of the whole bunch. Marlin is a typical Texas town in appearance, with low, one-story stores and one main street. Saddle horses and mules are tied in front of the offices and stores, while the broad-brimmed thatched owners saunter around the streets and transact their business.

The people here are all anxious to see the prominent players and the whole town turned out at the depot this afternoon. The Giants' visit has caused a sensation all through this part of Texas.

—Sam Crane, New York *Evening Journal*

MARLIN SPRINGS, Feb. 20—Marlin is a pretty little city of 8,000 inhabitants, situated on a broad prairie. There is a little excitement now and then. On Tuesday night a Texan used his artillery on three colored persons. The white went on his way unharmed and the colored gentlemen were taken to the hospital for repairs.

—Sid Mercer, New York *Globe*

{A comment by former St. Louis Cardinal pitcher Eddie Murphy:} Donlin is a fine fellow. His mother was killed in the Ashtabula Bridge horror, Mike found in his mother's arms. His brothers and sisters were placed in orphanages. Mike was taken into our home and we became chums. While still quite young we decided to go out and see the world. We struck out and drifted South, but soon after going to New Mexico I decided to return home. Mike kept going. He finally reached California and the next thing I learned he was playing ball out there. A year or so later he was picked up by the St. Louis Nationals and he has been in the limelight ever since. Just because he makes a lot of noise on the field and has a peculiar stride, people look upon him as rowdy.

—*The Sporting News*

——◇ FRIDAY, FEBRUARY 21 ◇——

MARLIN SPRINGS, Feb. 21—Real business was started yesterday. Training stunts were gone through, but footballs were brought into play to do the limbering up. There was any amount of leg work in kicking and chasing the leather sphere, and arms and shoulders were loosened up in throwing the ball around in the college style of passing the pigskin.

It was Winter weather for this part of the country, for thin ice formed on water in the gutters and was enough to set the natives to shivering and turning up their coat collars, while the poorly clad negroes hunted the sunny sides of their shacks and longed for watermelon time.

—Sam Crane, New York *Evening Journal*

———◇ **SATURDAY, FEBRUARY 22** ◇———

The time-worn cry of "more hitting" is heard again, and to help along the slugging several members of the joint rules committee will try to make a change that will bring the pitcher's box on a level with the home plate. Just now the pitcher hurls from a mound fifteen inches high. This, say committeemen who want the rule changed, gives the pitcher just enough advantage to cause the so-called falling-off in batting.

—J. J. Karpf, New York *Evening Mail*

———◇ **MONDAY, FEBRUARY 24** ◇———

MARLIN SPRINGS, Feb. 24—With the arrival of Manager McGraw the Giants' training camp seems to ooze pepper and ginger. Roger Bresnahan has done wonderfully well during the short period he had the youngsters in charge, but it remained for the big boss himself to pull the work out of the boys Sunday, yes, Sunday.

Contrary to all precedent, McGraw ordered the entire bunch for morning practice, and would doubtless have done the same in the afternoon, but the bath house was closed.

—Sam Crane, New York *Evening Journal*

MARLIN SPRINGS, Feb. 24—One subject that always crops out when fans discuss the Giants is the probable arrangement of the infield. Devlin and Tenney are conceded third and first base, but there is much uncertainty about Bridwell and Doyle. There's going to be so much rivalry for short and second that the lucky individuals finally chosen will squarely please the Polo Grounds patrons. Bridwell and Doyle have the inside track, but their positions are not guaranteed, and Fred Merkle and Charley Herzog will have to be reckoned with. Merkle has been doing most of his work here at second and short, and is a fellow who uses intelligence in everything he does. The only thing that will stop Herzog is his brief experience and lack of an infield opening.

—Sid Mercer, New York *Globe*

———◇ **TUESDAY, FEBRUARY 25** ◇———

Fred Tenney is the originator of the type of fast left-handed first baseman. He instituted the idea of clever and rapid double plays from first to second and back to first, through his ability to field the ball perfectly and snap it with sufficient speed and accuracy to second to permit a return throw to first.

The new Giant is in the best of physical condition. During all his service on the diamond he has been a member of the conservative element, devoting all of his time to baseball and little to frivolities. He is abstemious in his daily life, his sole indulgence being tobacco. "I suppose I could get along without that," he remarked last Winter, "but like a great many other athletes I like to chew something while I am at work, even if it's only a toothpick. Keeps my nerves settled."

—New York *Evening Telegram*

———◇ **WEDNESDAY, FEBRUARY 26** ◇———

The spit ball has been a source of a great deal of annoyance to catchers. Because of the quick and unexpected shoots that this delivery takes it is most difficult to gauge its course, and many a finger has been broken and shin bruised because of the inability of a catcher to intercept the ball with his mitt. {"Nig"} Clarke, of Cleveland, however, believes he has solved the problem by inventing a new mitt, which, he claims, will make handling a spit ball as easy as a fast or curve ball. Just what this mitt is like is being kept secret by Clarke.   —New York *Evening Mail*

——◇ THURSDAY, FEBRUARY 27 ◇——

MARLIN SPRINGS, Feb. 27—All the training paraphernalia, such as medicine balls, a new home plate, bases, balls, uniforms and the big pushball came yesterday from New York, and a variety was added to the regular routine. The pushball, a new institution to the young players, was the source of much amusement and excellent practice. The embryo stars of the diamond ran the big leather sphere from one end of the grounds to the other, playing "follow the leader" in leaping onto and over the ball as it rolled over the field.

The pushball was of infinite interest to the spectators, especially the "chocolate babies" delegation, the darkies rolling over and over on the grounds in paroxysms of laughter whenever a player lost his balance while on the ball and pitched forward on all fours or floundered flat and hard onto the field in a sitting position.

—Sam Crane, New York *Evening Journal*

How can any sane person believe, for an instant, that the Giants have even a slight chance to win the pennant? Why, boys, don't overlook the fact that McGraw's pitchers are weaker than Griffith's ever were, and Larry Doyle is a failure as a second-sacker.

Barring Mathewson, the Giants haven't got a single up-to-date twirler. McGinnity began to hit the toboggan in 1906, after he had pitched his arm off the previous year. Last season his efforts at times were painful. Luther Taylor was all in early last Spring and was a joke thereafter. Ames (who wants to be called "Red") cannot be depended upon because of his erratic work and his temperament. Wiltse lost his grip in 1906, because he was overworked.

Will anybody say it is good managerial judgment to go all Winter without picking up a couple of first-class pitchers and a second baseman? Instead of letting Bowerman, McGann, Browne, Dahlen, and Ferguson go for Tenney, Bridwell and Needham, why didn't McGraw make a deal for a pitcher? If Merkle is the coming first baseman, as McGraw says, why was the deal made for Tenney?

Take it from me, gents, the Giants will slide down pretty close to the second division simply because of these weak points. There's nothing to it, and by the time Memorial Day rolls around you'll be ready to take off your hats to me.   —Joe Vila, *The Sporting News*

————◇ **FRIDAY, FEBRUARY 28** ◇————

There was a joint meeting of the major leagues' rules committee yesterday, and it was agreed that the words "except the pitcher" after "player" in section 4 of rule 14 should be stricken out. This means that the pitcher must not discolor a new ball by rubbing it on the ground. {Prior to this amendment, Rule 14, Section 4 read, "In the event of a ball being intentionally discolored by rubbing it with the soil or otherwise by any player except the pitcher, the umpire shall, upon appeal by the captain of the opposite side, forthwith demand the return of that ball and substitute for it another legal ball and impose a fine of $5.00 on the offending player."}   —New York *Sun*

MARLIN SPRINGS, Feb. 28—Texas ladies drive to the grounds in carriages, and some come on horseback. One beautiful young lady rode to the grandstands in a most fetching costume, which included a wide-brimmed hat, and she attracted the attention of players away from their practice. The equestrienne stationed herself along the first-base line. It was remarkable how badly the players wanted to play the initial position. She sure was a peach.

Card playing is a diversion that ball players are accustomed to on Spring training trips, and what some of the old-timers will do to pass away their leisure time here is a question, for Texas laws on card playing are very strict. Gambling of any kind is a State's prison offense, and card playing, whether for money or marbles, is not allowed even in one's own home.

Dominos are allowed and that is the game played by the boys in the hotel. This with weird ragtime music played and sung by a quartet of darkies, is the only amusement here. The streets are deserted after dark and there is not a thing in town to distract or lure the players from their training.

That is one reason why McGraw likes the place so much as a training camp. But it is slow, oh, so slow at times. One can't spend a picayune after dark if he wants to.   —Sam Crane, New York *Evening Journal*

———◇ SATURDAY, FEBRUARY 29 ◇———

The mooted question as to the wisdom or folly of Southern training camps and extended Spring exhibition tours has received its usual Winter threshing—without changing conviction or methods; and so, as usual, all major league teams will start their rehearsals for the Big Show of 1908 in the so-called Sunny South. Following is a list of training places:

NATIONAL LEAGUE	AMERICAN LEAGUE
Chicago, Vicksburg, Miss.	Detroit, Pine Bluff, Ark.
Pittsburgh, Hot Springs, Ark.	Philadelphia, New Orleans, La.
Philadelphia, Savannah, Ga.	Chicago, Los Angeles, Cal.
New York, Marlin Springs, Tex.	Cleveland, Macon, Ga.
Brooklyn, Jacksonville, Fla.	New York, Atlanta, Ga.
Cincinnati, St. Augustine, Fla.	St. Louis, Shreveport, La.
Boston, Augusta, Ga.	Boston, Little Rock, Ark.
St. Louis, Houston, Tex.	Washington, Galveston, Tex.

          —*Sporting Life*

———◇ SUNDAY, MARCH 1 ◇———

By far the most pretentious training season undertaking will be that of {Charles} Comiskey's White Sox. Last night a special Pullman train departed from Chicago conveying 32 players and many relatives and friends of the club to Los Angeles. It is the first time that a baseball club has had its own train for a Spring trip. A year ago the White Sox went to Mexico in special cars, but they were attached to regular trains.

          —New York *Times*

◇ TUESDAY, MARCH 3 ◇

MARLIN SPRINGS, March 3—A broad-shouldered young man walked into the Arlington Hotel at noon yesterday, set down his grip, and in a neat hand wrote S. Strang Nicklin on the hotel register. The cub Giants spotted him for a ball player, but the name on the register puzzled them. Mike Donlin walked up, seized his hand, and said, "Hello Strang." "No more Strang, please," replied the man from Tennessee. "That fellow has been waived by all clubs in all leagues, and has retired.

"Allow me to introduce myself, Capt. Donlin. I am Strang Nicklin."

"Turn over on your back, you're dreaming," replied Mike.

"This is straight goods," said Sammy. "I have decided to use my real name. Not long ago I was thinking I would like to meet some of my old friends whom I knew in my college days. They don't connect Sammy Strang with Strang Nicklin, and a lot of them don't know that I am playing ball. If there is anything coming to me in my career I want it credited to my family name."

And so it will hereafter be Utility Man Nicklin. {Nicklin had played in the National League during nine seasons, for four teams, under the name Strang, used because of the low status formerly given to professional baseball players.}   —Sid Mercer, New York *Globe*

◇ WEDNESDAY, MARCH 4 ◇

MARLIN SPRINGS, March 4—All the Giants regulars are here now. The party that left New York by the steamer *Momus* arrived yesterday afternoon. Luther Taylor arrived at noon, and could not get out to the ball park quick enough to get into the afternoon practice.

Taylor on every training trip I have been with him has been the life of the camp, and yesterday he was more full of life, good nature and ginger than ever. Bresnahan began to spar with him at once, but Luther {a deaf mute} is pretty good with his hands, and knocked off Bresnahan's dicer the first crack out of the box. This pleased the amiable Luther immensely, and then there was more finger lingo than could be furnished in a deaf and dumb asylum. All the old players are adept at the deaf and dumb language, especially Bresnahan. Needham tried to break in with it, but Luther looked at Tom's knotted digits and spelled out on his fingers: "Another Bowerman; I'll bet he has a brogue."

—Sam Crane, New York *Evening Journal*

——◇ THURSDAY, MARCH 5 ◇——

MARLIN SPRINGS, March 5—{Spike} Shannon, Tenney, Donlin, {J. Bentley "Cy"} Seymour, Bresnahan, Devlin, Doyle, Bridwell and Mathewson— this will be the Giants' batting order this season. And allow me to whisper it is as nifty a bunch of slapstick artists as there is in the country. Just try to pick out any weak spots.

What looks good to me, too, is the spirit shown by the players. They all seem imbued with an inspiring confidence that presages winning results. One of the most prominent players said: "Yes, the old winning spirit is there all right. It is the same feeling we had three years ago, which we lost after winning the world series."

—Sam Crane, New York *Evening Journal*

——◇ FRIDAY, MARCH 6 ◇——

MARLIN SPRINGS, March 6—Marlin yesterday showed the Giants what genuine Southern hospitality really is. Thirty prominent merchants met the players after the day's practice with buggies, carriages, traps, automobiles and other vehicles and drove them to the Falls of the Brazos, a beautiful resort about four miles from town.

Luther Taylor can ride a horse like a Texas cow-puncher, but this can't be said about Mathewson. The big pitcher has been desirous of learning, and he was induced to straddle one of the broncos in making the trip to the Falls.

Matty's long legs made his pony look like a goat. Taylor took extreme delight in making Matty's life miserable, and would dash by him at a fierce gallop, which caused Matty's mount to coast wildly. All hands arrived safely all right, but it was noticed that Matty took his barbeque standing up.

Social affairs were not allowed to interfere with daily practice. Mathewson and McGinnity warmed up together, and I don't remember ever seeing two pitchers show better form so early in the season. Matty fairly made the ball talk, and had almost perfect control. McGinnity appeared to have more speed than ever. Joe has developed his "Old Sal" so that he can make it take an inshoot as it raises. {McGinnity called his favorite pitch, which he is credited with inventing, Old Sal. It was also known as a raise ball because, delivered underhanded, it rose as it approached the batter.} He said of this new delivery, "I have been practicing it this Winter and think I have it down fine enough to be effective. Us old pitchers must dig up something new, you know, to keep in the game."

The ball looked to me as if it took an incurve, but Joe still persists that no right-hand pitcher ever got an incurve to a ball.

"It is not possible for a right-hand pitcher to so twist his hand as to curve the ball in. It would require a man without any bones in his fingers to do it," said Joe. "Matty's fadeaway does not curve," continued Joe, "no more than this raise ball of mine."

—Sam Crane, New York *Evening Journal*

———◇ **SUNDAY, MARCH 8** ◇———

{On this day Sam Crane left Texas to join the New York Yankees, with whom he spent the remainder of spring training. Until their return to the Polo Grounds, Sid Mercer would be the only New York writer covering the Giants.}

DALLAS, March 7—The Giants played their first real game of the season today, defeating Dallas of the Texas League, 2 to 0. McGraw gave orders that McGinnity, Ames, and Mathewson, who trotted out in turn for a three-inning stint, could depend on speed as much as they liked, but so far as bending them or putting on the "jump" or any other twist was concerned, there must be absolutely nothing doing.

—New York *Times*

─────◇ **THURSDAY, MARCH 12** ◇─────

MARLIN SPRINGS, March 12—The other day at the dinner table Luther Taylor wrote on the back of the menu and passed it to McGraw. "This is a quiet town," was what the manager read. Coming from Taylor this is surely a recommendation of Marlin's virtues as a peaceful resort.

—Sid Mercer, New York *Globe*

─────◇ **MONDAY, MARCH 16** ◇─────

DALLAS, March 16—Manager McGraw has decided that Marlin as a training point is about the best place in Texas, but as a headquarters for a team playing exhibition games in larger cities it is inconvenient, on account of bad train schedules. He will therefore move his big squad this week and establish headquarters in Dallas.   —Sid Mercer, New York *Globe*

PITTSBURGH, March 16—Every indication is that Hans Wagner will never again play baseball. Satisfied that no ordinary contract would receive a second thought, Pittsburgh mailed him an offer of $15,000 a year and agreed to permit him to cut the Spring training trip, but the largest salary ever offered a ball player was turned down. Another, signed by the club, but with the salary line left blank, then was sent him. It was also refused, Wagner saying that there is not enough money in the world to induce him to play ball this year. He told a friend recently that his private business had grown to such proportions he can't afford to play.

—New York *Evening Mail*

─────◇ **WEDNESDAY, MARCH 18** ◇─────

One big item in the annual expense list of a big league ball club accrues from traveling over the circuit throughout the season. The sixteen teams will travel 188,287 miles between April 15 and the first week of October. The American League teams will cover 95,772, while National League clubs will cover 92,165 miles. At the rate of two cents a mile, each club carrying an average of eighteen men, the expense for railroad fares alone figures close to $68,000. And this does not include expenses for berths, meals and other incidentals.

One of the most remarkable features of traveling by baseball teams is the way in which they steer clear of accidents. In recent years there has been only one bad smashup in which players have figured. This was when a special train, carrying the St. Louis and Cleveland Americans to St. Louis in 1904, was wrecked. A few players were cut up, but the game the next day was played as scheduled.   —New York *Evening Mail*

——◇ FRIDAY, MARCH 20 ◇——

DALLAS, March 20—This city looks as big as New York to the Giants, who quit the bush league circuit after one day's experience. The discomforts attending the game at Calvert yesterday {in which the Giant regulars defeated the colts (rookies), 5 to 3, with McGraw umpiring} and the hotel accommodations were almost the limit. The players were so anxious to get out of the place they accepted upper berths in two sleepers without grumbling. Anyone who has ever heard a diamond star roar when an upper is handed him can appreciate how anxious the McGrawites were to get out of Calvert.

The town turned itself inside out to attend the game, all stores closing at 4 o'clock. The game was not started until all the school children had arrived {at 4:30}. The players rode to and from the game in a hay wagon and played on a field surrounded by strips of coarse bagging stretched on fence posts. The boys on the outside saw through this easily, but their elders paid cheerfully to get a look at the Giants.

—Sid Mercer, New York *Globe*

——◇ SUNDAY, MARCH 22 ◇——

Recent developments had led fans to believe that Chicago, the probable pennant winner, is not so sure of the flag, and that Pittsburgh will have a hard time finishing in the first division.

Chicago stock has depreciated since news came out of Vicksburg,

Miss., that Manager "Husk" Chance had to leave for Chicago to see about his injured hoof. Men who know assert that Chance will be lucky to play ten games in succession at any stage of the race. With Chance out, the world's champions will lose an aggressive, enthusiastic leader, who is one of the best pinch-hitters in the business, a grand base runner and a splendid fielder. {In this context a pinch-hitter is a batter who is dangerous in crucial situations.}

Hans Wagner, the Demon Dutchman, always has been considered the backbone of the Pittsburgh outfit, and if he persists in his determination to keep out of the game, the Pirates will be greatly weakened.

—New York *Press*

"You can't win without pitchers," is a baseball axiom. John McGraw expects the Giants to win this year. So he must have pitchers.

Known all over the country, Christy Mathewson returns for his eighth year at the Polo Grounds. He is easily the star of McGraw's staff. Over six feet in height and weighing about 190 pounds, he has an ideal build for a pitcher. "Matty" is a right-hander, and last year he played in 41 games, won twenty-four and lost twelve, and led his league in strikeouts with 178. He is one of the best fielding pitchers in the league. "Matty" is a warm-weather pitcher, reaching his best form in the Summer.

Luther (Dummy) Taylor is the oldest player with the Giants in point of service, this being his ninth year. He is also right-handed. Last year he won eleven games and lost seven, with three shut-outs. The "Dummy" is always ready to take his place in the box, and is one of McGraw's most useful men. He is a great favorite with fans because of his antics on the diamond.

Joseph "Iron Man" McGinnity begins his sixth season with the Giants. He is 5 feet 10 inches and tips the scales at about 175 pounds. The bulk of the work fell on his shoulders last year. Several seasons back he made the great record of winning both games of four doubleheaders within one month. {The month was August of 1903, when McGinnity won three, not four, doubleheaders.} McGinnity is a right-hander, won eighteen and lost the same number of games, and struck out 130 last year.

"Red" Ames starts his fifth year as a Giant. Last year he won ten and lost twelve. He needs a steady man to catch for him, as he is inclined to be wild. Although he struck out 146, he also gave 108 passes. Ames is still young, and McGraw expects this to be his best year.

The last of the veteran pitchers is George Wiltse, a southpaw, who wears a New York suit for the fourth year. He is 6 feet tall and weighs 170 pounds. Last year his health was poor. Out of 25 games he won thirteen, five of them shut-outs, and struck out 79.

Of the youngsters trying to win places as pitchers the most promising at present are {Roy} Beecher, Malarkey and McKinney.

—New York *Tribune*

———◇ **TUESDAY, MARCH 24** ◇———

JACKSONVILLE, Fla., March 24—Today Nap Rucker {of Brooklyn} sprung the new-fangled knuckle ball, which seems to be causing a considerable stir in professional ball. It had the opposing batters guessing all the time.

—New York *Evening Mail*

The knuckle ball is what its name implies. It is thrown with the hand all double, not unlike a pig's knuckle, and merely floats to the plate without a twist or turn. No speed can be put on it, the cramped position of the hand preventing that. It is safe to use only with a change of pace from a swift ball, and then when a pitcher has the batter in a hole.

—New York *Evening Journal*

———◇ **THURSDAY, MARCH 26** ◇———

DALLAS, March 26—To show how busy McGraw is it is only necessary to outline a day's work. Yesterday, for instance, he put the Dallas players through signal practice and infield work for two hours. Then his own players arrived on the field, and until nearly 1 o'clock McGraw worked with them. After a respite of an hour and a half, during which the Giants had dinner at the Hotel Oriental, McGraw had them out again. The game with the Dallas team started at 4, and was over at 5:30. When the last man was out, McGraw sent his colt team out to practice, and kept them

at it half an hour. He finished his supper at 7:30 and still seemed as fresh
as a daisy.   —Sid Mercer, New York *Globe*

It is seldom that a minor league recruit in his first year in fast company shows enough class to win a regular position, but this may be the
fortune of Charley Herzog. He covers considerable ground around short
position, is a sure fielder, and a fast and accurate thrower. He also has the
knack of touching a base runner without getting spiked or cut up, and is
clever at the bat and a good base runner.

Doyle and Bridwell have shown up well in their respective positions,
but they have nothing on Herzog in fielding; besides he outclasses them
with the stick. McGraw is puzzled just what to do, as he says the youngster is too good to be kept on the bench.   —New York *Globe*

———◇ SUNDAY, MARCH 29 ◇———

When the Giants open the season New York baseball enthusiasts will
watch with much interest the working of the infield. John McGraw has
made many changes, and the biggest have been in the infield.

At first base, where Dan McGann reached for wide ones and scooped
up low ones for years, Fred Tenney will be in command. The veteran
Boston player is a left-hander and one of the best first basemen in the
game. Though a fast man in the infield, he is at his best at bat and on the
bases. All the fine points of the game are at his command, and he is a past
master at advancing a runner.

At present it is undecided who will cover second base. It lies between
two youngsters, Larry Doyle and Fred Merkle. In build they are entirely
different. Doyle is short and stocky, Merkle tall and lanky. Doyle played
second with the Giants in sixty-odd games last year. He was green, but his
work was satisfactory. Since he has been in the South he has shown much
improvement. Merkle plays best at first base, but that position is well
covered. McGraw likes Merkle. He will find something for him to do,
and second base is the weakest point on the team. Therefore Merkle is
getting his chief practice there. Doyle will probably be the regular and
Merkle general utility man.

Al Bridwell will play shortstop. In the territory where Bill Dahlen held forth so many years the young Boston player is expected to do some fast work this year. He outclasses Dahlen in every department of the game. Bridwell is coming, while Dahlen has almost reached his limit of usefulness.

The only veteran Giant in the infield will be Arthur Devlin, at third base. For steady, reliable playing he has few superiors. This is his sixth year in a New York uniform, and he is faster than ever. Devlin is a hard worker, and his playing is filled with ginger.

—New York *Tribune*

◇ MONDAY, MARCH 30 ◇

The shinguard is to be the fashion this summer among the big base-ball men. The latest from the South is that {Kid} Elberfield {New York Yankee shortstop} and {Harry} Niles {Yankee infielder} are to decorate their legs with the guards, wearing them under the stockings, of course. Elberfield is always colliding with a base runner's spikes because he is so aggressive he will take all sorts of chances to get a runner stealing. Niles, too, has had sad experiences with spikes, and believes the guards will prevent further injury. —New York *Evening Mail*

◇ TUESDAY, MARCH 31 ◇

Chance has joined the Cubs again in the South and believes he will be able to continue practice with them and report in Chicago in good order to begin the season.

A special shoe has been made for his injured foot. The spike plate has been taken off the sole of the shoe, and in its place is a special arrangement of nails on the edge of the sole which do not press upon the affected portion. Eliminating the plate, it is believed, will put an end to his suffering. Its rigidity prevented the shoe from giving, and whenever he ran briskly and threw his weight upon his foot the pain was so intense he sank to the ground and had to give up completely.

Someday somebody will come along with an arrangement which will do away with the old-fashioned shoe plate. More men have been seriously hurt by cuts resulting from shoe plates than by almost any other source in baseball.   —John B. Foster, New York *Evening Telegram*

———◇ **WEDNESDAY, APRIL 1** ◇———

ATLANTA, April 1—Many contradictory stories have been published on why Honus Wagner has been holding out, but Frank Chance says the correct story has never been given the light of day.

According to the "peerless leader" of Chicago, Wagner's refusal to play was due to trouble with Fred Clarke, the Pirates' manager. Chance got this information from a Pittsburgh player.

"All this talk about Wagner quitting on account of rheumatism, chicken farm and other things is incorrect," said the boss of the world beaters.

"According to my information the whole trouble started over a play at the Polo Grounds last summer. Wagner has always been known as a player who worked for his individual record more than for the welfare of his team. In that game Clarke is said to have told Wagner to make a play in a certain way to help in getting a much-needed run. Honus at first refused, but when ordered to do so went to bat, made one effort as directed and then did exactly opposite from what Clarke told him. His effort failed, and Clarke called him good and hard.

"From that day to this they have been enemies. I understand that Wagner at first refused to join the Pirates unless Clarke was released, and held out until a few days ago. That Clarke wasn't going was a cinch; it was only a question of what could be done to placate the ire of the big German. That something will be done is evident, and I expect that President Pulliam is taking a hand in getting Wagner in line."
                    —New York *Evening Mail*

———◇ **MONDAY, APRIL 6** ◇———

McALESTER, Okla., April 6—For the first two weeks of the season at least, and perhaps much longer, the Giants must struggle along without the services of Joe McGinnity {who was suffering from a severe fever}.

McGraw does not believe that Mac will be out for more than three weeks, but it is the opinion of several players that the Iron Man will be lucky to report by the time the team reaches St. Louis on the first trip West. —Sid Mercer, New York *Globe*

——◇ WEDNESDAY, APRIL 8 ◇——

Players are learning to take almost all kinds of hits so that the gloved hand bears the brunt of the effort. Realizing the great advantage in playing with a glove, they face the ball in such a manner that the glove acts as a receiving cushion and the ungloved hand is the lid of the trap which insures the ball being held.

When reasons are sought for a presumable decline in batting it is hardly worthwhile to go further than consideration of the glove. Many a base hit is smothered in leather and padding.

—New York *Evening Telegram*

——◇ THURSDAY, APRIL 9 ◇——

{Quoting Chicago Cubs' pitcher Orval Overall:} I believe the rule prohibiting the pitcher from soiling a glossy ball will greatly increase the hitting department of the game. I also see trouble for umpires in enforcing it, as every pitcher will try to invent a way to get around the rule. You can't curve a glossy ball, and in my judgment there will be more pitchers knocked out of the box the coming season than ever before. Unless I am very much mistaken the hitting averages will go soaring. Supposing a pitcher has two strikes and three balls on a batsman and the next one is fouled over the stand. That means a new, slippery ball. The pitcher wouldn't dare try to curve it on account of its glossy surface, which prevents getting a good grip. He has no choice but to stick the ball over the plate with the prayer that it be knocked no farther than the back fence.

—*The Sporting News*

◇ FRIDAY, APRIL 10 ◇

WHEELING, W. Va., April 10—A topic of much discussion among the Giants this morning is the "dry spitter," a new pitching delivery of which Christy Mathewson claims to be the originator. Matty calls his freak the "spitless spitter," for he does not moisten the ball, yet it breaks like a spitter. He used it in Columbus yesterday, and it fooled several batters.

The "dry spitter" differs radically from the common spit ball not only because the ball is not moistened, but because it is a slow instead of a fast ball. Speed and a quick break have been the essential qualities of the spit-ball delivery, but Matty throws his deceiver without any effort.

In yesterday's game the ball floated up to the plate without any force behind it, and just as the batter would take a healthy swing the sphere would suddenly waver and drop dead into Needham's mitt. It was like a piece of paper fluttering along and encountering a puff of wind from the opposite direction. —Sid Mercer, New York *Globe*

ST. LOUIS, April 10—Hans Wagner would take first, second and all the rest of the prizes offered in an off-again-up-again contest. According to the very latest, as served out by the great Honus himself while passing through here last night, he will play for Pittsburgh this season. He was cornered, and after being well pumped admitted he will "probably consent to help the team out." —New York *Evening Mail*

◇ SATURDAY, APRIL 11 ◇

New York fans whose appetites have been whetted by glowing reports of the new Giants down in Dixie will get lots of action at this afternoon's doubleheader at the Polo Grounds.

The main wing of McGraw's army rolled into Jersey City this morning at 9:15 after an all-night ride from Wheeling, posed for the snap shotters, hurried across the ferry, and hiked to Harlem. After a hasty lunch they will don uniforms for the big reception which will formally open the baseball season in the greater city.
—Sid Mercer, New York *Globe*

——◇ SUNDAY, APRIL 12 ◇——

Half a hundred baseball players entertained 10,000 enthusiasts at the Polo Grounds yesterday afternoon, when the Giants were welcomed home. A doubleheader was the opening attraction of the season, the colts, or young recruits, playing the New York Athletic Club, and the real Giants lining up against Yale. John McGraw's men won both games, the first, a four-inning affair, 14 to 2, and the second, which went the full nine innings, 9 to 1.

Not in years has there been such a crowd at the Polo Grounds at a preliminary game. It augured well for a prosperous season.

—New York *Tribune*

{Included among the National League managers' statements at the opening of the season were the following:} John McGraw: The Giants will show New York what wonderful things can be accomplished by a few changes in personnel. We are going to be every bit as strong as we were in 1904 and 1905. This year we will have a team far ahead of last year's in every department, batting, fielding, and pitching. The Giants have just one team to beat this year, the Chicago Cubs. If we beat that outfit, and I am confident we will, New York will get another pennant.

Frank Chance: There is only one thing for the world's champions to do this year, and that is to repeat. We have taken two pennants straight with this team, and there is nothing to indicate we will not make it three in a row. We are now on top, and the others are doing the uphill fighting, so it looks all the more certain for another world's pennant in Chicago.

Fred Clarke: Without Hans Wagner I must admit I am worried. The Dutchman's decision to leave may have a very bad effect on the team, and may bring about other disappointing consequences. Pittsburgh's team, on pure dope, seems good enough to finish in the first division. As for reaching the top, I would have hopes if Wagner was with us.

—New York *Sun*

———◇ MONDAY, APRIL 13 ◇———

Good old Mike Donlin has been dubbed Turkey. Turkey lay down on three strikes the first time up Saturday, but maybe he didn't clout the leather after that. And who ever said Donlin has a bum leg? He appears faster now than at any time in his career. The season's layoff appears to have done Donlin a lot of good.

—New York *Evening Mail*

When fans reach the new Washington Park {Brooklyn's ball park} tomorrow they will realize what the improvements on the grounds mean. President Charles H. Ebbets of the Brooklyn baseball club states that the improvements have cost $22,000. He feels that the support accorded the Superbas {the principal nickname of the Brooklyn team} deserves recognition, and the new stand and grounds, with every convenience for patrons and players, is a model plant.

The new twenty-five-cent seats in centerfield are substantially built and will afford an excellent view of the game. They are far and away ahead of any similar seats on the circuit. With the additional seats, and with the arrangements made to handle an overflow on big days, 20,000 people can be comfortably accommodated. The boxes, of which there are 42, will provide for 252. There are over 5,200 seventy-five-cent seats and 600 more can be placed around the grandstand on the inside of the field in three raised rows. There are 8,500 fifty-cent seats and over 1,500 twenty-five-cent seats. With benches in the outfield and standing room, almost 4,000 more spectators can get in the grounds.

The "dugouts" of the new-fangled players' benches have been put into good shape. They are in their old positions but are made of cement foundations sunk into the ground about ten inches. They will not interfere in any way with the spectators' view. The roof is covered with tar paper, and a comfortable bench has been placed in each.

—Brooklyn *Eagle*

──◇ **WEDNESDAY, APRIL 15** ◇──

{On April 14, Opening Day, in Philadelphia, the Giants won 3 to 1. Winning pitcher, Mathewson; losing pitcher, McQuillan.}

From 16,284 throats there rose a mighty roar of blissful anticipation when a white leather sphere dropped from Mayor Reyburn's hand yesterday as he stood in the upper pavilion at the Phillies' grounds, and {manager Billy} Murray's men started the season's pennant race.

When the sun began to show a disposition to vanish and the wind began to send the faithful into overcoats, those throats were congealed with gloom, and there were few who did not sorrowfully admit that Mathewson had bunked those Phillies. The score was 3 to 1. In a nutshell, the Phillies could not connect with Mathewson. The stellar twirler, whose elusive curves have led the Giants so often to victory, was in fine form, and his mighty arm spelled disaster for Murray's men.

When the curtain was rung up on the show by the Mayor's ball-tossing stunt, grandstand and bleachers were filled by a great crowd. So rapidly did the mad ones arrive on the scene of carnage that a slice of the field on the north edge of the outfield was roped off and immediately stormed by those who came late, only to find the unwelcome "standing room only" sign to freeze their hopes.

There were the usual ceremonies before the battle began, ceremonies dear to the faithful. The peanut vendor was on hand, the waffle man did a land-office business, and the score card and the lemonade men were equally happy. They were on the job for the Summer, and they found the fans as willing as ever to part with nickels and dimes. While the early ones waited for the opening stunt they whistled, keeping time with their feet. They munched peanuts, snared waffles and speculated as to which batteries would be selected.

They were all on their feet in an instant when the blare of a brass band heralded the customary march and countermarch of contesting players on the field of battle. In their white uniforms the Phillies made a gladsome showing in the bright sunshine. McGraw's men also received a noisy salute from a delegation of crazed ones who had journeyed from Manhattan. The Gothamites bought a large piece of the upper pavilion, and from this point of vantage yelled themselves hoarse.

The game began with Mayor Reyburn facing a dozen cameras, the manipulators of which had followed him to the upper pavilion. He good-naturedly posed for the snapshot battery and then prepared to perform the customary ball-tossing stunt that invariably ushers in a new season of baseball.

The momentous time came when Umpire Klem {the only umpire for the game} stood in front of where the Mayor was seated and signaled him to toss down the ball. No sooner did the ball reach the umpire's hand than he in turn tossed it to Pitcher {George} McQuillan, the Phillies' new twirler. The latter carefully rubbed the new ball on the ground near the box, swung his arm with a mighty movement and drove the sphere over the plate, where Shannon stood waiting.

The first ball of the National League season in this city went wide of the plate. Twice did McQuillan drive the ball towards the plate, but it was not until the fourth time that Umpire Klem filled the fans with good cheer by yelling "Strike!" There was a great cheer when Shannon fanned twice again and the season began with a strikeout. As the game dragged on, it had its thrilling episodes, but usually favorable to the Giants. The Phillies simply could not touch Christy Mathewson. That's the whole story. They could not fathom him and until the last inning drew blanks with a regularity which caused the faithful to groan in anguish. Mathewson had them all buffaloed, and he fanned some Quakers with ridiculous ease.   —Philadelphia *Inquirer*

PHILADELPHIA, April 15—There is no more antitoxin in Christy Mathewson's system. The wise M.D.'s of the South squirted a lot of this dyphtheria killer into Matty's system two years ago, with the result that "Big Six" was weak around the knees last year, and everybody mistook this as a sign of Matty's decadence. {Mathewson gained his nickname when Sam Crane, principal baseball writer for the New York *Evening Journal*, likening Mathewson to New York's most famous fire engine, called him the Big Six of Baseball.} But all this medical juice has lost its effectiveness, and Matty jumped in yesterday and, defying cold winds, pitched a game of the kind that made him famous as the greatest pitcher in the land.

The game brought out the significant fact that the Giants are to be feared this year. The men, new and old, worked so well together that McGraw must be congratulated. The infield was like a stone wall. Bridwell and Tenney played the kind of ball that helps win pennants. Doyle handled himself admirably, and Devlin looks even better than last year. Most important of all was the teamwork displayed by this quartet.

—New York *Evening Mail*

Tonight the New York and Philadelphia teams will be special guests of the management of "The Merry-Go-Round" at the Lyric Theatre. Mabel Hite, Mrs. Mike Donlin in private life, is the star of the production, soon to be seen on Broadway. —New York *Globe*

——◇ FRIDAY, APRIL 17 ◇——

{On April 16, in Philadelphia, the Giants lost 6 to 3. Winning pitcher, Hoch; losing pitcher, Ames.}

PHILADELPHIA, April 17—Like the little boy, the Giants are awful good when they're good, and when they're bad a cheese factory hasn't anything on them. They certainly were bad yesterday.

Well, it was coming to them. It was the first defeat of the season, and nearly everybody contributed a foozle to the lost cause. It may have been a good thing to have crowded them all into the one session. The Giants ought to feel better with that nightmare out of their system. Every good team has these spells; they show that the players are human. The Giants made more errors than they commit in a half dozen ordinary games, but it's a waste of time to weep over these things, and the Giants are not doing it.

Out of something like 35 games this Spring it was the first decision the Giants lost, so it isn't hard to forgive them.

—Sid Mercer, New York *Globe*

─────◇ **SATURDAY, APRIL 18** ◇─────

{On April 17, in Philadelphia, the Giants won 14 to 2. Winning pitcher, Wiltse; losing pitcher, Moren. Giants' standing: 2 wins, 1 loss, tied with Brooklyn for third place.}

PHILADELPHIA, April 17—The National League's first slug-fest of 1908 turned up this afternoon, the Giants snowing the Murrayites 14 to 2. The Giants banged to all corners of the yard the slants of {Lew} Moren, {Harry} Covaleskie, and {Charles "Buster"} Brown, ripping off fifteen safeties. {The name was actually Coveleski, but as we shall see, it was variously spelled.} George Wiltse kept the Quakers from the plate for seven rounds and then eased up, the Phillies playing against a team with four substitutes.

Outside of Wiltse, Devlin was the New York player who deserves more than superficial comment, the whole team's work being so splendid it is hard to particularize. The third-sacker got three hits and stole two bases. His licks were for one, two and three cushions.

The knuckle ball got a bad advertisement, Moren, its inventor, being knocked out in the fifth inning.

The Giants were speedy in all departments and stole seven bases.

—New York *Press*

PITTSBURGH, April 18—Hans Wagner yesterday attached his name to a Pittsburgh contract, and left for Cincinnati in personal charge of President Barney Dreyfuss, who announced that the big fellow would be in the game there today.　　　　—New York *Evening Journal*

─────◇ **SUNDAY, APRIL 19** ◇─────

{On April 18, in Brooklyn, the Giants won 4 to 0. Winning pitcher, Mathewson; losing pitcher, Pastorius. Giants' standing: 3 wins, 1 loss, tied with Chicago for second place.}

There's gloom in Brooklyn. Yesterday before 20,000 howling fans the Giants took the Dodgers on their own lot and literally wiped it up with them. Christy Mathewson pitched for the big fellows, and he stood out like a crane on an ant hill. He was never in better form, and he sent twelve Brooklyn lads back to the bench in disgrace after they had swung their floating ribs out of shape trying to hit his benders on the snoot. The best hitters on the team fell before the magic of Matty's wonderful delivery.　　　　　　　　　　　　—Hype Igoe, New York *American*

Although enthusiasts who were present were not aware of it, Mathewson pitched the last three innings barely able to stand on one foot. In running to first base to cover a throw from Tenney he turned his ankle and McGraw was ready to take him out, but Mathewson decided he would fight the game to a finish. He limped decidedly when he left his uniform in the Brooklyn clubhouse and started his return to New York.
　　　　　　　　　　　　—New York *Herald*

CINCINNATI, April 18—"I was convinced by the management and the players that the team needed me," said Hans Wagner, "and so after considerable cogitating I made up my mind to get back into the game."

Seldom has joy appeared on Fred Clarke's face as that which showed up at the Havlin Hotel when the team arrived from St. Louis this morning. When he found Wagner tears almost came to Clarke's eyes, and Wagner seemed in about the same condition. With Wagner in the van the Pirates' strength is increased fully 25 percent.
　　　　　　　　　　　　—Pittsburgh *Dispatch*

◇ MONDAY, APRIL 20 ◇

{On April 19, the Giants were not scheduled to play because professional baseball was not permitted on Sundays in the state of New York.}

--------- NATIONAL LEAGUE STANDINGS ---------

	W	L	PCT.	GB		W	L	PCT.	GB
Chicago	4	1	.800	—	Brooklyn	2	2	.500	1½
New York ...	3	1	.750	½	Cincinnati ...	1	3	.250	2½
Pittsburgh ...	3	1	.750	½	Boston	1	3	.250	2½
Philadelphia .	2	2	.500	1½	St. Louis	1	4	.200	3

◇ TUESDAY, APRIL 21 ◇

{On April 20, in Brooklyn, the Giants won 4 to 1. Winning pitcher, Ames; losing pitcher, Rucker. Giants' standing: 4 wins, 1 loss, in second place.}

There may be nothing in the oft-disputed theory of the power of mind over matter as applied to baseball, but it does seem that there is always something doing when John McGraw goes on the coaching lines. He may not pull in the runs, but whenever he takes his stand at third base he seems to possess the uncanny ability of hypnotizing the pitcher and drawing base runners toward him. It was that way in Brooklyn yesterday.

Over in Philadelphia the other day Manager Billy Murray of the Quakers accused McGraw of mesmerizing one or two of his pitchers. Mac's coaching was directed toward the spot where it did the most good—or harm—and though the spectators could hear little of it, the Philly pitchers soon began to exhibit strange symptoms.

McGraw started to tell Murray's pitchers what to do, and they did it. He informed them that they were about to make wild pitches, that certain batters were going to hit, and that certain base runners would steal. He called the turn a few times and soon had the rival boxmen guessing. When you get 'em guessing the game is half won.

The Giants are weaklings before left-handers, did you say? Yes, that's so. Covaleski, Pastorius, Rucker—three southpaw victims already, and the season just a week old. {Because six of their regulars were left-handed batters, there had been some question about how well the Giants would perform against southpaw pitchers.}

Next!

—Sid Mercer, New York *Globe*

Brooklynites seem to prize highly balls which go into the bleachers. During the preliminary practice McGraw grew tired of seeing balls knocked into the stands never to return. He finally sent a policeman after them and they were thrown back. Mathewson picked out a man whom he charged with stealing a ball and the culprit was arrested.

—New York *Tribune*

Umpire {Hank} O'Day is strictly enforcing the new rule which provides for a player's expulsion from the game if he leaves his position to protest a decision. O'Day pulled a couple of bum decisions yesterday, but the Giants shouted their comments without rushing up to the umpire, who was waiting for a chance to serve some bench warrants.

—New York *Globe*

◇ WEDNESDAY, APRIL 22 ◇

{On April 21, in Brooklyn, the Giants won 6 to 1. Winning pitcher, Wiltse; losing pitcher, Bell. Giants' standing: 5 wins, 1 loss, tied with Chicago for first place.}

Pie—apple, mince, custard or any other kind—have the Superbas proved to be for the fast-going Giants. "Why couldn't we have those fellows all the year round?" wailed "Muggsy" McGraw after yesterday's game. "There would never be any doubt as to the championship. We'd win in a walk."

"Yes," chimed in "Larry" Fassett, once owner of the Albany team and a thirty-third-degree Giant "rooter," "it's all over now. The championship is already won. Who ever said Chicago could play ball is crazy. As for Brooklyn, Ebbets wants to get a real baseball team! And St. Louis? Why, they have no right to be in the National League."

Suddenly Bresnahan, with feet foremost, tore into third base, ripping {Whitey} Alperman's trouserettes with his spikes, and Tenney was put out of the game for disputing {umpire} "Bob" Emslie's decision on first, whereat "Larry" got into an argument with a spectator, and to show how strong a thirty-third-degree "rooter" he is he went off and sat in a se-cluded spot of the grandstand. —New York *Herald*

It is evident that McGraw has instructed his men not to bow meekly to the rulings of umpires. They have shown a disposition to scrap from the start but had no occasion to break loose until yesterday. {Harry} Pattee was declared safe by a whisker in the sixth, whereupon Tenney said things to Umpire Emslie and Fred was banished, whereupon McGraw uncovered a wonder in Merkle, who covered first base in great style. The new Giant had six put-outs and appeared to feel at home. He was all to the merry at bat and in his first trial knocked out a pretty safety between short and third. On his next appearance he laid down a neat sacrifice.

—Brooklyn *Eagle*

Today at 3 o'clock the Philadelphia and Boston National League teams will open the season at the South End grounds, the oldest baseball park in the country, formally opened to professional baseball in 1873. The South End grounds have been the home of 11 world's champion teams, a remarkable record that will probably never be equalled.

—Boston *Globe*

———◇ **THURSDAY, APRIL 23** ◇———

{On April 22, Opening Day at the Polo Grounds, the Giants beat Brooklyn 3 to 2. Winning pitcher, Mathewson; losing pitcher, McIntire. Giants' standing: 6 wins, 1 loss, tied with Chicago for first place.}

As a fitting climax to a game brimful of interest, Captain Mike Don-lin aroused 25,000 enthusiasts to a frenzy of excitement at the Polo Grounds yesterday by driving the ball into the right-field bleachers for a home run, which brought in two runs and gave the Giants a victory over Brooklyn 3 to 2.

It was the opening game of the season under Coogan's Bluff, and the biggest crowd which ever saw a game in this city filled every stand, circled the field and lined the viaduct and surrounding points of vantage. The Giants had trailed throughout the game, although mighty Matty was in super form and mowed down visiting batters like a machine gun. The Superbas scored one run, however, in the fourth inning and another in the eighth, while the Giants had one lone tally to their credit.

Brooklyn had taken its last chance at the bat. The crowd had inched onto the diamond so that the players were almost swallowed up. There was one continuous roar which drowned out even the crack of bat meeting ball. The crowd would have been satisfied with a single tally. McGraw sent in Merkle to bat for Mathewson, the first man up. Two strikes were called, and then Merkle picked one he liked and sent it sailing into the right-field crowd. It counted for two bases because of the ground rule. Shannon's sacrifice advanced him to third.

The crowd begged and implored Tenney to knock it out of the field. The former Boston captain hit hard, but the ball was fielded quickly, and Merkle was caught between third and home. Tenney went to second on the play, but with two out things looked gloomy to New York rooters.

Happy Mike Donlin then strode to the plate as nonchalant as if he were facing a "prep" school pitcher and the score was 30 to 0 in favor of the Giants. {Harry} McIntire sent the first ball straight and true. Mike never moved. The umpire bellowed "Strike, one!" The next was a ball. Then a strike was called, and gloom settled down on 25,000 rooters. Was Mike nervous? He didn't show it. "Ball, two!" roared Emslie.

Two balls, two strikes, two out, and two runs needed to win the game! It was a combination you often read about, but seldom see. Donlin grasped his bat tight, stepped close to the plate and waited for the next ball. After years of waiting, as it seemed to the anxious throng, it finally shot for the plate. There was a sharp crack, and the next instant the little sphere was sailing through the air, and finally dropped into the scrambling hands of right-field bleacherites. Tenney raced home and Donlin wended his way through the crowd, which by this time had taken complete possession of the field. The Giants had pulled out a victory with the odds almost 100 to 1 against them.

To say that the crowd went wild is putting it mildly. It went clean crazy. Hats and cushions were tossed in the air; old men slapped their companions on the back and laughed and cheered like undergraduates. It was one of the greatest sights ever seen at an athletic contest, and those present will never forget it. —New York *Tribune*

Mabel Hite up in a private box in the grandstand, with flushed face and happy glistening eyes, as her husband, Mike Donlin, made that game-winning home-run wallop yesterday, took me off my feet. It was not the cheering thousands so anxious to do Mike Donlin credit that impressed me the most.

It was the little woman with tears of joy trickling down her cheeks and so wildly clapping her gloved hands (I'll bet she has not the same gloves this morning) that got my goat.

And cheering as she did, so exultant over her husband's grand hit, still there was a shade of anxiety over her pretty countenance as she saw enthusiastic fans try to carry Mike to the clubhouse.

"Oh, I hope they don't hurt him," she said, and as Mike darted away from his too exultant admirers, pale of face and utterly exhausted, the little woman sank down in her seat with a little gurgle of delight that would have made a hit behind any footlights.

—Sam Crane, New York *Evening Journal*

The only thing at the Polo Grounds greener than the grass was a squad of almost officers doing business under the firm name and style of "Holmes Private Police."

Long before the game hundreds of rooters ranged themselves in a crescent around the front of the grandstand and gradually worked their way up toward the home plate. Secretary Knowles and Manager McGraw entreated the new policemen to force the crowd around the outfield, but when the crowd discovered that the officers were afraid to interfere or were otherwise incompetent, the crescent grew and grew, until it stretched out from the right-field bleachers clear around to the bench of the visiting players.

Thousands in the stands begged and threatened alternately, but the unruly ones refused to budge. As a result many hundreds sitting in the lower sections of the grandstand could not see more than an occasional glimpse of the game. This will never do. In the words of the statesman from Minnesota, "something must be did." {The "statesman from Minnesota" was John Johnson, the popular, colorful governor of Minnesota. The son of Swedish immigrants, Johnson was a dark horse candidate for the Democratic presidential nomination. He is mentioned again in the last May 5 entry as "Yohn Yohnson."}

—William F. Kirk, New York American

A lady with a "Merry Widow" bonnet, trimmed with several acres of foliage, perched herself on the shelf in one corner of the press stand. A few score unlucky individuals behind her, finding their view of the game cut off, amused themselves by making the hat a target for wads of newspapers and hot peanuts. So many minions found the mark that two men stood up beside the lady, withstood the bombardment, and incidentally cut off the view of several more people.

—Sid Mercer, New York Globe

———◇ FRIDAY, APRIL 24 ◇———

{On April 23, in New York, the Giants lost to Brooklyn 4 to 1. Winning pitcher, Wilhelm; losing pitcher, Ames. Giants' standing: 6 wins, 2 losses, in second place.}

Yesterday at the Polo Grounds was different from the day before.

> *They whopped it up for Donlin*
> *With a rooter-tooter blare;*
> *They rooted him,*
> *They tooted him,*
> *And boosted him for fair,*
> *But Donlin's bat was busted*
> *And he never did get there.*

Which means that yesterday wasn't Donlin's day. The Suburbas {the *Times* regularly referred to the Brooklyn Superbas as Suburbas} simply put it all over the Giants from start to finish, and gathered four runs as easy as falling off a log, two in the fifth and two in the ninth.

Ten thousand or more were on the grounds to see the show, and, unlike Wednesday's audience, they saw it, because the crowd didn't feel like walking out in the field and taking possession. Plenty of Merry Widow hats were along the upper front row, and one in particular had so wide a brim and a bunch of lingerie on top that a hot cigarette dropped into it would have called for four alarms and the Chief's gasoline go-cart. The weather was ideal, and brought out as many hillbillies {those who watched free of charge from atop Coogan's Bluff} as the day before. Coogan's Bluff looked like a full hand.

—W. J. Lampton, New York *Times*

New York is the only city where regular policemen are not on duty at ball parks. The lack of this protection injures the reputation of the city, for on every big baseball day there is always a riot or a near-riot. In some cities baseball clubs engage policemen who are off duty, paying them for the extra work. If no other way can be provided here it should be tried. There is no use talking. New Yorkers will not respect any uniform but that of New York policemen.   —Sid Mercer, New York *Globe*

{Irwin "Kaiser"} Wilhelm's whirlers had too much dampness on them yesterday, and they were altogether too slippery for the Giants.

Spit-ball pitchers are scarce in the National League. Consequently when one does appear, he is a troublemaker. Yesterday even Mike Donlin lapsed from up-to-date baseball and forced out Tenney on three separate occasions. When Donlin is fooled, the pitcher surely has something on his ball.

Miss Mabel Hite, Mike Donlin's pretty and talented little wife, who is to star in the "Merry-Go-Round" opening on Broadway tomorrow, was at the game accompanied by a bevy of enthusiastic stage-beauties, who occupied a private box and were primed from the tops of their dainty shoes to their Merry Widow hats for another celebration such as Captain Mike provided on Wednesday, but they were doomed to bitter disappointment.   —Sam Crane, New York *Evening Journal*

——◇ SATURDAY, APRIL 25 ◇——

{On April 24, in New York, the Giants lost to Brooklyn 4 to 1. Winning pitcher, Pastorius; losing pitcher, Crandall. Giants' standing: 6 wins, 3 losses, in second place.}

As it was Thursday, even so it was Friday. The earnest ball tossers from across the Bridge came back yesterday with another 4-1 score. Really, you know, Mr. Donovan {Brooklyn's manager, "Patsy" Donovan}, it isn't quite clubby.

We never like to mask the truth, and must concede that Brooklyn played better ball and deserved to win the victory. But we are all praying for the Giants to develop their normal hitting gait, because this thing is getting on our nerves. If we cannot win the next game, we must at least lose it by some other score than 4-1.

Without any paddock information, it is safe to state that Manager McGraw will summon his athletes shortly after we go to press and deliver an able lecture on the manly art of hitting. The Giants weren't hitting yesterday, and they weren't hitting the day before, and when a team isn't hitting that team invariably presents a poor front to the hopeful rooters. Every play looks stupid, every error seems flagrant, every attempt to score is derided when the scheme goes amiss. All of these things come to pass when a team isn't hitting. Let us hit.

—William F. Kirk, New York *American*

That boy {Al} Burch made a catch off Cy Seymour that ought to go down in baseball history as the best clutch ever.

In the sixth inning, when Cy leaned up against the bulb, the Superbas had accumulated two tallies and the Giants had one lone dot on their tally sheet, so a home run would have been very "peachy." Cy evidently awoke to the interesting and important situation and swung for one of his real old-time lambasters. He connected all right on the Spalding trademark. The ball shot off his chopstick on a loop-the-loop message for the clubhouse. The ball was labeled a sure enough homer, and that boy Burch evidently thought so, too, for he turned tail and tincanned so fast for the outer bulwark his red top-knot looked like a fiery streak.

He took one despairing glance at the horsehide through one corner of his offside lamp (I wish he had been crosseyed), saw that he had no possible chance of stopping the ball as a legit, and then, as if he had been on springs, he launched himself upward and forward, stuck out his gloved hand backward, and blamed if the ball didn't stick to the mitt. The force of the ball threw Burch forward and, being off his trolley, he pitched face downward and then turned a complete somersault, his nose ploughing up the ground for a city block as if a four-tongued barrow had been his proboscis.

Pitcher {Otis} Crandall, although beaten in his first game, really pitched a winning game. Not a run the Superbas made was earned, and six hits were all the victors made during the eight innings he was in the box. Crandall showed enough to warrant McGraw putting him in to take his regular turn hereafter. In my opinion, he made good—he "showed."

—Sam Crane, New York *Evening Journal*

————◇ **SUNDAY, APRIL 26** ◇————

{On April 25, in New York, the Giants lost to Brooklyn 4 to 1. Winning pitcher, Rucker; losing pitcher, Wiltse. Giants' standing: 6 wins, 4 losses, tied with Pittsburgh for second place.}

There is something magic in that combination, 4 to 1. It will go down as a record in baseball. After losing four straight the Superbas turned around and took three by the same score. It is a remarkable coincidence not likely to be repeated for years to come.

To Nap Rucker for his superb pitching and timely hit in the eighth, and {second baseman} Harry Pattee's brilliant fielding, base running and hitting is the victory chiefly due. Rucker was touched for four hits in the first three innings, and was then invincible. Pattee accepted ten chances, and time and again cut off apparently safe hits back of first and second. He stole three bases, two thefts being the third sack. {Pattee's brilliance was momentary. His major league career would be confined to eighty games in 1908, with a batting average of .216.}

Wiltse was on the firing line, and the elongated southpaw was in trouble in every inning but the second and third. In the ninth Wiltse was replaced by McGinnity, who made his first appearance of this year. The Iron Man was given a great ovation, but the Superbas scored two runs.

—Brooklyn *Eagle*

When Messrs. Ebbets and Medicus decided last Winter to raise the price of their bleacher seats to four bits (a slang expression signifying half a bean) there were those who opined that Messrs. Ebbets and Medicus had committed a strategic blunder, not because there aren't plenty of half dollars floating around in Brooklyn, but because the Brooklyn ball club had shown little cause for a boost in their drawing qualities. If Messrs. Ebbets and Medicus could evade the Sunday law and pull off a game this afternoon they could charge, and get, a dollar per head for standing room in centerfield. To back this assertion we are laying four to one.

—William F. Kirk, New York *American*

———◇ MONDAY, APRIL 27 ◇———

BOSTON, April 27—This city of culture and beans is mildly excited— which is as far as Bostonians allow themselves to go—over the prospect of what will happen when McGraw's team, strengthened by former Boston players, meets the revamped Boston outfit, bolstered by five ex-Giants this afternoon at the South End grounds. Though Monday is a bad baseball day, it is a safe bet that a big crowd will see the fun.

{Manager} Joe Kelley has made a hit with the fans here, and so has good old Frank Bowerman, who, like Bresnahan, has caught every game so far. And maybe George Browne, Bill Dahlen, Dan McGann, and Cecil Ferguson are not waiting to get a crack at the Giants! They feel they must show up McGraw for trading them. Did you ever see a transferred player who didn't have a grudge against a club that released him?

—Sid Mercer, New York *Globe*

——— NATIONAL LEAGUE STANDINGS ———

	W	L	PCT.	GB		W	L	PCT.	GB
Chicago	7	2	.778	—	Boston	5	5	.500	2½
New York ...	6	4	.600	1½	Cincinnati ...	5	5	.500	2½

| Pittsburgh ... | 6 | 4 | .600 | 1½ | Philadelphia . | 4 | 6 | .400 | 3½ |
| Brooklyn .... | 5 | 5 | .500 | 2½ | St. Louis ..... | 2 | 9 | .182 | 6 |

CINCINNATI, April 25—President Dreyfuss, of the Pittsburgh club, and Hans Wagner are having a tough time convincing the public that financial questions did not enter the decision of Wagner to retire some time ago, nor move him to come into the fold. "For some time," Dreyfuss said, "Wagner has had the privilege to name the figures in his contract, and the same privilege was extended when he was asked to sign this Spring. However, he did not care to avail himself of this offer when we talked some months ago. He was determined to retire, and the financial end of the game cut no figure with him. And so it was when he came into the fold. Finances did not come up for discussion. He simply made up his mind that he would rather play than not, and there was no argument about the figures in his contract." It has been reported that Wagner's salary was raised from $7,500 to $10,000, but neither Mr. Dreyfuss nor Wagner would discuss this matter. "There are only four people who know what my salary is," said Wagner, "and that is quite enough. My salary is satisfactory to me, and my great aim every year is to make it satisfactory to the people who pay me. If I thought I could no longer deliver an equivalent for the coin that is given me semi-monthly, I'd have my salary cut or quit the game."   —Charles H. Zuber, *Sporting Life*

◇ TUESDAY, APRIL 28 ◇

{On April 27, in Boston, the Giants won 2 to 0. Winning pitcher, Mathewson; losing pitcher, Young. Giants' standing: 7 wins, 4 losses, in second place.}

Sixty-five hundred fans witnessed a great game at the South End grounds yesterday between the Doves and the Giants. {Boston's team was called the Doves after its owner, George B. Dovey.} It was wonderfully well-played, lasting only an hour and 16 minutes, New York winning 2 to 0, both runs coming in the eighth inning on a lucky combination of two hits, one a scratch, a sacrifice, and an excusable fumble by {second baseman Claude} Ritchey, playing close to cut off a run at the plate.

No two teams ever displayed keener rivalry than Boston and New York did yesterday, and it was a rivalry exemplified by splendid sportsmanship. Both teams hustled for everything in sight, and both were aggressive, but a cleaner, more satisfactory game could not have been played.

Fred Tenney was given a royal reception by the fans, besides being the recipient of a handsome traveling bag. Fred was full of ginger, and that he is free from care was shown by the masterly manner in which he played the bag at which he was stationed so long in Boston.

—Boston *Globe*

BOSTON, April 28—With Joe McGinnity hardly able yet to pitch a full game, and Leon Ames ill in New York, the Giants are somewhat short of pitchers.

"If Ames was here and in shape to work," said McGraw this morning, "I am sure we would win every game. I left Leon behind under a physician's care. He has some sort of kidney trouble which started from a cold, and I fear he may be out for a while. It's tough to lose him. It seems that I can't get all my pitchers together at one time. At that, if Crandall pitches as good a game as he did against Brooklyn, he'll be a winner."

—Sid Mercer, New York *Globe*

———◇ **WEDNESDAY, APRIL 29** ◇———

{On April 28, in Boston, the Giants won 3 to 2. Winning pitcher, Malarkey; losing pitcher, Dorner. Giants' standing: 8 wins, 4 losses, in second place.}

The New York Giants made another eighth-inning finish yesterday, winning 3 to 2 in a game in which the locals did more hitting {9 hits for Boston, 4 for the Giants}, but were cut off from two runs by throws by "Cy" Seymour to the plate after base hits on which a runner tried to score from second base.

—Boston *Globe*

——◇ THURSDAY, APRIL 30 ◇——

{On April 29, in Boston, the Giants lost 7 to 6. Winning pitcher, Young; losing pitcher, Malarkey. Giants' standing: 8 wins, 5 losses, in third place.}

BOSTON, April 29—There was a merry mix-up at the Copley Square Hotel last night shortly after midnight. Dan McGann, now of the Boston Nationals, and his old manager, McGraw, were in a clinch taker. They were pulled apart by the players before McGann could be subdued.

At the end of yesterday's game when McGann went to bat and hit into a double play, McGraw made some slurring remark about McGann being an ice wagon {a slow runner}, which got to the ears of McGann. He is stopping at the same hotel where the Giants are housed. During the evening Dan walked impatiently up and down the corridor, waiting for McGraw to return from the theater.

McGraw came in with Mathewson and went to the billiard room. McGann followed, and in spite of Mathewson's intervention, struck at McGraw. Hats were spilled and there was a hot mix-up but no damage was done except to rile McGann's Kentucky blood. The scrap broke up the billiard game after the players separated the combatants.

McGraw went upstairs and was soon followed by McGann, who made a vicious pass at the Giants' manager. McGraw got the blow on his shoulder. Players had anticipated trouble and were on hand to interfere in time before any blood was spilled.   —New York *American*

BOSTON, April 30.—McGraw's noodle allowed Matty to get properly warmed up yesterday when Wiltse was pulled out. {Umpire} Emslie demanded a pitcher, and as Matty was not ready, McGraw walked out and announced himself as the twirler. He claimed the customary privilege of throwing five balls to warm up. He had just tossed up the first one when Matty came running out. McGraw should therefore figure in the tabulated scores as one of the Giant pitchers.

—Sid Mercer, New York *Globe*

———◇ FRIDAY, MAY 1 ◇———

{On April 30, in Boston, Boston beat the Giants 3 to 2. Winning pitcher, Flaherty; losing pitcher, Crandall. Giants' standing: 8 wins, 6 losses, in third place.}

BOSTON, April 30—Frank Bowerman, who has been working like a beaver to show John McGraw that a mistake was made when the Romeo {Bowerman's home town in Michigan} receiver was traded last winter, hammered an Otis Crandall offering over the left-field fence in the ninth inning, with Bill Sweeney on first base, and the rap gave Boston a victory, 3 to 2. Bowerman is the happiest man in the Hub, even though he gets credit only for a two-bagger, as Sweeney had scored before Frank reached third.

New York's pitching department is in such bad trim that McGraw had no veteran he could call on and so entrusted the job to Crandall. The Cedar Rapids recruit showed his mates how to hit by banging the ball out of the lot in the fifth inning, but unfortunately did not instruct them how to field, and the poor support he received allowed the resident athletes to win. —New York *Press*

The Giants ought to have had yesterday's game done up and iced for Youngster Crandall. All that Crandall brought back to New York was vain regret, a sigh for useless labor, an order for a pair of shoes, and a promise of a new hat the next time he goes to Boston. {A pair of shoes and a hat were given by local merchants to National Leaguers who hit home runs in Boston.}

Crandall's homer was one of the longest and highest round-trip belts ever seen in Boston. The New York, New Haven and Hartford tracks run just outside that fence, and yesterday a work train ran up alongside the fence and the crew got on top of the cars to watch the game. Crandall's hit sailed high over the heads of the trainmen and disappeared in a pile of junk. —Sid Mercer, New York *Globe*

——◇ **SATURDAY, MAY 2** ◇——

PITTSBURGH, April 29—Pittsburgh will spring a novelty this season. The Pittsburgh baseball club proposes to solve the "wet grounds" problem. A contract was signed yesterday by Dreyfuss with the Pittsburgh Waterproof Company for a tarpaulin to cover the entire playing field. The tarpaulin will contain 1,800 yards of brown parafinned duck and will cost $2,000. The center of the tarpaulin will be attached to a truck 10 x 15 feet and 3 feet high. Before and after a game in threatening weather, the truck will be run out and the playing ground covered with the tarpaulin. The tarpaulin will protect the field, and there should be no more deferred games on account of wet grounds, unless rain should fall during the progress of a game. —*Sporting Life*

——◇ **SUNDAY, MAY 3** ◇——

{On May 2, in New York, the Giants lost to Philadelphia 2 to 1. Winning pitcher, McQuillan; losing pitcher, Taylor. Giants' standing: 8 wins, 7 losses, tied with Philadelphia for third place.}

To the keen disappointment of about 10,000 fans, Philadelphia defeated the Giants yesterday 2 to 1. As the spectators went home after the game they meditated on what might have been had not Umpire Emslie reversed his decision twice in the sixth inning.

The trouble came over a decision by Emslie, who called balls and strikes, in the sixth inning. With the score 2 to 1 in favor of the visitors, Seymour made a safe hit. Bresnahan followed at the bat, and on the third ball pitched Seymour started to steal second. {Catcher Fred} Jacklitsch threw to {second baseman Otto} Knabe and caught Seymour. To the majority of spectators, as well as to Seymour, it seemed like Emslie called a foul. Rigler declared Seymour out, and pandemonium broke loose. McGraw was up in arms and engaged in a heated conversation with Emslie. The latter changed his ruling and said it was a foul ball. This brought a protest from the Quaker horde. {Philadelphia coach } Kid Gleason outargued McGraw, and Emslie, after a conference with Rigler, declared Seymour out. —New York *Times*

——◇ **MONDAY, MAY 4** ◇——

McGraw has sent an official protest to President Pulliam of Saturday's game on the claim that Umpire Emslie shouted "Foul!" on a strike by Devlin when he should have said "Strike!" The call of "Foul!" did without doubt cause Seymour, stealing second at the time, to slow up so that he merely ran into Knabe's arms "standing up."

Umpires are not called on to officiate as a general thing until the regular season begins. They have no preliminary training or exercise. They are heavy and logy physically and mentally. The players, on the contrary, by a month or six weeks' training in the South, are full of life, snap and ginger, and I don't blame them for getting hot, sore and mad to have well-made schemes go astray by slow thinking, slow moving umps.

An umpire can outlive his usefulness just as a player can, and the sooner Presidents {Ban} Johnson and Pulliam appreciate this the better off the national game will be.

Spring has "came" and something ought to be "did."

—Sam Crane, New York *Evening Journal*

—————— NATIONAL LEAGUE STANDINGS ——————

	W	L	PCT.	GB		W	L	PCT.	GB
Chicago	11	3	.786	—	Boston	8	8	.500	4
Pittsburgh ...	8	4	.667	2	Brooklyn	7	9	.437	5
New York ...	8	7	.533	3½	Cincinnati	5	7	.417	5
Philadelphia .	8	7	.533	3½	St. Louis	3	13	.188	9

——◇ **TUESDAY, MAY 5** ◇——

{On May 4, in New York, the Giants beat Philadelphia 12 to 2. Winning pitcher, Mathewson; losing pitcher, Sparks. Giants' standing: 9 wins, 7 losses, in third place.}

Well, sir, you should have been at the Polo Grounds yesterday, if you were not "among those present," for there was the finest piece of vivisection ever witnessed in a ball lot when the Giants suddenly got out the "big stick" and swatted the ball about with such continuity and vigor that they piled up an even dozen runs against the deuce the Murrayites scored in the last gasp of the game.

Mighty Mathewson appeared in the box for the home talent, bright-eyed and rosy as a flower of June, and his performance was of the high-grade kind which glistens with quality and comes only in five-pound boxes. He toyed with the sphere as a cat would with a ball of yarn, putting it where he pleased, and in the six innings in which he officiated he let the Quakers have three hits, but he presented these at such long intervals they were in no way associated with the two feeble runs made.

—New York *Herald*

Maybe Taft will get the Presidential nomination, and maybe Roosevelt will reconsider his rash declaration and do a little running himself. It is even possible that Yohn Yohnson, of Minnesota, will put some Scandinavian wallpaper in the East Room of the White House. But we don't care; we don't care. "Big Six" is his old grand self, and we're after the pennant.　　　　　—William F. Kirk, New York *American*

———◇ WEDNESDAY, MAY 6 ◇———

{In New York, the Giants beat Philadelphia 4 to 0. Winning pitcher, Wiltse; losing pitcher, Richie. Giants' standing: 10 wins, 7 losses, in third place.}

For the first time this season the whitewash banner was flung to the breeze of the Polo Grounds, George Wiltse hoisting it at the expense of the Phillies. New York played a brilliant defensive game behind their left-handed flinger and Bridwell and Tenney, by spectacular plays, boosted Boston as a place to learn how to field.

There was nothing quiet or pastoral about this last battle between representatives of the Empire and Keystone States, Manager McGraw and Captain Donlin being fired from the coaching lines for violating the Pulliam code and {Phillie catcher Charles "Red"} Dooin for informing Bob Emslie he was blind.　　　　　—New York *Press*

Now we will have what we have been looking for since snow flurry times, when that famous deal was made whereby the Giants were immeasurably strengthened by the accumulation of Tenney, Bridwell and Needham.

Yes, the Giants and Boston will meet this afternoon for the first time in Manhattan since the shift was made that caused that friction in the Hub between McGraw and McGann.

It goes without saying that the rivalry occasioned will make the hot series just finished with the Phillies look like a lawn tennis match with a pink tea climax.　　　　　—Sam Crane, New York *Evening Journal*

———◇ **THURSDAY, MAY 7** ◇———

There was no game yesterday at the Polo Grounds because rain interfered. "Old Jupe" and the grouchy weather man combined and made an enemy of every fan in Manhattan.

The fans were dead sore, and they had a right to be. Here was a series they had talked about all Winter and gloated over, only to be side-tracked by the aerial sponge squeezer who apparently doesn't know a base hit from an error.　　　　—Sam Crane, New York *Evening Journal*

I predicted several weeks ago that the Giants would finish sixth. Now I'll say they have an excellent chance to wind up in seventh place, if not in the tail-end division!　　　　　—Joe Vila, *The Sporting News*

PITTSBURGH, May 6—Making the claim that the Pittsburgh club had raised its third-base line illegally, to the detriment of visiting hitters, the Chicago team registered a vicious kick during and after the game today.

The raising of the line was so palpable that bunts toward third base could hardly remain on the diamond, and several times Chicago players were worsted by this. The Pittsburgh club admits the third-base line is higher, but says this was done for draining.

After the game Umpire O'Day asked Secretary Locke of the Pittsburgh club: "Will you fix the diamond to conform with National League rules or must I report to President Pulliam by wire?"

"We will fix the diamond," said Locke.

—New York *American*

———◇ FRIDAY, MAY 8 ◇———

The new unglossed baseball cover does not seem to bear out predictions that it would knock spit-ball pitching. All the saliva artists seem as adept with this style of delivery as usual. Chesbro has experienced no difficulty, and big Ed Walsh, of the White Sox, seems better than ever. {Walsh would have his best season in 1908, with 39 victories.}

—New York *American*

———◇ SATURDAY, MAY 9 ◇———

{On May 8, in New York, the Giants' third straight game with Boston was postponed because of rain.}

CHICAGO, May 2—An agent of the pitching machine in use at Yale and Harvard for several seasons took his brass howitzer to the park yesterday morning and fired off its repertoire for the Cubs to hit at. The thing resembles a cannon mounted on a wooden frame and does everything but chew tobacco, soil new balls and kick at the umpire. Compressed air shoots the ball at the batsman fast or slow, high or low, and applies the in and out curve, the fadeaway, and the raise curve, the gravity drop, smoke ball, grape vine sinker, and fooler. The addition of a metal gland of the breech containing a wad of loose chewing gum would enable the machine to throw the spit ball, it is said.   —*Sporting Life*

———◇ SUNDAY, MAY 10 ◇———

{On May 9, in New York, the Giants beat Boston 7 to 3. Winning pitcher, Mathewson; losing pitcher, Young. Giants standing: 11 wins, 7 losses, in third place.}

Old playmates mingled on the rain-soaked grass of the Polo Ground yesterday afternoon, and the present Giants beat the old Giants and beat them handsomely. Beat them with their pitcher, par excellence, "Young Cy" Young in the box; yes; more than that, knocked him out of the box. {"Young Cy" Young was Irving Young and should not be confused with the legendary Denton "Cy" Young, who in 1908 pitched for the Boston Red Sox in his nineteenth major league season.}

Two runs were made off the great Mathewson, the terror of the baseball world, in the first inning, and those with little faith groaned inwardly or prepared to revile the Giants outwardly because they felt they might be deprived of their mess of pottage by being present when Mathewson lost his first game in 1908. But Mathewson did not lose.

—New York Herald

◇ MONDAY, MAY 11 ◇

The Giants started West yesterday for the first long trip away from home, and will open at Pittsburgh today. The games this week mark the first clash between Eastern and Western clubs, and they are important as furnishing an opportunity to judge where the chief strength lies. This Western trip will go a long way toward settling how close the fight in the National League will be this year.   —New York Tribune

NATIONAL LEAGUE STANDINGS

	W	L	PCT.	GB		W	L	PCT.	GB
Chicago	13	5	.722	—	Philadelphia	10	9	.536	3½
Pittsburgh	10	6	.625	2	Cincinnati	6	10	.375	6
New York	11	7	.611	2	Brooklyn	7	13	.350	7
Boston	10	9	.536	3½	St. Louis	6	14	.300	8

◇ TUESDAY, MAY 12 ◇

{On May 11, in Pittsburgh, the Giants lost 5 to 2. Winning pitcher, Leever; losing pitcher, McGinnity. Giants' standing: 11 wins, 8 losses, in third place.}

The Giants came, they saw, they clouted and were vanquished 5 to 2.

Captain Clarke and his clever cohorts outguessed the McGraw maulers and landed a close-cut victory. In order to accomplish this highly commendable and fan-pleasing result they had to play the best kind of baseball they had in stock.

While the score was officially 5 to 2 in favor of Pittsburgh, a rooter with a red face and a Seed plate in his eyeglass pretty nearly called the turn as he made his way from the grandstand at the conclusion of the contest. "It was 5 to 2 in favor of Hans Wagner," he put it, and all within hearing applauded the sentiment.

Hans Wagner was pretty much the whole works, anvil, boiler shop and all.

In the field he played perfectly, at bat he drove spikes into the fond hopes of one J. McGraw, while on the bases he cut cute and game-winning capers.

In the second inning Wagner looked so dangerous McGinnity passed him down the deadhead route. Abby {Abbaticchio, a.k.a. Battey} accidentally tapped the ball along the first-base line where it was recovered by the astute Monsieur Tenney for an out, which placed Wagner on second. {Harry} Swacina next bounded the ball to the diligent Doyle, who made a low throw to Tenney. Wagner said farewell to second, hiking for third as fast as his parenthetical pins would carry him. Noting that the ball had escaped Tenney's grasp Hans kept on toward the plate, which he reached by a great slide. It is doubtful if any other player could have scored from second on such a play; few base runners would have taken such a chance, but Wagner is ever ready to take advantage of an opening.

No more runs were made until the sixth, when, with two out, Clarke held a brief conference with himself and decreed that it was time to be up and doing, and he promptly uped and dooed.

With a swish of his sphered spanker Fred sent a triple to right. Again did McGinnity discover a devilish gleam in the Wagnerian orbs and purposely sent Hans down over the fourball highway.

And the doughty German again showed his right to be classed as the great and only. Instead of trying the time-honored double steal Wagner and Clarke sprang a new one on the Giants, standing the latter completely on their heads.

Naturally the Giants expected Hans to break for second on a pitched ball. Instead, the big Teuton waited until Bresnahan had just returned the bulb to McGinnity, when, with head down and legs spread like this ( ), he started for second. McGinnity, taken completely by surprise by the boldness and suddenness of the action, heaved the ball to second. Wagner continued his wild dash until within a few feet of Doyle, when he suddenly turned and hastened back toward first, never letting up in his speed. The ball was thrown to Tenney, who awaited the arrival of the Flying Dutchman. When within a yard of the Giant first-sacker Wagner wheeled and scudded back over the route to second. Tenney started to give chase, but seeing that Clarke had started for the plate turned and threw to Bresnahan. The latter got the ball all right, but the Pirate chieftain, by a cleverly manipulated bit of contortion, evaded the touch and slid over the plate in safety, while Wagner smiled from his perch on second.

That play alone was worth the price of admission.

—C. B. Power, Pittsburgh *Dispatch*

——◇ WEDNESDAY, MAY 13 ◇——

{On May 12, in Pittsburgh, the Giants won 8 to 2. Winning pitcher, Wiltse; losing pitcher, Maddox. Giants' standing: 12 wins, 8 losses, in third place.}

Muggsy McGraw's Giants gave the Pirates an 8 to 2 slap in the face yesterday. George Wiltse had the knack of slanting them over so that Smoketown swatters turned them into unsafe territory, while Nick Maddox could not overcome his wildness during the four innings he lasted.

Hans Wagner twisted his foot in the fourth inning of Monday's game, and the injury made it necessary for him to remain out of the contest, and the absence of the German seemed to dishearten his teammates. —Pittsburgh *Post*

——◇ THURSDAY, MAY 14 ◇——

{On May 13, in Pittsburgh, the Giants lost 5 to 1. Winning pitcher, Camnitz; losing pitcher, Mathewson. Giants' standing: 12 wins, 9 losses, in third place.}

Christy Mathewson was clouted from the slab in the fifth inning at Exposition Park yesterday, while Howard Camnitz held the hard-hitting New Yorkers powerless until they were hopelessly trounced. Crandall, the Cedar Rapids twirler, finished for the Giants, and was more effective than Mathewson, but it was too late. It was the fastest game here this season, played in only an hour and 25 minutes. It was Mathewson's first defeat of the year. —Pittsburgh *Post*

Business Manager Frank Bancroft and members of the Cincinnati team are apprehensive that the doors of the Boston hotel where they have been stopping for several seasons may be closed to them this year as a result of the fight in that fashionable hostelry between McGraw and McGann. The incident may lead to the eviction of well-behaved as well as rowdy players. The spirit of rowdyism with which McGraw has imbued the Giants bids fair to live as long as do the men whom he taught to bulldoze umpires and behave like Bowery roughs, on and off the diamond. For several years the New York club has done more to lower the position of professional ball players than all other major league teams put together. No matter how well other clubs comport themselves, all players are classed with the Giants.

—Cincinnati *Post*, quoted in *The Sporting News*

————◇ **SATURDAY, MAY 16** ◇————

{On May 15, in Cincinnati, the Giants won 9 to 2. Winning pitcher, Taylor; losing pitcher, Campbell. Giants' standing: 13 wins, 9 losses, in third place.}

One fearful round, in which a vast amount of bad baseball was displayed, robbed the Reds of the first game of the New York series at League Park. For seven innings our boys played sterling ball behind the accurate and skillful pitching of William Campbell. Only two hits had been peeled off by Giant sluggers, and Cy Seymour, who doubled with two down in the seventh, was the only member of the New York crew to see second base up to that time. The Reds had a run to go on, and it was simply a question of retiring six more Giants and then making a dash for the dinner table. But McGraw's men are great finishers, and a lead of one run was never known to frighten them into hysterics.

Our noble athletes were suddenly seized with an attack of the wobbles. The strain of the close contest, the eager anxiety of the multitude in the stands and the fearlessness of McGraw and his men in their continuous conversation with that dignified official, Mr. Hank O'Day, worked on the nerves of the Red youngsters. It was a fine day for a balloon ascension, and the boys put one on exhibition.

Arthur Devlin opened the eighth with a lucky bounding hit over second base, of which {Miller} Huggins made a brilliant stop but could not quite get the ball to first in time. Then Campbell, steady Bill, gave his only base on balls to Nicklin, formerly Strang. Next was a fumble of Bridwell's bunt by Billy Campbell, and before the inning ended there had been six hits, five errors, a base on balls, good for nine tallies.

—Jack Ryder, Cincinnati *Enquirer*

CINCINNATI, May 16—You can never tell, as Bernard Shaw would say, just what that John McGraw person will spring next. When the Reds were seeing pinwheels, roman candles, spit-devils and other fireworks, a la the Fourth of July, the little Celt pulled an entirely new stunt on the dazed 4,000 witnessing the ruthless treatment of their pets.

McGraw began his assault by yanking Dummy Taylor off the batting order and substituting Merkle. Naturally it was expected that if Merkle had another chance to bat in this eighth round, he would be allowed to try it again. That's where McGraw sprung his new stunt.

Instead of sending Merkle to bat a second time, he sent Herzog to bat for him, thus establishing a precedent of having a man who had batted for another man having a man bat for him, making the {box} score read "Merkle batted for Taylor in the eighth. Herzog batted for Merkle in the eighth."   —Sid Mercer, New York *Globe*

———◇ **SUNDAY, MAY 17** ◇———

{On May 16, in Cincinnati, the Giants lost 3 to 1. Winning pitcher, Coakley; losing pitcher, Mathewson. The Giants' standing: 13 wins, 10 losses, in fourth place.}

Christopher Mathewson had plenty of time to play his favorite game of checkers yesterday. {Mathewson was probably baseball's best checkers player.} There were the long hours of the morning, the beautiful moonlit evening, and all but a very few moments of the glorious afternoon. Matty had been expecting to stay at the ball yard from lunchtime until the dinner gong sounded its raucous but pleasant tone, but he was not detained so long. The kind Reds, knowing his earnest love for the checker board, refused to keep him away from his pleasant pastime. Owing to their thoughtfulness, the great pitcher was at liberty after the second round of the Saturday show. He left the yard without saying "Thank you," and did not seem highly delighted at the hospitality of our boys. But great men are not always grateful. It did not take many hits to give Matty his freedom, for the Reds secured only two singles off the famous artist. These two, however, were peacherinos, and they were mixed with two errors and a base on balls, a combination which gave the Reds three runs right off the reel. Though our boys were not getting a very large number safe, they were feeling Matty so freely that Manager McGraw, always a quick shifter, yanked him at once, and substituted Leon Ames. The change killed off the Reds, who were unable to do anything with the auburn-topped athlete, nor with Young Crandall, who pitched the last inning, after Ames had been taken out to let Herzog bat for him. Lucky that Matty started this one. Dr. A. J. Coakley worked for the Reds with great effect. The heavy-hitting Giants just couldn't get them safe off the eminent dentist's tony pitching.

—Jack Ryder, Cincinnati *Enquirer*

————◇ **MONDAY, MAY 18** ◇————

{On May 17, in Cincinnati, the Giants lost 7 to 2. Winning pitcher, Weimer; losing pitcher, Wiltse. Giants' standing: 13 wins, 11 losses, in fourth place.}

Tales of great feats of old-time ball players, who were always performing marvelous stunts in the last half of the ninth inning, were blotted from the memories of several thousand enthusiasts at League Park yesterday, when big John Ganzel, with the bases clogged and the contest nearly over, leaned heavily on one of George Wiltse's offerings and laced a lovely homer to the left-field corner. The tender footsies of {Johnny} Kane, {Hans} Lobert and {Mike} Mitchell pressed the pan in rapid succession, followed by the Captain's generous hoof, hot from its fast trip around the sacks. Ganzel's great drive cinched a victory that had already been won by the nervy batting of his predecessors in the line-up, but it was no less creditable for that. A man who can crack out such a hit, with the bases full, is entitled to all the candy, cigars, booze, household goods and other paraphernalia that comes to the four-base hitter on the home lot. Mr. McGraw was so rattled he forgot to take Mr. Wiltse out of the box. —Jack Ryder, Cincinnati *Enquirer*

A number of thoughtful women removed their expensive millinery creations during the game, gaining the gratitude of many spectators. At a ball game you can tell whether a woman is a real lady or just a plain female by noting whether she has her hat on or not.

—Jack Ryder, Cincinnati *Enquirer*

NATIONAL LEAGUE STANDINGS

	W	L	PCT.	GB		W	L	PCT.	GB
Chicago	15	7	.682	—	Boston	13	13	.500	4
Philadelphia	13	9	.591	2	Cincinnati	11	12	.478	4½
Pittsburgh	12	9	.571	2½	St. Louis	10	17	.370	7½
New York	13	11	.542	3	Brooklyn	9	18	.333	8½

◇ TUESDAY, MAY 19 ◇

{On May 18, in Cincinnati, the Giants lost 9 to 5. Winning pitcher, Spade; losing pitcher, Mathewson. The Giants' standing: 13 wins, 12 losses, in fourth place.}

Oh, you Reds! Oh, you Giants! Oh, you Matty! Especially, oh, you Matty! The great Giant twirler, by many judges still ranked the ablest twirler in the business, went in against the Reds yesterday for the second time in the series, and for the second time was knocked sky-high and forced to retire before a bountiful bevy of beautiful bingles {base hits}. Matty plays a grand game of checkers. The Reds are stronger at poker, bridge, whist and baseball. If Christy could inveigle Bob Spade into a bloody combat on the checkerboard he would probably whale the everlasting tar out of the Atlanta recruit. But checkers is too rough a game to be allowed in the refined atmosphere of League Park, where baseball has the call. So Spade confined his attention to the national sport yesterday and made the great Matty look like a sucker.

—Jack Ryder, Cincinnati *Enquirer*

———◇ **WEDNESDAY, MAY 20** ◇———

ST. LOUIS, May 20—The Giants escaped from a mass of rumors in Cincinnati last night, and landed here early this morning.

Among the prominent rumors squashed was one that Mike Donlin had fallen off the water wagon with a dull thud. Donlin has lots of friends in Cincinnati {where he played in 1902–1904}, and he did not lack for invitations to dally with the flowing bowl. But he waved them all away and accepted distilled water and cigars instead. However, that did not prevent the rumormongers from circulating a story that Capt. Mike was pickled Monday night.

Cincinnati is a great town for rumors, but McGraw is harboring no boozers, the Giants are a splendidly behaved bunch, and their losing streak cannot be charged to dissipation.

—Sid Mercer, New York *Globe*

{The rumors concerning Donlin are not surprising. Consider the following quotation from an editorial in *The Sporting News* on March 22, 1902, when Donlin was a member of the Baltimore Orioles.}

"In Baltimore last Thursday {March 13} Mike Donlin assaulted an innocent, modest young lady on the street, cutting her face badly. On Saturday night he was arrested in Washington with two other thugs for assaulting a streetcar conductor. He was immediately taken to Baltimore to stand trial for the first offense. When arraigned in court for striking

Miss Minnie Fields, an actress, and Ernest Clayton, her escort, Donlin pleaded guilty and said that as he was drunk at the time he didn't know what he was doing. Miss Fields told of the assault, showed her bruised and blackened face, and said the blow felled her to the ground and rendered her unconscious. Clayton's blackened eyes were also in evidence as to the weight of the ruffian's fists. Judge Ritchie sentenced Donlin to six months in jail and a fine of $250." {Donlin served five months in the Baltimore city jail and was released on August 20, when he joined the Cincinnati club.}

—————◊ **THURSDAY, MAY 21** ◊—————

{On May 20, in St. Louis, the Giants lost 1 to 0. Winning pitcher, Raymond; losing pitcher, McGinnity. Giants' standing: 13 wins, 13 losses, tied with Boston for fifth place.}

When Manager John McGraw strayed out to Springfield, Ill., to pick a peach from the Three-Eye {minor league} baseball orchard, he evidently took a bridle path instead of the highway, and wound up in a lemon grove. He is reported to have paid something like $4,000 for the privilege of plucking a particular fruit named Doyle, and he thought he was just taking advantage of a "rube" management.

Since that time doubts as to the character of his purchase have arisen in his mind. Mr. Doyle has been analyzed, assayed, dissected and microscopically scrutinized to the end that the peach part of him is entirely absent.

In fact, even to the naked eye Mr. Doyle's appearance at League Park yesterday was positively citric. He contributed a bunch of fat-headed work that would drive a real manager like McGraw to the woods to think it over.

In the opening round, with one down, {Raymond "Chappy"} Charles hit to Doyle, and the latter played imaginary cup-and-ball for a time sufficient for Charles to get his base. A base on balls and a scant single threatened to bring home a tally, but McGinnity stiffened and retired the side.

In the second Doyle shone. {Bill} Ludwig smashed a two-bagger down the third-base line and was sacrificed to third by {Billy} Gilbert. {Arthur "Bugs"} Raymond then hit an easy bounder to Doyle, who promptly mutilated the play, which was the easy retirement of Ludwig at the plate. Instead, he did an act of prestidigitation, following which he tossed the runner out at first. He escaped an error, but he cost the game.

One more count before we are through with the gentleman. He not only lost the game, but lost a chance to win it. In the second inning Seymour led off with a safety to left. Needham flied and Devlin put him on second with an infield out. Seymour kept up the good work by stealing third as Doyle walked. Then a double steal was started and {catcher} Ludwig hurried the ball down to {second baseman} Gilbert, hoping to get Seymour on a quick return to the plate. This would have happened and Seymour would probably have been safe with a tally, owing to a fine lead, had not Doyle kept pounding down to second, instead of halting and forcing the second baseman to make the throw home. But he kept right on and insisted that he be put out—and he was.

—John E. Wray, St. Louis *Post-Dispatch*

CINCINNATI, May 21—Members of the New York team predict that checkers will be the downfall of mighty Christy Mathewson if he does not curb his passion for the game. Just before leaving for St. Louis McGraw complained to one of the Reds that Matty's limited success in recent games was due to checkers.

"Matty has been besieged by checker players ever since we came on this trip," said he. "They come from far and near at all hours of the day and night to play with him, and he accommodates them all. If he doesn't cut it out he'll go to pieces as a pitcher." —New York *American*

◇ FRIDAY, MAY 22 ◇

{On May 21, in St. Louis, the Giants won 8 to 4. Winning pitcher, Crandall; losing pitcher, Karger. Giants' standing: 14 wins, 13 losses, in fourth place.}

Manager John McGraw may not need his well-advertised pitcher, Christy Mathewson, as badly as he supposed if a certain Mr. Crandall continues to pitch the kind of baseball that helped the Giants beat the locals yesterday.

Beginning in the second half of the fourth inning, this youngster twirled and the Cardinals were closed up like a jack-knife. But one single was made off Crandall.

"Dummy" Taylor is evidently not at his best, like McGinnity and Mathewson. The man responsible for the most unique signal code in baseball gave up two runs in the first inning. In the third, the Cardinals scored two more runs and "Dummy" was chased in favor of Crandall.

If "Dummy" never does another thing he will be worth doing in oil and hanging in the Brush mansion. Since his advent to the team {in 1900} it has become necessary for every member of the aggregation to acquire a working knowledge of how to talk with the hands. In a game Taylor's only method of communicating with his captain or manager has been through the mute's finger language, and so all his team members have become familiar with the employment of this means of communication.

Realizing the value of this in running his team, McGraw has had the men pay special attention to it until now all plays from the bench are described in digital terms.

It was for failure to follow signals thus delivered in the first Giants–St. Louis game here that Doyle was taken off the regular team at the outset of yesterday's game and replaced by Nicklin.

—St. Louis *Post-Dispatch*

———◇ **SATURDAY, MAY 23** ◇———

Not one umpire officiating in either big league is in the touch he ought to be with the fast style of the game now being played. The game has progressed so far and fast that the umpires have been left behind.

Now, in my opinion, umpires should be out in the Spring practicing just the same as the players. They should exercise down South, or somewhere else, to get the cobwebs off their think-tanks, as well as to limber up their anatomical departments. Ball players get charley horses of the

legs, but umpires can get the same charley horse in the head.
—Sam Crane, New York *Evening Journal*

President Murphy, of the Cubs, says he wouldn't protest a game, no matter what happened. Good for Murphy! There are protestors enough as it is. —*Sporting Life*

——◇ SUNDAY, MAY 24 ◇——

{On May 23, in St. Louis, the Giants lost a doubleheader 6 to 2 and 2 to 0. Winning pitchers, Lush and Sallee; losing pitchers, McGinnity and Wiltse. Giants' standing: 14 wins, 15 losses, in sixth place.}

The first game evoked the pathos of fans who have seen and known "Iron Man" McGinnity when he was at his best. McGinnity has not been himself these many days and this year has not been himself at all. Yesterday he was target for Cardinal batsmen who returned his delivery to all parts of the field in two innings, getting ten hits and scoring five runs. Malarkey, who succeeded him in the sixth, was invulnerable.

In the second contest three singles and a wild pitch by Wiltse gave up two runs in the first, after which neither team scored.
—John E. Wray, St. Louis *Post-Dispatch*

——◇ MONDAY, MAY 25 ◇——

{On May 24, in Chicago, the Giants won 6 to 4. Winning pitcher, Taylor; losing pitcher, Fraser. Giants' standing: 15 wins, 15 losses, in fifth place.}

There is nothing more exciting than a ninth-inning batting rally when a club is way behind—a rally that snatches victory out of the fire, or comes so near it that the multitude has an excuse for going crazy. The finish of yesterday's game, bitter as was the final disappointment, drove the populace dotty, and men who haven't yelled in years split the ether with uncouth sounds and waving arms.

The first half of the ninth was exciting enough, for Roger Bresnahan poled out a smite that went far down the lea, and Roger made four bases by terrific sprinting. This feat caused the populace to arise and prepare to go home.

The exits were jammed when {Harry} Steinfeldt drew four balls. Then {Jimmy} Slagle awaited one, and hundreds, going forth, stayed their steps and strove to return. {Johnny} Kling walked; the sacks were full.

Joe Tinker could have done great things. He hoisted a pop foul for Bresnahan. Del Howard batted for {Chick} Fraser, got a ticket, and a run was forced in. At this juncture McGraw, who seemed to be gradually getting interested in the game, yanked Taylor and sent in Joe McGinnity. The Iron Man had zinc in his curves and {Johnny} Evers hit one. It rose and came right down in Shannon's hands, but just as the ball arrived Shannon thoughtfully turned his back and fled. The sun had blinded him and he feared that the ball would fall on the vacuum that terminated his neck.

Two runs in, bases still full, one gone. {Jimmy} Sheckard worried McGinnity for a pass, and in came another run. Bases still full; a hit would tie, a long drive would win. Ah, look who's here, handsome Frank Schulte! The game will surely terminate as soon as he wallops the pill. Frank hit—and raised a little fly that Donlin grasped with a cruel leer. All up to Chance. On the Heap Big Bear depended the fortunes of the afternoon. Bing. Plunk, and the grotesque apparition in centerfield had it clinched tighter than an oil king's grip upon a dollar.

Aside from the great rally and Bresnahan's homer, the feature of the day was {right-fielder} Schulte's work in the eighth, when he performed the hitherto unheard-of feat of hurling out two men at the plate in a single session. It was a wonderful thing and not likely to happen again in twenty years. —W. A. Phelon, Chicago *Journal*

NATIONAL LEAGUE STANDINGS

	W	L	PCT.	GB		W	L	PCT.	GB
Chicago	18	9	.667	—	New York	15	15	.500	4½
Philadelphia	15	13	.536	3½	Boston	15	16	.484	5
Pittsburgh	13	12	.520	4	Brooklyn	13	18	.419	7
Cincinnati	15	14	.517	4	St. Louis	13	20	.394	8

——◇ TUESDAY, MAY 26 ◇——

{On May 25, in Chicago, the Giants lost, in 10 innings, 8 to 7. Winning pitcher, Brown; losing pitcher, Wiltse. Giants' standing: 15 wins, 16 losses, in fifth place.}

There have been ball games and them some, but such a game as yesterday's struggle doesn't often happen. Exciting? Beyond the limit of deliriums. Ten innings of the wildest, fiercest battling; five pitchers beaten to a lemon meringue; batting and fielding feats of every variety, and the right people winning just as darkness settled down—how could you tie that combination?

C. Mathewson, who is very handsome, assayed to pitch at the kickoff, and the Cubs warmed to him as if he were homelier than a mud fence. A young man named Malarkey, who has a swinging in-shoot as his chief stock in trade, came next and did well—for a while. Then the hits seemed to rise right out of the ground all about him, and he retreated in great confusion. Long Wiltse followed, and all was going nicely with him, when a black bat, wielded by a black-haired man, batted a black ball into the black dark, and put black scowls all over Muggsy's countenance.

{Jack} Pfiester tried to fool the Giants, but they batted him to a lamb stew in short order. Brown took up the burden, and got slammed plenty, but pulled it through just the same. The umpiring was hideous. Both teams were well soaked, umpirical errors being pretty evenly divided. To hear Chance tell it, New York was given six runs, and the Cubs had nine taken away from them. According to McGraw, the Cubs were presented with seven tallies, and New York was robbed of nineteen.

The grand razoo came in the tenth. New York had been retired runless, and Slagle came up. Wiltse wove them over, but some went askew. The ump said Slagle walked. The Giants said he fanned, but it is what the ump says that goes on the score sheet. {Pat} Moran laid down a bunt, and having done his duty, went back to the bench walking on air.

Joe Tinker had the one great chance, and took it. He stood swinging the bat, when an agonized voice piped down from the stand: "Hit it, you pigeon-toed orang-outang!" The ball was black and the sky was blacker. To use the words of a long-haired poet making pretty verses in section D, "Night cast a sable seal upon the darkling field." At this moment Joe hit it, and Cy Seymour saw something go over, past, and beyond. The ball is alleged to be going yet, but this is probably an exaggeration.

—W. A. Phelon, Chicago *Journal*

Manager McGraw watched most of yesterday's game from the clubhouse. He was chased by Umpire Emslie in the second inning, because, after a heated argument with Blond Robert, he turned to the crowd and begged someone to send out a hairpin to Emslie for his wig. As the umpire is given to the toupee habit, the shaft struck home and he banished McGraw instanter.

—New York *American*

When Moran was passed in the third after Slagle had fouled, McGinnity ran from the bench and claimed an out on the ground that Moran was batting in Tinker's place. Emslie pulled out his score card and showed that Pat was batting in his own place. As a matter of fact, Tinker batted in Pat's place in the first inning and Pat in Tinker's place in the second, and if the Giants had noticed it they could have prevented those three Cub runs, but the rule is not retroactive. The opposing team loses the right to claim an out when the pitcher delivers a ball to the succeeding batsman.

—I. E. Sanborn, Chicago *Tribune*

———◇ WEDNESDAY, MAY 27 ◇———

{On May 26, in Chicago, the Giants won 7 to 4. Winning pitcher, Crandall; losing pitcher, Reulbach. Giants' standing: 16 wins, 16 losses, in fifth place.}

You can talk till the silver moon gets a copper lining about the beauties of scientific ball and the pretty features of 2 to 1 games, but if the crowd gets a chance to express itself, it will rise up and yell for games where home runs skip down the lea and two-baggers rake their way amid sylvan lanes. There is something enchanting about the music of a long, hard drive.

Action, energy and uproar—that's what a crowd wants in every branch of sport, and in baseball most of all. That is why the three New York games at Cub park have been feasts of joy to the beholders, and why the attendance yesterday was the largest any Tuesday has seen in the old grounds for many and many a year.

It was the most joyful slugging bee anyone could want. The Cubs and Giants walked up, shook heavy bats at the pitchers, and then jammed the sphere athwart the muzzle. The managers refused to rescue the suffering slabmen, and Reulbach and Crandall had to stand on the slab and take it all. They liked it too. Liked it the way a man does when he is being scalped. Between whiles they punctured the batsmen, just to get even.

After Reulbach had hit four of the enemy, it got so that he couldn't throw within two feet of a batter without having the man threaten to lick him and assert that it was a direct attempt at murder.

During the hot, tempestuous afternoon Tinker, Tenney, and Seymour all drove home runs down the yard and circled the sacks amid delirious approval. It was a gleeful day of mighty hitting, but the Giants hit the harder.　　　　　　　　　　　　　—W. A. Phelon, Chicago *Journal*

———◇ THURSDAY, MAY 28 ◇———

{On May 27, in Chicago, the Giants won 1 to 0. Winning pitcher, Wiltse; losing pitcher, Pfiester. Giants' standing: 17 wins, 16 losses, in fifth place.}

Neither Cubs nor Giants had much swat left in their systems after their batting jamboree of the previous three days, and they hooked up in an airtight game in which New York scratched a 1 to 0 victory.

Wiltse accomplished what fans beg every pitcher to do when he comes to bat with the score against him. George won his own game literally, for he held the Cubs to three hits and batted home the only run in the seventh round. A dizzling double between {third baseman} Steinfeldt and his base was the instrument with which Wiltse hooked the victory.

The Cubs hammered Wiltse much harder than the Giants did Pfiester, but the Giants performed some circus stunts behind their hurler. Little Herzog, just out of the minor incubator, was prominent in some of the plays which killed Chicago runs and behaved so feloniously in the way of stealing hits that he had the rooters applauding his every turn. Bridwell was not there to see his sub perform, as he was on his way to New York to shake the malaria acquired in St. Louis. If Herzog can hold that gait for any distance, Bridwell can have all the malaria he wants and McGraw won't turn a hair about it. —I. E. Sanborn, Chicago *Tribune*

CLEVELAND, May 28—The Giants en route to an exhibition game in Buffalo. The team has braced up wonderfully since leaving St. Louis, but the loss of Bresnahan {who was injured in Monday's game} will be a serious handicap. The big catcher had his sore finger placed under an "X" ray machine Tuesday, and it was discovered that one of the small bones was fractured. Bresnahan's physician thinks that Roger will not catch for at least two weeks.

The one mystifying feature of the trip just ended is Mathewson's loss of form. He showed nothing, and got his bumps in all four Western cities.

The series gave some youngsters a chance to make good. Charley Herzog has more than fulfilled predictions made about him this Spring. Malarkey and Crandall proved their right to be seriously considered as regular pitchers, and Larry Doyle came out of the trance that almost lost him his job. —Sid Mercer, New York *Globe*

"It's hitting that wins," said John McGraw yesterday. "They say the White Sox won a flag {in 1906} without hitting, but I know better. Their grounds prevent anyone from hitting heavily, and as they played 77 games there, it made their averages look very small. On the road they hit as hard as anybody. {Known as the Hitless Wonders, the 1906 world's champion Chicago White Sox had a team batting average that was the lowest in its league and second lowest in the majors.}

"Have you noticed how much Mike Donlin improves our lineup? He is hitting as he always did and Mike is one of the greatest natural batsmen of the business. He can slam left- and right-handed pitchers the same way, and I don't see any deterioration in his fielding or his base running.

"Shannon is beginning to hit and Devlin is bound to come back stronger. That will give us the best batting outfit in the league, and if we can find one more pitcher how are you going to hold us?"

—Chicago *Journal*

Poor McGraw! His lot will indeed be sad if the peerless Mathewson blows up, for Christy is the only real pitcher on his staff. McGinnity is a has-been, Ames a never-was because of inordinate wildness, Luther {Taylor} a mediocre man and Wiltse a fair southpaw. Crandall has done well, but McGraw hasn't shown real confidence in him. The Giants' other new twirlers don't amount to much.

—Ralph Davis, *The Sporting News*

The Giants? Well, I said "about the seventh" for them, didn't I? Well, how about the tail end? Drubbed by Cincinnati and St. Louis, McGraw's misfits look pretty small now. The once great Matty is a "soft mark." The supposed sluggers cannot hit a pumpkin, while McGraw has publicly pronounced Doyle a pinhead. Just as I told you, the Giants are outclassed simply because McGraw didn't get new and competent players when he had the chance.

—Joe Vila, *The Sporting News*

———◇ SATURDAY, MAY 30 ◇———

{On May 29, in Brooklyn, the Giants won 1 to 0. Winning pitcher, Mathewson; losing pitcher, Rucker. Giants' standing: 18 wins, 16 losses, in fourth place.}

Guess he was just holding back for bets, this Mathewson person. He drove into Brooklyn yesterday and unloaded the choicest collection of knockout drops dealt since Amos Rusie was doing a specialty.

"And they said he'd gone back," said Charley Ebbets, with tears in his eyes as big as rain checks.

"They say that about every great man," said James Corbett, who promenaded very prettily along the upper concourse. "I remember very well, myself, one time a guy got to me on a fluke, but when I had recovered—" {The former heavyweight boxing champion (1892–97), Corbett was an avid Giant fan.}

The only run came in the fourth as the result of some very hitful endeavors by our returned wanderers. Donlin hit clean to center, advanced on Seymour's sacrifice bunt, and when Needham banged out two bases, Donlin scored.

Donlin, two innings later, retired from activities. He had hit to {third baseman Tommy} Sheehan, who whipped it to first. Donlin allowed he was safe. Umpire {Frank} Rudderham spoke up in a still, small voice, saying this impression was erroneous. Over on the grounds at Highland Park or 155th street, Donlin might have used language, but in the peaceful stretches of Washington Park, he never forgot his bringing up. "Have you, by chance," he asked, "an acquaintance with Old Doctor Georgen, the oculist?"

"Such is not my good fortune," returned Mr. Rudderham, "why do you ask?"

"I should advise you to visit him," said Mr. Donlin. "Your eyesight appears defective."

"Possibly you are right," agreed Mr. Rudderham. "I cannot see you for the rest of the game."

Which is the Brooklyn equivalent for a benching.

—W. W. Aulick, New York *Times*

———◇ **SUNDAY, MAY 31** ◇———

{On May 30, in Brooklyn, the Giants won the first of two scheduled games, played in the morning, 5 to 0. Winning pitcher, McGinnity; losing pitcher, Pastorius. The scheduled afternoon game was postponed because of rain. Giants' standing: 18 wins, 15 losses, in third place.}

Over in Brooklyn they don't bet that the home team will win—they make book on how much the opposing forces will win by. This sport furnishes the only uncertainties of the entertainment. The answer yesterday was five.

The game was very fast. It had to be, for it was a match race with the rain, and the pair ran to a head for nine innings. Sheehan flied out to Shannon just on the stroke of noon and ended the engagement. Then the floods descended, and there wasn't an afternoon game, which meant an appreciable percentage loss to McGraw's pets, to say nothing of the sorrow represented by the failure to house a paying army in the grandstand.

—W. W. Aulick, New York *Times*

◇ MONDAY, JUNE 1 ◇

Boston, June 1—The Giants will be entitled to unusual credit if they win two of three games here. Several players are under the care of Dr. {James} Creamer, club physician. He is trying to drive malaria germs out of Bridwell's system and is prescribing for Leon Ames, ill in New York. Roger Bresnahan is here, but is not likely to catch as his bad finger is as stiff as a board.

Sammy Strang Nicklin will play the short field today. Herzog had to quit in Saturday's game. He played the day before against the advice of his physician, and in the Decoration Day game he suddenly became nauseated and was relieved by Nicklin. Herzog went home to Baltimore Saturday night and will remain there for a few days. Bridwell did not make the trip and is not expected to play until next Thursday.

Cy Seymour is on the job, but there is no telling when he will break down. Seymour is playing with a very obstinate "charley horse." Trainer Richards and Dr. Creamer have advised him to rest, but against his better judgment, Seymour is permitting his loyalty to the club to keep him in the game. —Sid Mercer, New York *Globe*

Once more we beg leave to repeat the old saying that Giants cannot beat left-handers. Rucker and Pastorius failed last Friday and Saturday and Pfiester lost twice in the Chicago series. The count is almost 2 to 1 against the port-flingers who have faced McGraw's men.

—Sid Mercer, New York *Globe*

NATIONAL LEAGUE STANDINGS

	W	L	PCT.	GB		W	L	PCT.	GB
Chicago	22	12	.647	—	Cincinnati	18	16	.529	4
Philadelphia	17	14	.548	3½	Boston	17	19	.472	6
New York	18	15	.545	3½	St. Louis	15	24	.385	9½
Pittsburgh	17	15	.531	4	Brooklyn	13	22	.371	9½

◇ TUESDAY, JUNE 2 ◇

{On June 1, in Boston, the Giants lost 4 to 0. Winning pitcher, Dorner; losing pitcher, Wiltse. Giants' standing: 18 wins, 16 losses, in fifth place.}

Gus Dorner was wild enough in the first half of the game yesterday to lose two games, but he gained the somewhat anomalous distinction of shutting out McGraw's so-called "Giants" 4 to 0.

New York had the bases full twice, in the first inning with none out and in the fourth with two gone, but could not score. Dorner held New York to three scattered hits, and while he had something good on the ball, he never would have applied the Kalsomine brush {"Kalsomine" is an alternate spelling for "calcimine," a whitewash. In baseball vernacular, to whitewash a team is to shut it out.} had not he received great support. He was so constantly in the hole on account of wildness that he had to "put them over," and the ball in consequence was hit very hard at times.

—Boston *Herald*

CINCINNATI, June 1—President {Garry} Herrmann and Manager Ganzel, of the Cincinnati Reds, began negotiations to secure Joe McGinnity, who has been placed on the market by the New York Giants.

—New York *Evening Journal*

◇ WEDNESDAY, JUNE 3 ◇

{On June 2, in Boston, the Giants lost 4 to 3. Winning pitcher, Flaherty; losing pitcher, Crandall. Giants' standing: 19 wins, 18 losses, in fifth place.}

BOSTON, June 3—Sammy Strang Nicklin has probably played his last game as a Giant. Nicklin performed in very poor style yesterday. He may have been trying as hard as he could, but it did not look that way. Sammy's inaccurate fielding cut a large gash in whatever chance the Giants had to win the game and McGraw was disgusted with him.

It is thought that McGinnity will quit the game. He has been a high-salaried man for years, and no club in either league is willing to take him and assume his present contract, which calls for something like $4,000 a season with a bonus of $1,000. Had it not been for this obstacle McGinnity could have been used in a trade, but wartime salaries are no longer in vogue. So waivers were asked on the pitcher who would have brought a small fortune not many seasons ago.

—Sid Mercer, New York *Globe*

———◇ THURSDAY, JUNE 4 ◇———

{On June 3, in Boston, the Giants won 3 to 0. Winning pitcher, Mathewson; losing pitcher, Young. Giants' standing: 20 wins, 18 losses, in fifth place.}

Christy Mathewson, better known as "Big Six" and the "Checker Champion" of Greater New York, pitched for the Giants, and for that reason the third game of the series did not result in a Boston victory. Matty was in great form. He allowed but three singles, fanned eleven batsmen and gave one pass. Two Boston players reached second, but not one got any farther.   —Boston *Herald*

After all the furor about Joe McGinnity, there is a large possibility that the "Iron Man" will not quit the Giants unless he does so of his own will. A shortage of effective pitchers at the Polo Grounds and McGinnity's recent work are the principal reasons why the original shift may not go through.

Incidentally there may be an inquiry into the publicity department of the Cincinnati club. That is where news of many National League deals leaks out. From Cincinnati came the announcement that New York had asked waivers on McGinnity. These things are supposed to be confidential.

Such a thing nearly always affects the work of a player, and the National Commission should provide a penalty for those who give out confidential matters.   —Sid Mercer, New York *Globe*

——◇ FRIDAY, JUNE 5 ◇——

{On June 4, in New York, the Giants lost to St. Louis 7 to 5. Winning pitcher, Sallee; losing pitcher, Taylor. Giants' standing: 20 wins, 19 losses, in fifth place.}

There was a ball game at the Polo Grounds yesterday, the first we have seen at the old park for many days. The sun shone brightly, a large crowd assembled, and the grass never looked greener. But the Gallant Giants were trimmed by Measly Missourians.

Mr. {Harry "Slim"} Sallee, pretty nigh as tall as those windmills we read about in the farm journals, did the flinging for the foreign fleet, and won. Luther Burbank Taylor, he of the quiet mouth and nimble fingers, worked for the home talent until replaced by Crandall along at the shank end of the game. It wasn't the mute's fault that he was yanked out of the contest. Had it not been for loose work back of him in the fatal eighth, Mr. Taylor might have beaten his foe. But he didn't, so why indulge in post-mortems?

Some things make delightful reading, and other things never should be put in print. The awful eighth is one of those other things:

{Bobby} Byrne singled. {John "Red"} Murray fanned. Spike Shannon dropped {Joe} Delahanty's long fly, Byrne scoring. {Ed} Konetchy hit to Devlin, who made an unusual heave, the ball going to the right-field bleachers, Delahanty scoring. {Art} Hostetter added to the gloom by singling and scoring Konetchy. {Joseph "Patsy"} O'Rourke made a Texas league two-bagger. Gilbert hit to Doyle, who tried without success to catch Hostetter at the plate. Four runs.

—William F. Kirk, New York *American*

Conversation on yesterday's game should be conducted with a clothespin adorning the nose. This is about the 'steenth game the Giants have tossed away this season. When they were champions they allowed the other teams to do this tossing act. The Cardinals once were obliging, but it is a terrible sight to see the Giants stealing the St. Louis "stuff," and on the Polo Grounds, too!

—Sid Mercer, New York *Globe*

———◇ SATURDAY, JUNE 6 ◇———

{On June 5, in New York, the Giants lost to St. Louis 4 to 2. Winning pitcher, Karger; losing pitcher, Wiltse. Giants' standing: 20 wins, 20 losses, in fifth place.}

"Rudderham," remarked the scholarly Master Donlin at the ninth stage of yesterday's performance, "is not an umpire. It is a verb. I recall very well on one occasion of my early youth, I was witness to the apprehension of two cut-purses on the public street, and I inquired for what these folks had been taken into custody. 'They are rudderhamers, Micky,' said my father, and I asked, then, 'What is a rudderhamer?' 'One who rudderhams, to be sure,' said my parent, briskly, and I have never forgotten his words."

Mr. Donlin then added more explicitly his views of Mr. Rudderham, and Mr. Rudderham snapped his fingers real hard and said to get off his ball ground. Mr. Donlin got, but not until he had walked right up to the umpire and given him an awful hard look. It must have taken a lot of courage to do this, because Mr. Donlin can't weigh more than 180, and Mr. Rudderham is almost a hundred-pounder. That is, counting his pad and everything.

A ninth-inning decision caused the excitement. Hostetter had gone out on Bridwell's fast run and admirable throw, and then O'Rourke batted one to Devlin, who made a wonderful stop and a quick throw to Tenney. Everybody said wasn't Devlin the grand third baseman entirely, and wasn't it nice to see 'em go fast-like, and then, "Safe!" calls this courageous Rudderham, and all baseball New York declares it's time for a justifiable murder.

Such demonstrations enliven the proceedings and take the critical mind off the final score. The Giants' bats seem on the bum, and eke the Giants' reason. For you don't win games by terrorizing a featherweight umpire. —W. W. Aulick, New York *Times*

When the heretofore despised St. Louis Cardinals can make the over-cocky Giants look worse than thirty cents there is surely something "rotten in Denmark."

In five innings yesterday the first Giant reached first base. Was he shoved along by the next batter? Not on your life. Not a Giant tried up-to-date baseball.

The Cardinals played teamwork yesterday and the Giants did not. The Cardinals have a team of hustling youngsters that are full of "good old ambish." I noticed that Billy Gilbert {the veteran Cardinal second baseman} had something to say all the time and wouldn't let a player fall asleep on the job for want of a little verbal prodding. But did the Giants open their mouths? If they did I failed to hear them. There is nothing like players shouting to one another. "Keep talking" has always been McGraw's idea, but Tenney, who has been a good popper-up fellow heretofore, has gone away down into his boots.

The Giants need a shaking up—there are no two ways about it. They cannot win unless they cut out their individual work and play for the team.   —Sam Crane, New York *Evening Journal*

No matter how the team slumps, Donlin keeps his hitting up to a standard. Donlin's hustling is the oasis in the desert of long deferred hopes of Polo Grounds fans. His aggressiveness and speed in running out hits is appreciated. On ground hits to infielders, Donlin is springing them out and sliding into first base. In this way he has registered hits that would have been outs had he loafed.

                              —Sid Mercer, New York *Globe*

The scarcity of good material for major league umpire staffs will make it necessary to change to the double-umpire system. With batting cut down to a minimum, the slightest error by an umpire often deprives a team of a victory. There is really too much for one man to watch in a ball game.   —*Sporting Life*

——◇ SUNDAY, JUNE 7 ◇——

{On June 6, in New York, the Giants defeated St. Louis 3 to 2. Winning pitcher, Mathewson; losing pitcher, Fromme. Giants' standing: 21 wins, 20 losses, in fifth place.}

The Giants experienced a change of heart and manner yesterday. With the inspiration of a big crowd {15,000} they played ball and won. They weren't inert as on the two preceding days. On the contrary they had partaken of pepper. The result was a snappy, well-played game. Mathewson pitched an evenly effective game, but the Cardinals gave him a stiff battle.

The eighth inning was bristling and critical. Gilbert bunted safely. Then Mathewson did something he rarely does. He passed two men in succession, {Bill} Ludwig and {Al} Shaw. Byrne flied to Seymour and Gilbert hotfooted it for the plate. Seymour's throw shot past Needham, and Gilbert scored. Had Ludwig been spry he too would have scored, but he lost time around third base. Mathewson had backed up cleverly and fielded the ball from Needham in time to catch Ludwig.

—New York *Sun*

——◇ MONDAY, JUNE 8 ◇——

Roger Bresnahan's return today ought to brace up the team, for when Roger works behind the bat there always seems to be more life and aggressiveness on the field. Tom Needham has done nobly in Bresnahan's place, and his timely hitting has helped win several games. His throwing has turned back base runners, but somehow Needham doesn't stir up the infield as Bresnahan does.

That vague thing known as baseball luck was with the Giants Saturday. Just as sure as Mr. Rudderham isn't a good umpire, the last two-bagger of Donlin's was at least a foot foul. This hit broke a tie and won the game. When Mathewson has to pitch one of his best games to get a 3-2 decision over St. Louis, and the Giants have to have all the luck to get the winning run, either the McGrawites are playing way below form or the Cardinals are a great team.

Mr. Rudderham was not so much to blame, however, as he was standing behind the pitcher's box with the sun shining in his eyes. The ball skimmered over the grass outside of third base, and Rudderham had to make a quick guess. He hesitated a moment and then took the cue from the coachers and started to follow Donlin around the bases. The umpire evened up in the eighth. Mathewson threw Shaw at least five strikes, but

Rudderham walked him and forced Gilbert around to third base, from where he scored on Byrne's sacrifice fly.

—Sid Mercer, New York *Globe*

──────── NATIONAL LEAGUE STANDINGS ────────

	W	L	PCT.	GB		W	L	PCT.	GB
Chicago	25	15	.625	—	New York ...	21	20	.512	4½
Cincinnati ...	23	17	.575	2	Boston	19	22	.463	6½
Pittsburgh ...	22	18	.550	3	St. Louis	19	27	.413	9
Philadelphia .	19	18	.514	4½	Brooklyn	15	26	.366	10½

──────◇ **TUESDAY, JUNE 9** ◇──────

{On June 8, in New York, the Giants defeated St. Louis 4 to 0. Winning pitcher, McGinnity; losing pitcher, Raymond. Giants' standing: 22 wins, 20 losses, in fourth place.}

The talk of Mr. McGinnity's projected release reached the ears of the Iron Man only yesterday, being somewhat delayed in transmission. "Oh, well," quoth this wondering marvel, "if they feel like that I'll give them something to release me for."

So he fanned seven scarlet socks and shut out St. Louis neat and systematic. If we don't want pitchers who practice this sort of specialty, now's our chance to make an advantageous deal. Who wants McGinnity? A neat dresser on and off, and we pay fares. Let's hear the bids.

—W. W. Aulick, New York *Times*

Manager Jawn McGraw made plenty of noise yesterday on the third-base coaching line. He yelped at {Cardinal pitcher} "Bugs" Raymond, he chided {manager John} McCloskey, he shrieked at the umpire, and he got away with it all. He got away with it because he has been reading *The Virginian* {Owen Wister's classic Western novel, published in 1902}, and every time he says anything to the umpire now he smiles. It's a good system.

—William F. Kirk, New York *American*

———◇ WEDNESDAY, JUNE 10 ◇———

{On June 9, in New York, the Giants defeated Pittsburgh 8 to 2. Winning pitcher, Crandall; losing pitcher, Camnitz. Giants' standing: 23 wins, 20 losses, in fourth place.}

A goodly crowd—10,000 or maybe more—made the pilgrimage to the ball lot at the end of the "L" {elevated train} and probably many were attracted by the one, only, and invincible Hans Wagner, whose prowess as a ballist is ringing over the nation.

But Hans suffered an eclipse practically total. He didn't knock seven or eight balls out of the premises, he didn't steal home from first base, nor did he, in fact, do anything to make Rome meow, let alone howl.

Instead, the gathering was treated to an old-time exhibition of baseball à la Giants—as they used to play it regularly in the misty past.

—New York *Herald*

Crandall sent up a lot of puzzling twisters, and it was hard for the Pirates to meet the ball solidly. He also cinched his own game by lifting the ball into the left-field seats in the fifth, with Devlin and Bridwell on base. —New York *Sun*

Samuel Strang Nicklin, who has served as utility player for the Giants for several years, was yesterday sold to the Baltimore club of the Eastern League. —New York *Times*

Some day it is to be hoped that baseball owners will enact a law placing fines on players who use profanity in public. Men in uniform have no right to insult patrons by careless language. How quickly a player would take the matter up if a spectator should heedlessly indulge in bad grammar and worse in the presence of the player's mother or sister. Chew gum and cut out the words in black letters.

—John B. Foster, New York *Evening Telegram*

———◇ **THURSDAY, JUNE 11** ◇———

{On June 10, in New York, the Giants lost to Pittsburgh 1 to 0. Winning pitcher, Leever; losing pitcher, Wiltse. Giants' standing: 23 wins, 21 losses, in fourth place.}

These Pittsburgh parties didn't terrorize us yesterday—they just out-speeded us a bit in the fourth inning and scratched in a run. These are the depressing details: Clarke hits past second. Then up comes Wagner, the extensively advertised shortstop. Mr. Wagner gives our tall young pitcher Wiltse such a hard look! Poor Wiltse quivers in every fiber. Cy Seymour, our charley-horsed centerfielder, moves to the fence limit, and wonders anxiously if this will be far enough. Mike Donlin edges out to the end of the bleachers. Everybody who hasn't had his breath bated before has it done now. And Wagner strikes out.

Pirates, eh?

The Pittsburgh second baseman, a gent with a serial name, called variously Abby and Battey {Abbaticchio}, goes out on a sacrifice. First baseman {Jim} Kane then drives the ball to Bridwell, who flops it to Tenney, not quite in time to nip the runner. Tenney slams it home, but Clarke is there ahead of it by a fraction of a second. If we had been a trifle fast and Clarke a trifle slow, our cherished plate would not have been passed.

—W. W. Aulick, New York *Times*

It isn't often that Hank O'Day is caught napping, but a young player just getting his "cup of coffee" in the league put one over on Hank and Mr. Klem yesterday.

Bresnahan hit a two-bagger down the left-field line. Klem {umpire at the plate} did not follow the runner as he squared around to note whether the ball went fair or foul. There being no play at first base, O'Day wheeled and moved toward second. With the attention of both arbitrators drawn away, {Jim} Kane mussed up Roger's sprint with a very palpable interference. Bresnahan stopped and stumbled, and then merely trotted down to second, not expecting that the incident had been overlooked. The ball beat him to the base by several feet, and he was touched out.

If two umpires are not enough to see all plays, why not hire a third umpire to sit in the grandstand and decide plays not covered by the other two? O'Day had no alternative but to call Bresnahan out as his back was turned to the interference. If Klem had seen it he should have so informed O'Day and in that case a reversal of the decision would have been proper. Perhaps Klem didn't see it. Many umpires will not disagree with a co-laborer even when they know he is making a wrong decision. Such dignity is unnecessary. The Giants did the only thing they could to get even. The few runners who got on first base after that trod on the toes of Mr. Kane. {This was Jim Kane's one moment of glory, for the 55 games in which he played for Pittsburgh in 1908 constituted his entire major league career.}

—Sid Mercer, New York *Globe*

In justice to Manager McGraw, I may say that he is not to blame for the rank treatment accorded "Iron Man" McGinnity. Just as McGinnity pitched a beautiful shut-out in Brooklyn, it became known that the club had asked waivers on him. At first McGraw came in for a roast because of this, but I soon learned on excellent authority that John T. Brush, with Andy Freedman behind him, was responsible for the strange move. {Andrew Freedman had preceded John Brush as president and principal owner of the Giants, and although he had sold his controlling interest late in 1902 he was still influential in club operations.} It seems that John and Andy have been trying to find a way to cut McGinnity's $5,000 salary ever since he was hurt at Waco. McGinnity has an iron-clad contract and has refused to accept a cut. So Brush decided to unload the famous pitcher, with the result that local fans are up in arms.

—William Rankin, *The Sporting News*

———◇ **FRIDAY, JUNE 12** ◇———

{On June 11, in New York, the Giants lost to Pittsburgh 5 to 2. Winning pitcher, Willis; losing pitcher, Mathewson. Giants' standing: 23 wins, 22 losses, in fifth place.}

It wasn't Matty's fault that he lost yesterday, any more than George Wiltse should be blamed for Wednesday's defeat. Both men pitched magnificent ball, and both went down to glorious defeat.

Old Honus Wagner was very much in evidence yesterday. The wonderful Teuton was everywhere, choking off sure hits and encouraging his comrades at any and all times when encouragement was needed. His huge bow legs carried him from third base to second base, and his large paws, the fingers of which seemed like tentacles of a devil fish, raked in everything that came within a mile of them. Oh, Honus, how could you do it?

—William F. Kirk, New York *American*

———◇ SATURDAY, JUNE 13 ◇———

{On June 12, in New York, the Giants lost to Pittsburgh 4 to 0. Winning pitcher, Maddox; losing pitcher, McGinnity. Giants' standing: 23 wins, 23 losses, tied for fourth place with Philadelphia.}

About 6,000 fans came to see the Giants win the final game of the series, and after the dust had lifted about 6,000 fans, accompanied by about 6,000 grouches, plodded wearily homeward.

To come down to cases, the Giants played like a lot of suffragettes. When the stern voice of duty called, with eager base runners on the bags, the local swatsmiths had their ears stuffed with cotton. More than once a good, clean single would have sent runs home, but the good clean single was not forthcoming.

To make a bad matter worse, Roger Bresnahan sprained an ankle in the second inning, and was carried from the grounds.

The accident to Bresnahan is a calamity indeed. Needham is a good, steady catcher, but he cannot infuse ginger into the local lads with anything like the skill shown by Bresnahan, and if there's anything we need now it is ginger. We had about as much ginger yesterday as a bowl of cold custard.

—William F. Kirk, New York *American*

———◇ SUNDAY, JUNE 14 ◇———

{On June 12, in New York, the Giants defeated Cincinnati, in 10 innings, 3 to 2. Winning pitcher, Crandall; losing pitcher, Ewing. Giants' standing: 24 wins, 23 losses, in fourth place.}

Our boys looked like sure winners during most of the game, holding a lead of 2 to 0 up to the ninth. But as has been frequently remarked the national game is an uncertain affair, and you can never be positive of anything until the last man is out. That is why 15,000 fans remained for the finish, and this is the reward they received for their patience.

Good old Mike Donlin {whose base running was spectacular} is playing like three or four men, and doing fully half of the Giants' aggressive work. —Jack Ryder, Cincinnati *Enquirer*

———◇ MONDAY, JUNE 15 ◇———

By the way, little old New York did itself proud in attendance figures. Whether a city is a baseball standby or not is shown by how it supports a losing team. What other city could or would have turned out 20,000 people in the face of three straight defeats of the home team, and the local players putting up bush league ball? —Sam Crane, New York *Evening Journal*

Manager McGraw has shaken up his batting order, dropping Bridwell out entirely. This will give Charley Herzog his first real chance to deliver the goods. —New York *Globe*

——— NATIONAL LEAGUE STANDINGS ———

	W	L	PCT.	GB		W	L	PCT.	GB
Chicago	30	16	.652	—	Philadelphia .	21	22	.488	7½
Pittsburgh ...	26	20	.565	4	Boston	22	26	.458	9
Cincinnati ...	26	20	.565	4	St. Louis	22	30	.423	11
New York ...	24	23	.511	6½	Brooklyn	16	30	.348	14

—————◇ **TUESDAY, JUNE 16** ◇—————

{On June 15, in New York, the Giants' scheduled doubleheader with Cincinnati was stopped in the fourth inning of the first game because of rain.}

Unless President Pulliam can find a way to transfer Umpire {James} Johnstone from the Polo Grounds and from the games the Giants play abroad, a scandal is liable to arise that will be detrimental to baseball.

Umpire Johnstone's inconsistency yesterday in his attitude on the rain should be brought to the attention of the National Committee.

The game was started under doubtful possibilities. The Reds made a run in the first inning and also in the second. It was raining in torrents even then. The Giants in the second made two runs. The Reds came back in the third with one more. The Giants accumulated five runs in the third and it was still pouring down. The Reds made no tallies in their fourth stanza.

Doyle started the fourth with a single, and Seymour walked. Then Mr. Johnstone got an attack of cold feet and motioned his associate, Umpire Rigler, to come to the plate for a consultation.

"What would you do?" asked the sole boss of the situation. Rigler replied, "You ought to have called time in the second inning." Then Johnstone shouted: "Time!"

But, mind you, it was not until the Giants were four runs to the good, with a prospect of making more.

That Johnstone had the original idea of making the players take the full count was evident when at the start of the fourth inning the Reds were showing dilatory tactics and he hollered, "You might as well get up here; you will have to play out the game anyhow."

Johnstone's sudden change of front can only be explained by the fact that the Giants were in the lead.

Umpire Johnstone has thrown out statements that he blames McGraw for being assaulted a year or two ago near the Polo Grounds after a clash on the field.

Captain Donlin, during the wait, after time had been called, asked

Johnstone, "Why did you decide to call time after the Giants got the lead?"

Johnstone replied, "If it had been a clear day you wouldn't have had a show."

Now is that a nice remark for one of President Pulliam's immaculate umps? If that does not show animus, I don't know what can.

—Sam Crane, New York *Evening Journal*

While the third inning was being played, Dummy Taylor appeared on the coaching lines wearing Groundkeeper Murphy's rubber boots. Johnstone failed to see the joke that was plain to everybody else and fined Taylor $10 and sent him to the clubhouse.   —New York *World*

McGraw's suspension went into effect yesterday. It was for three games, and had yesterday's doubleheader been played two-thirds of the sentence would have been served. Pulliam's order simply keeps McGraw off the coaching lines. In Johnstone's report the umpire averred that {on the preceding Saturday} McGraw had called him a piece of cheese. "And I can prove it," said McGraw.   —New York *Globe*

After it was all over Joe McGinnity, still in uniform, was sitting on the balcony of the clubhouse, smoking a pipe and basking in the favorable smiles of the multitude as they filed out in the rain. A special officer, after the manner of his kind, was hustling some small boys in a very determined manner. Joe asked the cop why he didn't take on someone of his size, and Mr. Cop replied that he would take him on if he would come down. The Iron Man accepted the challenge, descended and was hit in the eye by the officious guardian of the law. McGinnity came back strong, and it required the united efforts of McGraw and a special policeman to separate the combatants. The cop's coat was torn off his back and he also lost his job, but McGinnity will be able to pitch the next time he is called on.   —Cincinnati *Enquirer*

——◇ WEDNESDAY, JUNE 17 ◇——

{On June 16, the Giants' scheduled game with Cincinnati was postponed so that Yale and Princeton could use the Polo Grounds for their Ivy League championship game.}

——◇ THURSDAY, JUNE 18 ◇——

{On June 17, in New York, the Giants defeated Cincinnati in a doubleheader, 2 to 1 and 4 to 2. Winning pitchers, Mathewson and McGinnity; losing pitchers, Coakley and Weimer. Giants' standing: 26 wins, 23 losses, in fourth place.}

Revenge is sweet, and revenge is ours. The Ganzel Gang trotted to the Polo Grounds yesterday to win a doubleheader. They were met by McGraw's merry men, and the Polo Grounders handed them a double dose of disaster.

Mathewson was in fine form, so he was. The Reds were on his stuff all through the remarkably fast first game (it lasted only an hour and a quarter) and the nearer Cincinnati base runners got to home plate the steadier became "Big Six." Christy threw out his arm in the series between the Giants and Athletics two years ago, and now the poor fellow has to depend on his fielders.

In the second game McGraw handed a new white ball to Joe McGinnity, and Ganzel sent Weimer, known as "Tornado Jake," onto the firing line for the Reds. Weimer is a classy twirler, one of the best southpaws in the business. But he was outpitched by McGinnity, who never looked better.　　　　　　　　　　　—William F. Kirk, New York *American*

The Giants have been getting their bumps right along. The fans are wise to the fact that McGraw and his men have absolutely no chance to finish near the top. If the Cubs win the series this week, it will be all over.
　　　　　　　　　　　　　　　　　—Joe Vila, *The Sporting News*

———◇ FRIDAY, JUNE 19 ◇———

{On June 11, in New York, the Giants lost to Chicago 7 to 5. Winning pitcher, Lundgren; losing pitcher, Wiltse. Giants' standing: 26 wins, 24 losses, in fourth place.}

Fourteen thousand yesterday saw the Cubs play the waiting and bunting game. They saw the champions get a man on first base at the beginning of the fourth, fifth, sixth, and eighth innings, and they saw three of the five score. They also saw a sacrifice in three of the five innings.

The fans are criticizing the Giants more and more for not playing the sacrifice game. It is the only thing in a close game. They are getting weary of seeing Devlin come to bat and bang into a double play or raise a fly. For some reason Arthur never tries to lay down the ball any more, and he is not a bad bunter. He certainly can sacrifice better than he can hit. Seymour has done the same thing when a sacrifice was in order. Perhaps it is unjust to criticize these players, for they may be under orders to bat a certain way, but there is a lot of growling among the fans. When the Cubs were "laying 'em down" yesterday the remark was passed along, "Why don't the Giants play that game?"

—Sid Mercer, New York *Globe*

In the seventh inning when Schulte threw Doyle out at the plate with what would have been the tying tally, Doyle appeared to be a bit too wagonish in cavorting from second, but that was because Steinfeldt got in some funny work that escaped the argus eye of Umpire Hank O'Day. Steinie deliberately blocked the innocent Larry at third by doing the little shoulder stunt that will always slow a runner and throw him off his stride. Now, as Larry, notwithstanding the premeditated interruption, was barely nipped by Schulte's good throw, Steinie's little trick did what was intended.   —Sam Crane, New York *Evening Journal*

Although McGraw was not supposed to be directing his club, for he is under suspension, it made no difference in the tactics used by the Giants. The coaches were permitted by Umpire Klem to incite the fans to all kinds of hooting and jeering, and the players resorted to all kinds of tricks to upset Cub pitchers. One tenth of the antics performed by McGraw's troupe yesterday would have sent half the Chicago club off the field had it resorted to them in Chicago.   —Chicago *News*

——◇ **SATURDAY, JUNE 20** ◇——

{On June 19, in New York, the Giants defeated the Cubs 6 to 3. Winning pitcher, Crandall; losing pitcher, Pfiester. Giants' standing: 27 wins, 24 losses, in fourth place.}

Manager Jawn McGraw had his suspension lifted yesterday by the Hon. Mr. {Harry} Pulliam. Jawn didn't send a message of thanks to Haberdashery Harry, because he has had suspensions lowered and lifted so often the story is old indeed. But the little manager was on the coaching lines, sending suggestions to all corners of the diamond and hurling the harpoon into Manager Chance and Southpaw Pfiester, and the magnetism of the man went a long way before the final curtain dropped.

Otis Crandall, the fine young pitcher, won the hearts of Manhattan fans. The husky youngster showed his class by refusing to blow up. More than once the Cubs had men on the bags when a hit might have spelled disaster, and great was the yelping of Chance's coachers. Crandall, however, refused to be awed in the presence of greatness. His more seasoned rival, Pfiester, might have taken a few lessons from this recruit, so far as steadiness was concerned.

Before going any further, let us dwell on a phenomenal piece of fielding. In the fifth inning, Pfiester led off with a clean single and took second on Evers' sacrifice. Artie Hofman smashed one hard and cruelly toward the centerfield ropes. It looked like a certain home run. Seymour started with the crack of the bat, hurried over the greensward like a leopard, gave a great leap skyward at the "flycological" moment, and speared the ball with his bare hand. There was a hush for a moment until Seymour lit on the grass with the ball in his possession.

Then—well, you might buy a seat for every game during the rest of the season and never hear such an outburst of applause again. Even the hardened regulars got up in their seats and yelled like Roosevelt rooters.

Fair women in the upper tier waved their M. W. {Merry Widow} lids until the hatpins fell into the necks of the fanatics beneath, but the fanatics plucked out the hatpins and kept on shrieking. It was perhaps the greatest ovation ever given a ball player for a fielding performance.

—William F. Kirk, New York *American*

———◇ **SUNDAY, JUNE 21** ◇———

{On June 20, in New York, the Giants defeated Chicago 4 to 0. Winning pitcher, Mathewson; losing pitcher, Fraser. Giants' standing: 28 wins, 24 losses, in fourth place.}

The oldest baseball inhabitant remembers only one other game when more persons assembled on the Polo Grounds than yesterday, and he doesn't remember that very well. At 2 o'clock, an hour and a half before the time for play, they were selling nice, soft standing room, and nothing else.

Half an hour before post time the overflow broke through the confines and streamed out on the field. A band of special policemen had as much luck getting them off the green as Old King Canute had when he tried to boss the bounding main. So after a while the specials said the crowd could stay on the grounds, and the crowd said thank you for nothing. {This writer estimated that 25,000 were in attendance.}

Our esteemed Matty was all there. He threw 'em in fast and savage and plentiful, and every now and then Roger Bresnahan had to walk away from the plate or stoop down and pick up a little gravel, or stall in some other equally genteel way so's Matty wouldn't be so fast. But even at that, Christy was the Lightning Kid and struck out six Cubs.

Evers was a victim in the fourth. He was the first man up and had no more idea of what Matty was doing than Dummy Taylor has of that ventriloquist's turn over on the roof garden yonder. When Matty had puzzled him three times Umpire Klem made the customary decision. Mr. Evers then spoke. He spoke eloquently, pointedly, and for a long time.

"Is that all?" asked Mr. Klem.

"It is all I can think of now," admitted Mr. Evers.

"Perhaps if you had a little leisure you could think of something more," said the umpire kindly. "Suppose you go over to that nice, quiet clubhouse for the rest of the afternoon and think up some more things. You may tell them to me Monday."

—W. W. Aulick, New York *Times*

To players and faithful fans yesterday was by far the hottest of the season. The sun was scorchingly blistering and coats and some collars were peeled off in quick order. During the second inning someone in the grandstand back of the plate turned on the fire hose. The crowd in the closely packed aisles for a distance of forty feet received enough water to wet them to the skin before it was turned off.

—New York *Evening Telegram*

In New York's seventh on Saturday, Fraser tried to work Tenney on bad balls and passed him, filling the bases with two out, preferring to take a chance with Doyle. While Tenney was being passed, McGraw grasped the situation and its psychological possibilities. He sent Mathewson from the bench to murmur instructions to Doyle, waiting his turn at bat. No sooner did Doyle step to the plate than those instructions were plain. He palpably tried to get hit by the first ball pitched, but failed. Then Donlin, who was coaching, made it all the more palpable by showing Doyle how to stick out his hip. The youngster proved an apt pupil and on the next ball, which would have been a strike, he turned his back, standing almost on top of the plate, and stuck out his hip so that the ball glanced off it. The trick was done amateurishly, was palpably intentional and did not even have the element of surprise in it. Klem was not unprepared for the trick, as Kling called his attention to Doyle's purpose the first time it was tried. Yet Klem sent Doyle to first and forced in the only run needed to win the game. Klem dared not do otherwise. He knew that if he refused to allow the trick McGraw & Co. would make a frantic demonstration and would infuriate the crowd, which already had once broken away from the helpless Pinkertons in an effort to get nearer the play. He knew that the crowd would attack him before or after the game, and he would have as much protection as the 25-cent bleachers in a cloudburst, and not half as good a chance to make a getaway. And McGraw knew that Klem knew it, and hence Doyle had only to get hit in order to win the game.

—I. E. Sanborn, *The Sporting News*

———◇ MONDAY, JUNE 22 ◇———

If Mike Donlin keeps up his present rate of gaining in the batting average race, he will finish as did the old yacht *America* which beat the British yachts so badly that the Englishmen were forced to admit "there was no second."

Donlin has a percentage of .329, leading {John} Titus of Philadelphia by 11 points. Seymour is the next Giant to Donlin, with .272, and then Tenney with .263.   —New York *Globe*

——— NATIONAL LEAGUE STANDINGS ———

	W	L	PCT.	GB		W	L	PCT.	GB
Chicago	32	19	.627	—	Philadelphia .	23	26	.469	8
Pittsburgh ...	33	22	.600	1	Boston	24	30	.444	9½
Cincinnati ...	29	24	.547	4	St. Louis	23	34	.404	12
New York ...	28	24	.538	4½	Brooklyn	20	33	.377	13

———◇ TUESDAY, JUNE 23 ◇———

{On June 22, in New York, the Giants beat Chicago 7 to 1. Winning pitcher, Wiltse; losing pitcher, Lundgren. Giants' standing: 29 wins, 24 losses, in fourth place.}

Even as in Chicago a few weeks ago, so it was at the Polo Grounds. The wonderful Champions of the World got another kick in the slats, and started for their native haunts much chastened in spirit. When twilight began to tint the edge of Coogan's Bluff, a person named Francois Chance propelled his bow legs toward the clubhouse, thinking thoughts we dare not put in type. The Chicago invaders came here with bells on, growling awful threats. They went away peaceably, pathetically, like nice, well behaved little Cubs.

The Giants outplayed the visitors in every department of the game. One of the biggest Monday crowds that ever swarmed into the yard sat back and gloated. They gloated when Frank Chance struck out, they gloated when Wiltse outpitched Mr. Carl Lundgren, they gloated when Kid Bridwell pulled off his sweet shortstop plays, and most of all they gloated when the final score was hung up on the old blackboard in left field. In fact it was the gloatingest gang you ever saw.

There are a few little boosts to be distributed.

Boost No. 1. Mr. Bresnahan was all there, lame leg or no lame leg. His throwing was beautiful and his batting timely.

Boost No. 2. Mr. Frederick Tenney was in grand form. Fred is certainly playing a sugar brand of ball for Manager Jawn, and seems to improve with age.

Boost No. 3. George Wiltse was steady at all stages, and won his game easily. George will win many more this season. Watch him.

Boost No. 4. Little Mr. Bridwell is playing splendid ball in the short field. He is fast, graceful and steady, and when it comes to a pinch, we'd just as soon see him up there as anybody.

Boost No. 5. Larry Doyle performed like a Lajoie. {A major leaguer for 20 years (1896–1916), Napoleon Lajoie is still regarded as baseball's best second baseman, and in 1908, in his fourth season as player-manager for Cleveland, he, along with Honus Wagner, was one of the sport's two greatest superstars.}

Boost No. 6. Manager Chance done his derndest.

—William F. Kirk, New York *American*

The Giants have up to date this season won as many games from the Cubs as they did all last year. The record stood at the end of last season: Chicago, 15; New York, 6. Now it stands: New York, 6; Cubs, 2.

—New York *World*

It was announced yesterday that Johnny Evers has been suspended by President Pulliam for three days. This was scarcely a surprise to Manager

Chance or any of the Cubs, but it angered them clear through. Umpire Klem has the reputation of being the most cordially disliked umpire on Pulliam's staff. Almost every player in the league would back up Chance's opinion on such a statement. Klem takes advantage of his position and the immunity given him by Pulliam to deride players to the point where they say and do things for which they are suspended and fined. But this does not reach the ears of the league president. The evidence on which players are punished is strictly ex parte, for the man sentenced is never heard in his own behalf. The umpire is judge, jury and prosecuting attorney and is well termed "the autocrat of the diamond."

—Chicago *News*

Cincinnati walloped Pittsburgh yesterday in a close game. Among the Pirates' few hits was a lone little bingle by Honus Wagner that had no effect on the result of the contest; but, at the same time, it established a record that will probably live after yesterday's game, the 1908 pennant race and even the National League are forgotten.

Wagner's unnoticed single completed a record of 2,000 hits in his 12 years of service in the big league. Two thousand hits! Just think about it for a minute! This is a record that will probably stand as long as baseball is the sport of Americans. How many youngsters are there in the game today who can set out with any confidence to equal it? The Seymours, Donlins, Stones, Cobbs, and even Lajoies come and go, but leave the crown with the "Flying Dutchman."

In his twelve years of fast company Wagner has played in 1,505 games. He has been officially at bat 5,772 times, and his 2,000 hits therefore give him a grand average of .347. {By 1980, fifteen players had gained 3,000 hits, one of whom, Ty Cobb, twenty-one years old in 1908, ended his career with more than 4,000.}

—J. W. McConaughy, New York *Evening Journal*

———◇ WEDNESDAY, JUNE 24 ◇———

{On June 23, in New York, the Giants split a doubleheader with Boston, winning 6 to 3 and losing 9 to 7. Winning pitchers, McGinnity and Flaherty; losing pitchers, Dorner and Mathewson. Giants' standing: 30 wins, 25 losses, in fourth place.}

They played the kind of ball at the Polo Grounds yesterday that brings the crowds back.

The biggest inning was the seventh in the second game, when the Giants made five runs. It happens like this sometimes, even outside of fairy tales. With two men on base, the Giants four runs down, Merkle pinch-hits for Taylor. Strike lustily, good Merkle, and we shall be pleased with you.

Merkle smacks the ball over the top of the rail in the left-field bleachers and three runners trot home.

Everything is suspended for the minute. Some politicians in the front row voice the general sentiment when they say Merkle can have any office within the gift of a grateful electorate. They tell him about Denver {on July 7 the Democratic Party's national convention would open there} and ask him how he'd like to have Bryan as the tail of the ticket, and Roger Bresnahan almost kisses him. {In July, William Jennings Bryan would, for the third time, become the Democratic nominee for president.}

Boston finally won against Matty, but there is another day, and that day is today. Have a care, Hubsmiths.

—W. W. Aulick, New York *Times*

Shortstop Herzog has jumped the Giants. He is at his home in Ridgely, Md., and declares he will never again play with the Giants as long as McGraw is manager. The trouble came about Saturday night when the manager ordered Herzog to accompany the team to Elizabeth for a Sunday game, subsequently called off.

Herzog refused, saying his weak wrist would not permit him to play, and he didn't care to go along to view the game. McGraw is said to have applied an epithet to Herzog in the excitement of the mutiny. This wounded the sensitive youngster, who immediately packed for home when McGraw refused a personal apology.

The loss of Herzog will be keenly felt if anything happens to Bridwell. This leaves the Giants with but one utility man, Merkle.

—New York *Herald*

———◇ THURSDAY, JUNE 25 ◇———

{On June 24, in New York, the Giants defeated Boston in a doubleheader, 4 to 0 and 7 to 1. Winning pitchers, Wiltse and Mathewson; losing pitchers, Lindaman and Young. Giants' standing: 32 wins, 25 losses, in third place.}

The Gingery Giants copped two more yesterday, and Josephus Kelley led his band of braves to the Elevated train with not a sign of a smile on his freckled map. Crushed by their double defeat, they stumbled into their seats and cussed the guards all the way downtown.

It is well that we didn't have to do much shuddering, because the weather was so beastly sultry the nerves needed a rest. One rooter in the right-field bleachers was overcome, but he must have hailed from Boston, as he shouted "Summon a physician!" before he wilted. Eighteen or twenty needy young practitioners sprang to his relief before you could count twenty-three, and he was brought out of his trance in time to see the Bostonians getting their second lacing.

Wiltse pitched in the first battle and had Kelley's gang on his staff {slang expression meaning "had everything under control"} from beginning to end. Much outspoken criticism was heard in the stands before the game, as not a few of our brightest rooters allowed that Wiltse should not pitch so often. McGraw refused to change his mind and put George through his paces, showing the doubting tommies that he was crazy like a fox. Mac is winning back ever so many old friends. All the world loves a winner—if he can win every day.

Mr. {Vive} Lindaman started for the Kelley folks, but he didn't last. It was too hot for him to use his spit ball, so he substituted a new one, known in Boston as the "perspiration pellet." The formidable Mr. Lindaman, instead of forcing his salivary glands, simply rubbed the ball across his forehead, moistening it not wisely, but too well. He lasted three innings.   —William F. Kirk, New York *American*

I have heard of a player backing up his own throw, but I never saw it until Tuesday. Doyle, in an endeavor to get a slow bounder to first ahead of the batter, tossed the ball wide to Tenney. The batter passed first and then turned as if to dash for second, but Doyle followed the ball and got

it after it had passed Tenney and held the runner on first. So those who
saw the rare play can bet that Doyle backed up his own throw—and win.

—Sam Crane, New York *Evening Journal*

———◇ **FRIDAY, JUNE 26** ◇———

{On June 25, in New York, the Giants split a doubleheader with
Boston, losing 14 to 10 and winning 7 to 4. Winning pitchers Dorner and
Taylor; losing pitchers, Crandall and Lindaman. Giants' standing: 33
wins, 26 losses, in third place.}

Not even in the weird imagination of the Welsh Rarebit Fiend artist
has there been played a baseball game such as the first contest at the end
of the "L" yesterday.

That game certainly was of the pippin variety. Even fans who did
nothing but put dots alongside names of the run makers on their score
cards had a busy two hours and a half. They kept dotting dots on the
score card with such regularity that it looked like a contest in a polka-dot
shirtwaist factory.

One fellow in the grandstand undertook the monumental task of dotting down runs, hits and errors as the game proceeded. When he had
covered his score card in every available spot he used his cuffs, then his
shirt front, and finally he began to tear pieces from his newspaper, putting
runs, hits and errors in different pockets.   —New York *Herald*

{Harry} Smith, the Boston catcher, got hit in the arm yesterday and a
boy brought him a glass of water, and Roger Bresnahan, the batter, took
the glass and drank it, the jolly old cutup.

—W. W. Aulick, New York *Times*

———◇ **SATURDAY, JUNE 27** ◇———

{On June 26, in New York, the Giants defeated Boston 2 to 0. Winning pitcher, McGinnity; losing pitcher, Flaherty. Giants' standing: 34
wins, 26 losses, in third place.}

Honest Joe Kelley, the man who would be king, has left our lovely city. With two games out of seven, he has gone and left us—and his loss we deeply feel. We would like to have Joe and his aggregation of ex-Giants tenting on our old camp grounds all Summer, Kelley's the "nine of least resistance."

Iron Man McGinnity went into the game with everything, including his glove and his "Old Sal" curve. Joe showed numerous marks of old age. His arm was so shaky that visiting batsmen couldn't follow its motions, and his hand quaked so quakerish-like that the ball shook its way across the plate without meeting a bat on the nose more than three times. Poor old Joe! Nothing is more pathetic than the sight of a pitcher who still imagines he can win. Poor old Joe!

The game was a pitcher's battle until the sixth inning, when Artie Devlin slapped out a lovely home run. The luck was with Artie. The ball hit the greensward about fifty feet from the right-field bleachers and bounced into the home of the proletariat. {Until 1931, a fair ball that bounced into the stands was a home run.} A fellow about sixteen years of age, with freckles on his map, stole the ball and took it home to his mother, but Devlin didn't care. Devlin wants his new shoes, that case of spirits and all the haberdashery which belongs to home-run heroes.

—William F. Kirk, New York *American*

---◇ **SUNDAY, JUNE 28** ◇---

{On June 27, in Brooklyn, the Giants won a doubleheader, 4 to 3 and 5 to 2. Winning pitchers, Wiltse and Mathewson; losing pitchers, Rucker and Wilhelm. Giants' standing: 36 wins, 26 losses, in third place.}

Continuing their steady advance on the Cubs and Pirates, the Giants invaded Brooklyn and before the biggest crowd yet thrust into Mr. Ebbets' improved ball park, felled the Superbas twice in a long seance enjoyed by a few thousand Manhattan rooters and bitterly mourned by faithful adherents of the Brooklyn team whose slogan is "We care not how many games they lose to other teams just so they beat New York."

Mathewson was a hero to those who came across the river to cheer for their Giants. Not only did he go the full route in the second game, but he went to Wiltse's rescue in the first. The Donovanites had been touching up "Hooks" {Wiltse's nickname alluded to the shape of his nose} rather freely, and they finally established a tie in the eighth. After New York nosed ahead in the ninth, McGraw decided to take no more chances. He chased Matty to the box and before the dazed Donovanites knew they were being counted out he whiffed three in a row.

Mathewson continued to hurl the ball into Bresnahan's mitt during the short interval between games and then took up his pitching burden again. The second game was not as keenly relished by the spectators as the first, for Mathewson never lost control of the situation. He seemed to just breeze along under wraps. Whenever the foundation for a Brooklyn rally was laid, "Big Six" steamed up and made the batters miss.

—New York *Press*

◇ MONDAY, JUNE 29 ◇

Are some ball players being robbed of more base hits by a ruling of President Harry Pulliam than by fancy fielding stunts? This is being asked by many scorers and fans.

Pulliam ruled that when a ball is hit to a fielder, and that fielder attempts to force another player but fails, the batsman should be given a fielder's choice instead of a hit, unless it was clear that the fielder could not have thrown him out at first.

It seems like an injustice to say a batsman reached first on a fielder's choice when his wallop panned out to be as valuable as a hit. But President Pulliam says the batsman does not get a hit, so batting averages will be computed accordingly.

—Brooklyn *Eagle*

NATIONAL LEAGUE STANDINGS

	W	L	PCT.	GB		W	L	PCT.	GB
Chicago	37	21	.638	—	Philadelphia	26	28	.481	9
Pittsburgh	40	24	.625	—	Boston	27	36	.429	12½
New York	36	26	.581	3	St. Louis	24	40	.375	16
Cincinnati	32	30	.516	7	Brooklyn	21	38	.356	16½

———◇ TUESDAY, JUNE 30 ◇———

{On June 29, in Brooklyn, the Giants lost 11 to 7. Winning pitcher, Holmes; losing pitcher, Crandall. Giants' standing: 36 wins, 27 losses, in third place.}

More heat prostrations were at Washington Park yesterday than in all the rest of the city combined. When the Giants' outfielders crawled to the dressing rooms after the game they feebly asked for the score, and were told that Brooklyn had won 11 to 7. "Is that all?" asked Mike Donlin, as he tried to get under two shower baths at once. The Brooklyn players hit the ball so often and so hard that Donlin, Shannon and Seymour ran around with their tongues hanging out. Crandall, McGinnity and Malarkey took turns in the box, but each was hit hard.

—New York *Tribune*

———◇ WEDNESDAY, JULY 1 ◇———

{On June 30, in Brooklyn, the Giants won 3 to 0. Winning pitcher, Taylor; losing pitcher, Pastorius. Giants' standing: 37 wins, 27 losses, in third place.}

"Dummy" Taylor was opposed by Pastorius, and it was the Silent Man all the way. The Brooklyn twirler was not hit much harder, but he didn't have "Dummy's" control.

Taylor has not had a good season so far, and there were rumors of his being a "has been," but he fooled a few persons yesterday. He was never in better form, and the Superbas couldn't hit the ball where there wasn't a Giant fielder. Five safe drives was their total.

—New York *Tribune*

According to advice from Cincinnati, the New York National League club has just closed one of the greatest deals ever pulled off in baseball. It is authoritatively stated that Manager McGraw outbid several other major league clubs and will secure Pitcher {Richard} "Rube" Marquard of the

Indianapolis team of the American Association for $11,000, more than has ever been paid for the release of any single player.

The other player who figures in the deal is Jack Meyers of the St. Paul club. Meyers, a catcher, attracted so much attention this season he was sought by several American League managers. He is said to be a full-blooded Chippewa Indian. The price paid for Meyers is reported to be $6,000.

Information of the deal comes from Cincinnati because details of such deals must be filed with the National Commission, of which Garry Herrmann, owner of the Cincinnati club, is president. The papers were filed there yesterday.

Marquard is the twirling sensation of the year in minor league circles. His succession of victories has kept Indianapolis close to the top in the American Association, and among his victories are two no-hit games.

—New York *Globe*

———◇ **THURSDAY, JULY 2** ◇———

{On July 1, in Brooklyn, the Giants lost 4 to 0. Winning pitcher, Rucker; losing pitcher, McGinnity. Giants' standing: 37 wins, 28 losses, in third place.}

Rucker, Brooklyn's clever left-handed artisan, toppled the Giants at will and blanked them impressively. Rucker distributed eight strikeouts; he made the ball talk, hum and cut curious capers, and often hostile batters didn't know whether they were hitting at a baseball, a pea or an elusive streak. —New York *Sun*

Mabel Hite (Mrs. Mike Donlin) and a friend lunched at Washington Park yesterday. They captured two ham sandwiches and two bottles of soda from one of Harry Stevens' minions. {For many years Harry Stevens was in charge of concessions at the Polo Grounds, and at this time he also performed the same duty in Brooklyn.} No harm resulted, though Miss Hite's understudy was ready to step in at any moment during the performance of "The Merry-Go-Round" last night.

—New York *Globe*

——— ◇ FRIDAY, JULY 3 ◇ ———

{On July 2, in New York, the Giants defeated Philadelphia 4 to 3. Winning pitcher, Mathewson; losing pitcher, Foxen. Giants' standing: 38 wins, 28 losses, in third place.}

Christy Mathewson wasn't at his best yesterday, and the Giants have given better exhibitions of the great national game, but Christy and his teammates were good enough to win, and the victory will look just as good toward the shank of the season as a no-hit shut-out.

The terrible heat kept down the attendance, but those present witnessed one of the tightest struggles of the season. Matty was wilder than he has been for some time. Seldom does the big fellow pass two men in a row, but he did it in the first inning. He seemed uncertain in other innings, and his support was anything but superlative. Still we won.

Umpire Rigler, unaccompanied by the genial Mr. Johnstone, had his work cut for him, and held the unruly ball gainers fairly well in hand, considering he was out there all by his dear little lonesome. Nobody seemed to know where Rigler's pal Johnstone might be, and nobody seemed to give a gosh darn.

Our manager, Gentle Jawn McGraw, he of the shrinking, retiring disposish, had a terrible run-in with Rigler in the second chapter, claiming that Foxy {Bill} Foxen had done the balk act. Jawn put it to Rigler in a calm, statesmanlike way, never forgetting his dignity.

"Did you call me a piece of cheese?" demanded Rigler.

"By no means," retorted Manager Jawn. "I said you were the hole in a piece of cheese."

Umpire Rigler shuddered. It was the first time he had been called anything so insignificant as the hole in a piece of cheese. "Go home!" hissed Umpire Rigler. "Avaunt!" And Jawn avaunted.

—William F. Kirk, New York *American*

——— ◇ SATURDAY, JULY 4 ◇ ———

{On July 3, in New York, the Giants defeated Philadelphia 8 to 3. Winning pitcher, Crandall; losing pitcher, Sparks. Giants' standing: 39 wins, 28 losses, in third place.}

With their ambitions centered on passing the Pesky Pirates and Chesty Cubs, the Giants kicked the wind out of the Peculiar Phillies. Otis Crandall improved after a bad start and held Murray's men in the hollow of his hand after the fourth inning.

The difference in the play of the teams shows in the box score. The hits and errors were the same, ten and three, and yet the home crew scored five more tallies than its opponents. Manager Billy Murray thought part of this discrepancy was due to the desire of his players to keep their uniforms clean. Titus did not slide to the plate in the first inning and the failure to hit the dirt cost him {a fine of} $25. Two other sluggish athletes from the banks of the Schuylkill were also massacred at the fourth bag and died in an erect attitude.   —New York *Press*

————◇ **SUNDAY, JULY 5** ◇————

{On July 4, in New York, the Giants defeated Philadelphia in a doubleheader, 1 to 0 and 9 to 3. Winning pitchers, Wiltse and McGinnity; losing pitchers, McQuillan and Corridon. Giants' standing: 41 wins, 28 losses, in third place.}

The Giants twice defeated the Phillies yesterday, and last night started on the second Western trip. The Fourth of July celebration showed a new world's record in George Wiltse's retirement of the Quakers without a hit or run in ten innings in the morning game. In the past, hurlers have gone one round beyond nine without allowing hits, but something turned up to hoodoo the performance. Wiltse came within an ace of letting down his opponents in nine rounds without a man reaching first base. Unfortunately Charles Rigler, Pulliam's fighting umpire, suffered from an attack of astigmatism on the fourth serve to George McQuillan, the 27th Phillie who strode to the plate, and called a ball when Wiltse put a third strike over. Then the left-hander hit his rival hurler in the arm, and Philadelphia got its only man on base in the game.

—New York *Press*

In recognition of their clean-up of the series with the Phillies, President Brush gave each member of the team an order for a new pair of baseball shoes worth $7.50 each.   —*Sporting Life*

———◇ **MONDAY, JULY 6** ◇———

CINCINNATI, July 6—The Giants left New York at 9 o'clock Saturday night, and arrived here in time for supper last night, tired and thoroughly wilted. It was a fearful ride, and it was well that the start was made early, as a good night's rest has made the players fresh again.

—Sid Mercer, New York *Globe*

Ever since the Pirates paid a visit to the Polo Grounds June 19–21, the Giants have made teamwork the most distinguishable part of their games and have climbed consistently. I may appear egotistical, but ever since I brought attention to the woeful lack of up-to-date baseball the Giants were playing a month ago, their total lack of playing for one run by banging the ball into double plays and force-outs, instead of bunting by "suicide splash" methods, the Giants adopted the plan and have carried it through with the most successful results. I, of course, did not originate the idea, but I did assist in bringing to the notice of McGraw and the players their faults. It was like an outsider looking over the shoulders of card players and seeing mistakes they possibly could not.

—Sam Crane, New York *Evening Journal*

Mike Donlin and Hans Wagner are having a fight for batting honors in the National League. Turkey leads the league with the fine percentage of .342. The Flying Dutchman added fifteen points to his average last week and is second, with .336.   —New York *World*

CINCINNATI, July 6—Another move on the baseball checkerboard has landed Outfielder Harry McCormick in John McGraw's bandwagon once more. Following a conference between Manager Murray of the Phillies and McGraw last Saturday, title to McCormick passed to New York. He will report here tomorrow and will be a utility outfielder and emergency batsman.

New Yorkers will remember him as one of McGraw's outfielders in 1904, the first year the Giants won the pennant under McGraw's management. —Sid Mercer, New York *Globe*

Fred Merkle pulled up lame on the road from New York to Cincinnati yesterday and is nursing a badly swollen foot, the origin of which is not clear to him. —New York *Evening Telegram*

—————— NATIONAL LEAGUE STANDINGS ——————

	W	L	PCT.	GB		W	L	PCT.	GB
Pittsburgh ...	43	27	.614	—	Philadelphia .	27	34	.443	11½
Chicago	41	26	.612	½	Boston	31	39	.443	12
New York ...	41	28	.594	1½	St. Louis	27	42	.391	15½
Cincinnati ...	36	34	.514	7	Brooklyn	25	41	.379	16

——————◇ TUESDAY, JULY 7 ◇——————

{On July 6, in Cincinnati, the Giants won 2 to 1. Winning pitcher, Mathewson; losing pitcher, Ewing. Giants' standing: 42 wins, 28 losses, in third place.}

CINCINNATI, July 6—Steadily climbing the ticklish pennant ladder, the Giants used Cincinnati as a stepping stone today.

Larry Doyle kept up his brilliant work by which he enthused Polo Grounds fans last week. New York made six hits and Doyle got three of them. Also, Larry capered about second base in clever style, making five pretty assists and three put-outs.

To show how futile the home players' efforts were at bat, 22 put-outs were made by the New York catcher and infield.

—New York *Tribune*

———◇ WEDNESDAY, JULY 8 ◇———

{On July 7, in Cincinnati, the Giants lost 4 to 3. Winning pitcher, Spade; losing pitcher, Crandall. Giants' standing: 42 wins, 29 losses, in third place.}

Coming from behind with great speed, the Reds, who looked like certain losers for six rounds at League Park yesterday, nosed out the fighting Giants. Just when the pessimists were predicting a shut-out for our boys, said boys found their batting eyes, put them to the best possible use and turned a 3 to 0 defeat into a very ornate 4 to 3 win.

—Jack Ryder, Cincinnati *Enquirer*

———◇ THURSDAY, JULY 9 ◇———

{On July 8, in Cincinnati, the Giants lost 8 to 3. Winning pitcher, Weimer; losing pitcher, McGinnity. Giants' standing: 42 wins, 30 losses, in third place.}

With the utmost brutality, the Reds attacked the chesty Giants yesterday and blew them off the baseball map. Rapping one star pitcher after another with great freedom, our noble fourth-placers achieved a total of a dozen bingles.

Joe McGinnity lasted six rounds, and then sought a shady seat on the bench. The removal of the Iron Man brought George Wiltse on, stalking in stately fashion to the mound and modestly acknowledging the applause in recognition of his great no-hit game last Saturday. But Wiltse found the Reds a more difficult proposition than the Phillies. The southpaw remained for exactly one round.

The poor work of the Giants in the field was relieved by a wonderful catch by Mike Donlin, which saved several runs in the lucky seventh when he went back at great speed, did a few acrobatic stunts with his arms and legs, leaped seven feet into the sunshine and came down with the ball in his fin.

—Jack Ryder, Cincinnati *Enquirer*

Another surgeon was called in to treat Merkle last night. The operation yesterday left the big fellow resting easy, but he is not out of danger yet, and McGraw will take no chances. Merkle cannot be moved and will probably stay here until next week and then go to his home in Toledo. He has little chance to get back in harness this month.

—New York *Globe*

Rube Marquard is not swelled up in the least because a big bunch of money will be handed over for him. He says: "There is nothing to gloat over. If I am worth that amount of money to the New York club, I should get a good salary. I tried to break into the big company with the Cleveland club, but they could not see where I came in at all. When I start in fast baseball, I want to get a salary that will make it worthwhile." And they say he is a rube.

—New York *Globe*

◇ FRIDAY, JULY 10 ◇

{On July 9, in Cincinnati, the Giants won 2 to 1. Winning pitcher, Mathewson; losing pitcher, Coakley. Giants' standing: 43 wins, 30 losses, in third place.}

Mr. J. J. McGraw paid the Reds a high compliment yesterday by selecting Christopher Mathewson to twirl the final game of the Giant series. This desperate move was taken to avoid a third straight defeat. Matty was called on, instead of being saved for Pittsburgh today, as had been McGraw's intention.

The Reds could not do much with the great checker player. No team can when Matty is in form. Dr. Coakley was only a shade less effective than the great Mathewson. The eminent dentist had his famous slow ball frequently on exhibition, and it was a puzzler for fair. His work would have beaten any pitcher but Matty.

—Jack Ryder, Cincinnati *Enquirer*

Pittsburgh, July 10—Dave Brain has been transferred from Cincinnati

to the Giants. McGraw closed the deal with Manager Ganzel after yesterday's game. He takes Merkle's place as utility infielder. The deal was an
outright purchase, price not stated.

—Sid Mercer, New York *Globe*

———◇ SATURDAY, JULY 11 ◇———

{On July 10, in Pittsburgh, the Giants lost 7 to 6. Winning pitcher,
Leever; losing pitcher, Wiltse. Giants' standing: 43 wins, 31 losses, in
third place.}

A sizzling, sweltering, nerve-racking, now-you-have-it-now-you-
haven't game. That's the sort of seance the Pirates and Giants gave on
Exposition Field yesterday.

First the Giants took a big lead only to be overtaken. Clarke and his
men forged to the front, and again did McGraw coach his combination to
the tie-it-up stage.

In the eighth the Pirates went one to the merry, but they were overtaken again in the first of the ninth. Naturally all this whipsawing got on
the nerves of the panting push, and it was not to be wondered that more
than one spectator fell back and gasped for breath.

With the score standing 6 to 6 the Pirates prepared to make a flying
finish.

{Tommy} Leach was first up. On the way to the plate he was stopped
by Clarke, who whispered a few words of encouragement to his right
lieutenant.

Tommy nodded, smiled and pushed his little personality plateward.

Leach spat on his small, sun-kissed salary grabbers and faced the tall
heaver, Wiltse. Two balls and two strikes had been registered when Leach
crossed his toes and let fly at the next delivery.

There was a noise like the fall of a truck horse on a board sidewalk.
The ball and bat kissed and parted forever. "I am going on a long journey," shrieked the blistered bulb, and the bat chuckled, "On your way,
and I don't care if you never come back."

Mike Donlin and Cy Seymour hastened hence.

Around the bases sped the little Leach lad. Those short legs of his were moving like piston rods on a record-breaking electric engine.

Rounding first he hiked for second, Donlin and Seymour still in quest of the bounding bulb.

Passing second Tommy dodged under the dust and came up at third. Seymour and Donlin, still doing the sleuth act, were now near the fence in right center.

Leaving third Leach began to show signs of fatigue. His action was not quite so spirited, yet he was going some.

At this juncture the ball was retrieved and hurled with great haste in the direction of the shinguarded Mr. Bresnahan.

On came Tommy. Fans stood on the seats and yelled. Some of them may have stood on their heads. No one was seated.

When within ten feet of the plate Leach threw his frame to earth, it slid over the pan an instant before Bresnahan got his mitts on the ball.

So energetically had Leach exerted himself he was "all in" and could not have pushed a grain of sand out of his way if he had tried with both hands and feet.

Wagner, Clarke and other Pirates ran out, kissed Tommy, lifted him from the dirt, embraced him and then carried him to the bench.

After carrying the little one to the shade of the bench the Clarkesonians did an Indian dance, the spectators tried to get their nerves into working order and it was all over.

—C. B. Power, Pittsburgh *Dispatch*

CINCINNATI, July 11—Reports from the Good Samaritan Hospital, where Fred Merkle underwent two operations on his foot for blood poisoning, are to the effect that serious complications have arisen. Unless they are checked it is likely that the foot will be amputated.

The foot is about the size of a big pumpkin, and even the lower leg up to the knee is affected. —New York *Evening Journal*

——◇ **SUNDAY, JULY 12** ◇——

{On July 11, in Pittsburgh, the Giants lost 6 to 2. Winning pitcher, Willis; losing pitcher, Taylor. Giants' standing: 43 wins, 32 losses, in third place.}

The Pirates still are the Giants' hoodoos. The victory of the Pittsburghs was their seventh of the season over the New Yorks, who thus far have taken the Corsairs {the Pirates} only twice. The issue yesterday was again decided by the men on the firing line. Willis was eight times better than Luther Taylor, the sum total of the Giant clubbing attack being a three-bagger by Mike Donlin.   —New York *Press*

Game to the core and loyal to Pittsburgh is the Mighty Hans Wagner.
During the past week it was noticed that Wagner was missing chances and making more errors than had been chalked up against him in many months. Yesterday an explanation of Wagner's foozles was forthcoming. He has been playing with a finger so disjointed and inflamed that when he showed it to Manager Clarke the latter asked Hans to take a rest in order to have the injured member properly cared for. Hans declined, saying he believed the team needed his services and he would continue to do his best. How's that for gameness and loyalty?
                                      —C. B. Power, Pittsburgh *Dispatch*

Several ministers and two or three judges were spectators yesterday. Baseball appeals to all classes. It is the one real sport.
                                      —Pittsburgh *Dispatch*

{From an interview with Mr. and Mrs. Mike Donlin at their residence in New York's Hotel Cumberland:} "I've been before the public about ten or twelve years," Mike said, "and they have read a great deal about me. Several of my public appearances I deeply regret, and I have tried to atone for my foolishness.

"My best friends will tell you I could get in trouble easier than the man who invented it. If there was a scrap at the Battery and I was in Harlem it would be my misfortune to get to the scene of trouble just as the 'pat' wagon pulled up. But I don't take any more chances. I wouldn't stop to listen to a street organ for fear I'd get in wrong."

"Fifty-fourth street is the dead line for me now," laughed Mike, "and I never run out of the base line. I'd need a guide on Broadway. I've got a reserved seat on a crystal chariot and I'm not looking for a rain check either. Croton cocktails and cow juice is my limit."

"You look a great deal thinner than a year ago. Are you on a diet?"

"Diet!" screamed Mrs. Donlin in merriment. "If you saw him pull down half a dozen portions of corned beef and cabbage you wouldn't wonder where those home drives come from. He's the original cabbage kid."

"How about it, Mike?"

"She's got me by several feet," said Mike. "I think cabbage should be the national flower."

"Has he any other dissipations?" I asked.

"My mother's strawberry shortcake," said his wife. "The way he buries that double-deck delicacy is a caution."

"There's some talk about you going into vaudeville, Mike. Is there any truth in the story?"

"He's stuck on reciting 'Curfew Shall Not Ring Tonight,' " said his wife, "but I want to make a real actor of him."

"What do you expect to do when your playing days are over?"

"I hope to manage a team," said Mike, modestly.

"And he'll get his hope if I have to pay the players myself," said his plucky wife.

"And your ambition?" I asked her.

"I'm going to buy her a theater," was Mike's gallant response.

—Joe Fitzgerald, New York *World*

———◇ **MONDAY, JULY 13** ◇———

PITTSBURGH, July 13—There is absolutely nothing to do in Pittsburgh on Sunday, so it was a long, weary day for the players who were here.

—Sid Mercer, New York *Globe*

――――― NATIONAL LEAGUE STANDINGS ―――――

	W	L	PCT.	GB		W	L	PCT.	GB
Chicago	45	29	.608	—	Philadelphia .	32	37	.464	10½
Pittsburgh ...	46	30	.605	—	Boston	34	42	.447	12
New York ...	43	32	.573	2½	Brooklyn	29	43	.403	15
Cincinnati ...	40	37	.519	6½	St. Louis	28	47	.373	17½

――――◇ TUESDAY, JULY 14 ◇――――

{On July 13, in Pittsburgh, the Giants won a doubleheader, 7 to 0 and 7 to 4. Winning pitchers, Mathewson and McGinnity; losing pitchers, Leifield and Maddox. Giants' standing: 45 wins, 32 losses, in third place.}

PITTSBURGH, July 13—By winning both games from Pittsburgh, the Giants are in a fine way to crowd the Pirates out of second place and go to Chicago prepared to give the Cubs the battle of their life.

Mathewson continued his brilliant work by holding the Pirates to three hits and no runs in the first game.

Joe McGinnity and Maddox faced each other in the second duel. The Iron Man won easily.　　　　　　　　　　—New York *Tribune*

――――◇ WEDNESDAY, JULY 15 ◇――――

The feud between the Cubs and Giants is of ancient origin and has several causes. One of the chief ones was the temerity of the West Siders to win the National League championship in 1906. New York critics have never forgiven the Cubs for that and whenever Chicago's team gets into Gotham it is panned in proper style in nearly all newspapers. Another cause that hurt even worse was the way Chance "showed up" McGraw when the Giant manager locked Umpire Johnstone out of the Polo Grounds and gave out the statement that the police had locked him out for fear of trouble.　　　　　　　　　　—Chicago *News*

PITTSBURGH, July 14—Mike Donlin is the first player in either major league to make 100 hits this year. Mike reached the century mark yesterday, when, in the fifth inning, he made a three-bagger. Last year this honor was carried off by Wagner in the National League, and by Ty Cobb in the American League.   —New York *World*

————◇ **THURSDAY, JULY 16** ◇————

{On July 15, in Chicago, the Giants won 11 to 0. Winning pitcher, Wiltse; losing pitcher, Brown. Giants' standing: 46 wins, 32 losses, in second place.}

CHICAGO, July 15—The Cubs fell from the top perch to third place after being shut out by New York, 11 to 0.

The Giants knocked the pitching heart of Mordecai Brown, slammed Jack Pfiester to every part of the lot and stung Orvie Overall so hard it looked as if the Cubs' famous score of 19 to 0 against New York two years ago would be duplicated. {The Cubs' 19 to 0 humiliation of the Giants occurred in Chicago on June 7, 1906. The losing pitcher was Mathewson, who allowed six runs in the one-third inning that he pitched.}

Wiltse pitched in wonderful form, and the result tossed the three National League leaders into a merry jumble. The Pittsburghs gained the lead and New York took second place, both passing the champions.

—New York *Herald*

————◇ **FRIDAY, JULY 17** ◇————

{On July 16, in Chicago, the Giants won 4 to 3. Winning pitcher Crandall; losing pitcher, Reulbach. Giants' standing: 47 wins, 32 losses, in second place.}

CHICAGO, July 17—How would you like to be enjoying a fine bath under a shower, with no thought of anything except a big supper right ahead, and then suddenly have nine special messengers rush in and tell you that you had just two minutes to get on the baseball diamond and save a game which you thought was won when you started the bath?

Well, that's what happened to Mathewson yesterday. He was the man enjoying the bath, and the messengers were Giant ball players carrying urgent orders from McGraw to come back and stave off the final rush of the once-champion Cubs.

It came about in the final inning of the game. Crandall held Chicago safe until the ninth, and then went up long enough to fill the bases, with only one out and three runs needed to tie the score. In the din and confusion McGraw's voice could be heard yelling for Matty.

Five minutes before Matty had been warming up in deep centerfield, but when he was wanted it transpired that he had taken to the bath.

Wet as he was he pulled on a pair of somebody's trousers and another blouse, some stockings which were footless, and did not stop to look for socks. His feet were wet and he couldn't get his baseball shoes on, so he grabbed a pair of street shoes, and, without a cap, raced out to see why his name was being yelled so persistently.

In the meantime Manager Chance was protesting the delay and McGraw, Donlin, Tenney and Devlin were working every known trick to stall. The limit of Umpire Johnstone's patience was reached before Matty appeared, and McGinnity had to go into the box, and the first thing he knew a run was over with the bases still full.

Then Matty, in his makeshift uniform, waddled across the field. A lovely finish for the third act of a melodrama, with Mathewson, the hero, ready to work and lift the mortgage from the farm. And work Mathewson did.

He was entitled to put five balls over the plate before starting to pitch, but he only shot two over and nodded that he was ready. Everybody who saw that nod knew that the stuff was off for Chicago. One more run came in while a man was being put out at first on a little love tap, and then Big Six calmly struck out the last Cub batter.

Chance tried to pull off a trick yesterday which failed. When it was announced that Crandall would pitch, Chance told McGraw that Chicago would bat first. Under the rules the home team has a right to say when it will take its first inning. {Until 1951 major league rules gave the home team the option of starting the game at bat or in the field.} Chance figured that Crandall would line out a few hits, and perhaps a run or two. The scheme didn't work. Crandall was steady as a stone wall.

—Nie, New York *Evening Mail*

Harry McCormick is an addition to the college men on the New York team. Mathewson, Devlin, Shannon, {Fred} Snodgrass, and Tenney were "rah-rah" boys. {Like Mathewson, McCormick attended Bucknell and, like all of the Giants' other college men, he played football as well as baseball.} Mike Donlin also claims distinction along that line. "I went through Harvard," says Mike. "It was during my first trip there with the St. Louis team. One morning I went out to Cambridge, entered Harvard at the front door, went through, and came out a rear door."

—New York *Globe*

———◇ SATURDAY, JULY 18 ◇———

{On July 17, in Chicago, the Giants lost 1 to 0. Winning pitcher, Brown; losing pitcher, Mathewson. Giants' standing: 47 wins, 33 losses, in second place.}

The fans who came out yesterday grunting, disgruntled, sore, stung, and aching to vent their anger, went home pleased, flattered, satisfied and gleesome. They saw Brown pitch one of the greatest games of his career. They saw the Cubs, who had for a week played like Coshocton Gings {a Chicago juvenile baseball team} on the back lots, round into fighting trim and put up a defense that was magnificent, and they saw Joseph Tinker.

Mr. Tinker was the whole works in several innings. It was his stop and throw to the plate that started a double play killing off the Giants with the bases full and runs sprouting like alfalfa in Pasadena. It was his superb pickup and hurl to first that beat Bridwell to the base by the eightieth of a step and saved another bundle of runs, and finally Joe delivered the goods with one of the grandest wallops ever scored on any field.

That romantic biff {base hit} came in the fifth. Joe had two strikes called, and Matty was pitching a peculiar ball that came up with a high swing, then dropped suddenly and faded into the mitt of Rhino Bresnahan.

Joe aimed for the last of these, and got it. As the ball headed down deep left field, it was ticketed home run to a certainty, and the fans began to go insane.

As Joe turned third, artful Artie Devlin crossed his bows and delayed him some. He still had time and was keeping on, when H. Goat {Heinie} Zimmerman, coaching on the line, seized him and forced him back to third. Screams of rage rose from the people and the Cub bench. Joe took a look, saw that there still remained the slimmest sort of a chance, and shook H. Goat off furiously. He plunged for the plate and, Bridwell throwing with a strange slowness, beat the ball by the eighth of an inch.

The scene that followed was long to be remembered. People rose, smote one another, wailed, roared, guffawed and squalied {screamed}. Tinker steamed on to the bench; Chance rose, and called in Zimmerman. What happened in the doghouse, screened by red awnings, no one knows, but the awnings shook as if mighty whales were battling in the deep and strange sounds of lurid dialogue, mingled with the batting of heads against the woodwork, streamed forth on the people, who rubbered hard but could not see. Whatever happened, H. Goat Zimmerman came forth to coach no more. —W. A. Phelon, Chicago *Journal*

Mr. Mathewson went into the fray with a blot upon his bright escutcheon, whatever that is. Matty sat in a checker orgy the night before with Mr. Barnes, the local sharp, and was beaten 1 to 0. These fateful statistics followed him into the arena and were painted in large letters of lime where Matty's blue eyeballs couldn't help seeing them.

 —Charles Dryden, Chicago *Tribune*

CHICAGO, July 18—Mike Donlin had a narrow escape from being killed in an automobile accident here last night. A big sixty-horsepower machine in which he was riding on Michigan avenue skidded on the slippery street, turned completely around, and collided with a fast-moving automobile, the property of Mayor Busse. The mayor was driving his own machine. —Nie, New York *Evening Mail*

When Joe Tinker smashed out his home run for the Cubs on July 17, William Hudson, watching from the top of a four-story flat outside the park, was so excited he fell off the building and broke his neck.

—*Sporting Life*

PITTSBURGH, July 17—Today was celebrated as "Wagner Day" in honor of Hans Wagner. Before the Boston game, members of both teams gathered around home plate and Wagner, much embarrassed, was the center of attraction. He was presented with a gold watch and chain, valued at $700, as a token of esteem from admirers who subscribed one dollar each. Also the Carnegie Lodge of Elks, of which Wagner is a member, gave him a beautiful charm. Then a small boy came forward and, opening a box, handed him a rooster, which he said "could lick anything."

—*The Sporting News*

Mr. Rigler uses a hotel register inside his blouse instead of the wind-pad {umpire's chest protector, made of rubber and filled with air} used by most umps. The back of the book is worn outward to circumvent deadly foul tips. He stands in well with urbane hotel clerks, who supply him with all the registers he requires.   —*Sporting Life*

———◇ SUNDAY, JULY 19 ◇———

{On July 18, in Chicago, the Giants lost 5 to 4. Winning pitcher, Overall; losing pitcher, Wiltse. Giants' standing: 47 wins, 34 losses, in third place.}

Hero Tinker is a regular little third-rail athlete. His home run Friday led to the destruction of one fan, and a two-bagger yesterday skinned the Giants in the ninth round and caused an overwrought bug {fan} to throw a fit. The rest threw cushions in a riot of joy.

Joe's triple in the sixth shook Mr. Wiltse much. That blow led to our first tally. In the eighth Wiltse gave up two more runs and in the ninth he blew up completely, his remnants scattered around the diamond in the shape of steam-heated cushions. The black pads sailed out of the stands like a shower of buzzards turned loose by dotty bugs in an effort to pay homage to the greatness of Hero Tinker. A pass to Evers laid the fuse for the explosion. Moran whaled a double over third base and the Cubs were in position for Mr. T. to apply the match. Joseph leaned his faithful pestle against the first pitch and—bingorino! Away went the ball between left and center. McCormick and Seymour approached each other, but the bounding pill passed a given point long before they reached said point. Mac and Cy wheeled about and headed for the box stalls as Evers and Moran hustled the other way and it was all over but chucking the cushions. That final swipe meant another home run had it been needed. However, Mr. Tinker will not need the extra suit, especially since he has a magazine offer of $1 per word to write a story of his home run.

—Charles Dryden, Chicago *Tribune*

McGraw, distressed by the unexpected turn in events, poked a boy in the jaw on the way to the clubhouse. Police had to escort him off the field after he had dressed.　　　　　　　　　　—New York *Herald*

The boy who fell fifty feet from a stand on a roof yesterday is dead. The Building Department has condemned the stands which seat more than one thousand.　　　　　　　　　　—New York *World*

{The following appeared in "Inquisitive Fans," a column of letters to the sports editor, appearing each Sunday in the Chicago *Tribune*. The significance of this letter will come out later.}

Sports Editor of the Tribune: In the last half of the ninth, with the score tied, two men out and a runner on third, the batter hits to left and the runner scores. The batter, seeing the runner score, stops between home and first. The ball is thrown to first baseman, who touches his base before the runner reaches it. Can runner score on this? {Signed} Joseph Rupp, Chicago

Answer: No. Run cannot score when third out is made before reaching first base.　　　　　　　　　　—Chicago *Tribune*

———◇ MONDAY, JULY 20 ◇———

{On July 19, in St. Louis, the Giants won, in 16 innings, 6 to 4. Winning pitcher, Crandall; losing pitcher, Karger. Giants' standing: 48 wins, 34 losses, in third place.}

New York and St. Louis fought one of the most sensational battles of the season at League Park, with the Giants finally winning in 16 innings. Not only was yesterday's game as exciting as extra-inning contests usually are, but there was added excitement on the diamond and in the grandstand. Excitement on the diamond was furnished by the fact that the umpires lost control of the game and for a good part of the time players did pretty much as they pleased.

Some of the poorest umpiring seen in a good many days might have been overlooked, as officials are liable to make mistakes. There was no excuse, however, for the way Johnstone and Rudderham allowed the players to handle them. New York had the umpires under fire from the start and the climax was reached in the fifth inning when Donlin rushed up as though he was going to do Johnstone bodily harm and followed him around making remarks. Donlin repeated the trick of following Johnstone twice more on decisions he did not like. Bresnahan handed it to both umpires and McGraw and other members of the team also took a hand. New York finally got the Cardinals started, and for a while it looked like the players were running the game. New York violated nearly every coaching rule, even yelling derisive terms loud enough to be heard in the stands.

During the game a chap in the grandstand "rooting" for New York made some personal remarks to others around him. He was requested by {team} Secretary Beckamp to be more quiet and became defiant. He made a lunge at those standing around him and it looked like he was going after Police Commissioner Bland, seated back of him. He was finally led away by two policemen.   —St. Louis *Globe-Democrat*

McGrawism, to coin a word, seems effective if objectionable.

For years the rowdyism of McGraw teams has been proverbial. McGraw has stamped his own aggressive personality on every team with which he has been identified. He remolds staid veterans to his own ways and makes a success of it.

Today by adopting tactics almost obsolete, he has browbeaten his way nearly to the front. What is the quality of baseball that is peculiarly McGraw's? None can believe that mere talk, bluff and bullying can alone make a baseball team. McGraw knows baseball; and better, he knows how to impart it quickly. Give him the physical makings and he will put brains, technical excellence and ambition into the outfit and make something of it.

One has to lift the bonnet to a man like "Muggsy."

By his works ye shall know him, and there is surely no better test that can be applied to McGraw. We don't like his methods—they beat us; we don't like his taunts and sneers and umpire baiting—but they win for him, somehow.

—St. Louis *Post-Dispatch*

——— NATIONAL LEAGUE STANDINGS ———

	W	L	PCT.	GB		W	L	PCT.	GB
Pittsburgh ..	49	33	.598	—	Philadelphia .	39	38	.506	7½
New York ..	48	34	.585	1	Boston	37	45	.451	12
Chicago	47	34	.580	1½	Brooklyn	30	48	.385	17
Cincinnati ..	45	39	.536	5	St. Louis.....	29	53	.354	20

———◇ TUESDAY, JULY 21 ◇———

Larry Doyle got a telegram from President Pulliam telling him he had been suspended for three days for his run-in with Hank O'Day in Chicago. Doyle's suspension was brought about in the second game with the Cubs, when there was a lot of excitement over Crandall going out of the box, and McGinnity, and later Mathewson, going in. Doyle's kicking helped kill time so that Matty could dress and save the game.

—New York *Evening Mail*

Some time ago I noted that Mike Donlin was rapidly passing Hans Wagner for popularity and as a drawing card around the circuit. Today

Mike got a telegram from Chicago stating that the cup offered by a newspaper to the most popular ball player had been voted to him by a tremendous majority of Windy City fans.

—Nie, New York *Evening Mail*

Herzog is willing to return to the Giants, but McGraw resents the
Baltimore boy's hasty departure and refuses to make concessions. The
manager positively denies he used harsh language toward Herzog and is
sore because he has been put in a bad light by the young fellow. Herzog
has written and telegraphed his desire to rejoin the team, but his pleas
have not been answered.   —Sid Mercer, New York *Globe*

———◇ **WEDNESDAY, JULY 22** ◇———

{On July 21, in St. Louis, the Giants split a doubleheader, 4 to 2 (in 12
innings) and 1 to 3. Winning pitchers: Mathewson and Lush; losing
pitchers, Sallee and Taylor. Giants' standing: 49 wins, 35 losses, in second
place.}

St. Louis wound up one of the hardest-fought series of the season by
getting an even break in a doubleheader. Three games were played, and
with an even break in luck and umpiring, the Cardinals would have
taken all three. That is a fine record for a team at the bottom of the
league against one fighting for the lead.

—St. Louis *Globe-Democrat*

CLEVELAND, July 22—The Giants reached here this morning en route to
New York for the important series with Pittsburgh which begins at the
Polo Grounds Friday. By getting away from St. Louis a day earlier than
the other Eastern teams finish their engagements in the West they will
get a day of rest before tackling the Pirates.

Not all of the players are making this jump. Spike Shannon packed
his grip and took another train last night. He said farewell to the Giants

rather hurriedly, for during the second game of yesterday's doubleheader McGraw received a wire from Harry Pulliam notifying him that Pittsburgh had refused to waive claim on Shannon. Thus the player who cost the New York club $10,000 two years ago is disposed of for a paltry $1,500, the usual waiver price.

—Sid Mercer, New York *Globe*

───◇ **THURSDAY, JULY 23** ◇───

The real reason why Shannon was let go by McGraw on waivers to Pittsburgh was simply because "Spike" had shown no inclination to take care of himself and his batting and fielding fell off accordingly. His contract had what is known as a "booze clause," and it is claimed that he more than once broke that part of the agreement. Shannon is a fine ball player, and, if he takes care of himself, a great one. He is very liable to jump in and do splendid work for the Pirates, but his usefulness for the Giants was at an end. —Nie, New York *Evening Mail*

TOLEDO, July 23—Fred Merkle, unless complications set in, will report to the Giants ready to play within a week or ten days. He was on crutches for the first time yesterday and now that he can get around his recovery is expected to be rapid. —New York *Evening Mail*

Hans Wagner Says!!! "You can't play good ball without vim—you've got to be full of enthusiasm and energy and keep your brain going—always. You can't afford to take alcoholic stimulants or anything that has a 'let-down' effect. Coca-Cola is the only beverage I have ever drunk that had vim, vigor and go to it—that quenched the thirst and assisted my mental and physical activity."

—from an advertisement in
The Sporting News

———◇ FRIDAY, JULY 24 ◇———

With the Giants and Pirates clashing at the Polo Grounds this afternoon a series starts that may be the turning point in the National League race. The series has the big city baseball crazy. All boxes and reserved seats in the upper grandstand have been sold for today's game, and for tomorrow's contest there is a bigger demand. It would not surprise me to see all attendance records broken tomorrow, and this afternoon I look for a 20,000 crowd. That, for a common, ordinary Friday, will be going some.
—Sam Crane, New York *Evening Journal*

It is pretty well established that harmony does not exist in the ranks of the Chicago Cubs, at least not enough to call the champions a happy family. For some time rumors of dissension among the Cubs have been bandied about. Vague rumors have developed into reliable facts. The tale related here was told by two Chicago men close to the Chicago club, and verified by several players—not members of the New York club. Here are the alleged "inside" facts.

Just before the Cubs came East on their first trip it was announced that Sheckard's eyesight was nearly ruined by the explosion of a bottle of ammonia in the Chicago clubhouse. About the same time Zimmerman was sent to a hospital. Some excuse was made for his dropping out of the game so suddenly.

It has developed within the last few days that the injuries to Sheckard and Zimmerman were the result of a free-for-all fight in the Chicago clubhouse, in which Chance played a conspicuous part. According to our information, after a few hot words had been passed Zimmerman went at Sheckard. During the melee Sheckard threw something at Zimmerman.

Angered by this style of attack, Zimmerman picked up a bottle of ammonia and hurled it at Sheckard. The bottle struck Sheckard in the forehead between the eyes. The force of the throw broke the bottle and the fluid streamed down Sheckard's face.

Manager Chance, thoroughly enraged, buckled into Zimmerman, and the uproar continued. Chance is known for his fighting prowess, but it is claimed that Zimmerman stood his ground until Chance called on other players for help. Then, it is alleged, Zimmerman was borne to the floor by force of superior numbers, and while he was down he received such a beating it was necessary to cart him to the hospital for repairs. Afterward the players took sides on the matter and the affair created bad feeling all around.

Sheckard and Zimmerman were out of the game for two or three weeks. That weakened the team, and when Schulte had to quit on account of illness the Cubs could not gain ground.

—New York *Globe*

At a banquet in New York last December Johnny Evers declared that the absolute lack of friction between members of the Chicago team was responsible for its success, and that Frank Chance was like a father to the boys. Perhaps the lack of good feeling now keeps the Cubs out of first place. Perhaps Chance has become a stepfather. After a game lost this season Chance yelled at his men, "You're a fine lot of curs, you are." Not exactly the sort of talk boys expect from their father. Rumor has it that "curs" was not the word used, but it will do under the circumstances.

—New York *Evening Mail*

———◇ SATURDAY, JULY 25 ◇———

{On July 24, in New York, the Giants defeated Pittsburgh 2 to 1. Winning pitcher, Wiltse; losing pitcher, Willis. Giants' standing: 50 wins, 35 losses, in second place.}

Nothing prodigal, sonny, about the return of our Giants eh? No sneaking in the back way and seeking for sympathy. They drove right up to the front door, unloaded their wandering bats, and demanded respectful consideration. Being entitled to the same.

For they beat the bunch Piratic in a fashion most emphatic, and they'll drive 'em from the attic, never fear.

It was fine at the Polo Grounds yesterday. A gallus band was strewn over the greensward, and the merry musicians played all they knew about "Tannhauser" when Wagner went to bat, and every time we made a good play the drums beat joyously. When we finally won there was one last triumphant blare, something on the order of those that had been given out every time Larry Doyle went to bat.

For Master Doyle was the batting hero. In the first inning Tenney opened with a single, and then Larry cracked a three-bagger to the right-field bleachers, and Tenney could hardly see to cross the plate for the noise. That was Mr. Doyle's entrance. In the third inning he cleanly singled to right, and in the sixth he doubled to the right-field bleachers. Music cue. "Conquering Hero."

—W. W. Aulick, New York *Times*

The jam at 155th street is something to be avoided on a hot day. The runway is littered with pestiferous ticket speculators who insist on pushing their wares in one's face. More inconvenience is encountered inside. The wiseacres now come on big days with a pocketful of quarters to "slip" the various officials, who always bar the way to those who are not Joseph to their elaborate system of graft but step aside as soon as they see a flash of silver.

This graft idea is strong at both New York parks and is an institution founded on the habit of New Yorkers in reaching for small change the minute they run against opposition. Yesterday a fireman in uniform was taking "handouts" at the Polo Grounds. The back of the grandstand was packed, and this fireman was stationed at the head of an aisle. Those with business down the aisle found it difficult to break through, but anyone willing to drop something into the laddie's mitt was not held up. Those personally conducted passengers were steered down the aisle by the fire fighter, who brushed aside others in his haste to earn money.

—Sid Mercer, New York *Globe*

Good old reliable Honus Wagner has turned many a clever trick when opposed to the Giants, but never before anything quite so smooth as he sprang yesterday, in the third inning, when Willis issued his only pass of the day, to Wiltse. Tenney tried to sacrifice and the little pop fly looked good when {third baseman} Leach sat down as he started for it. But Wagner raced in like a streak of lightning over half the distance to the

plate and scooping it up with his bare hand an inch from the carpet fired
to Swacina for the grandest double play ever seen in New York.

—E. J. Lanigan, New York *Press*

The veteran baseball editor of the Boston *Globe*, Mr. Tim Murnane—
in his youth a major league player of note—never said a truer word than
when he uttered his protest:

"Bar big gloves from baseball and batting averages will bob up. The
real artist can play without gloves or mitts. The old-timers worked without gloves. Take the mitts off present players and see how many great
stars are left. The big mitt has made the ball player. Men break into the
game simply because they can hit. The big mitt does the rest. Sporting
goods manufacturers are responsible for the big gloves. Outfielders should
be compelled to catch in their bare hands or use very small gloves. The
only exceptions should be the catcher and perhaps the first baseman.
Without big mitts, batting averages would jump. More action and harder
hitting would make baseball more thrilling than it is now."

We have no desire to revert to the glove-less game, but there is a wide
margin between no gloves and the present huge mitts which enable the
veriest dub to face a cannon shot. The big mitt should be confined to the
catcher; the first baseman should be restricted to a small mitt; the pitcher
and infielders should wear only small gloves; and outfielders should wear
no gloves at all.   —*Sporting Life*

——◊ SUNDAY, JULY 26 ◊——

{On July 25, in New York, the Giants lost to Pittsburgh 7 to 2. Winning pitcher, Leifield; losing pitcher, Mathewson. Giants' standing: 50
wins, 36 losses, in third place.}

That baseball game at the Polo Grounds yesterday was a News Item.
Thirty thousand of our fellow-citizens were among those present.

And of course it wasn't long before the stands were too small to hold
the crowd. Then they spread over the ground, and half an hour before

play time was called they threatened to shove first base up to the pitcher's box and move third bag over to home plate. So Johnny McGraw, he gets him a bat, and he whales a lot of those fellows proper, and as fast as he drives back one bunch they're sagging out at another end, just like a bolster full of gas. And Fred Knowles, ripping off his coat and yelling "Who will stand by my right hand to hold the bridge with me?" rushes out and has as much luck as a man fishing in a bathtub.

But Joe Humphreys, the persuasive, throws himself into what he hopes to make a breach, and flitting from group to group, and pointing a terrible umbrella at each, entreatingly, "Don't crowd onto the field, fellows, or the game'll be forfeited. I ask you, please. It's up to youse." {A well-known "man about town," Joe Humphreys was perhaps the Giants' most enthusiastic and vociferous supporter.}

At which they crowd all the harder, and jump over the outstretched ropes, and from that time on there isn't any more boundary line than a rabbit, and it's two bases every time you fire into the crowd, and it's ten to one you don't catch a foul, and it must have cost the club something awful in lost balls, for giving anything back wasn't the specialty of fellows yesterday.

As for the game itself Larry Doyle won it and lost it. In the second, Wagner, first up, cracks a bad one into the crowd around left field, and that's two bases under the rules. Then he tries to steal, and Bresnahan throws to third, and everybody say it's an easy out, for Devlin doesn't have to move to catch the ball and tag the runner. But what does Hans do but jump about sixteen feet in the air, clean over the outstretched hands of Devlin, and make the base. There's something you never saw before, did you? Abby slams into the right-field crowd, and Wagner scores.

We got our runs in the fifth, when Bridwell walked, Matty hit to right and Tenney sacrificed. Then up comes Doyle, with that sheepish, sleepy look on his face that he wears whether making a record play or doing a fan, and he smashes brave and bold to left, scoring Brid and Matty, and the crowd is on the field calling for their Doyley. They do some more calling in the seventh, but it isn't the same. In that inning {Owen} Wilson singles for a starter, Swacina walks, and {George} Gibson hits into the crowd, scoring Wilson and tying the game, and then—

Leifield hits to Doyle, and lo! our Larry fumbled! What, lissome, lightning Larry? Yes, our youngster sure backslid. And what fell out when Larry missed? The grandstand and the bleachers hissed. And did that let the Pirates win? You bet your life it did. For, a minute later, Doyle makes another bad one, and Leifield scores the winning run.

—W. W. Aulick, New York *Times*

After the crowd and the importance of the game was the batting of Honus Wagner. He batted five times and five times he smote the ball safely, two of his hits being doubles. Such mighty swatting against a pitcher of Mathewson's caliber was worth the price of admission alone.

—New York *Tribune*

Each time he hit safely, after his second hit, Hans Wagner signaled to Mike Donlin in right field, "That's 3, Mike," "That's 4" and "That's 5."

—New York *World*

Fred Merkle, who had been threatened with blood poisoning, batted for Matty in the seventh. He looked pale and sick, not equal to a game yet. Herzog, the little shortstop, who had a disagreement with McGraw and quit the team, was also in uniform yesterday.

—New York *Tribune*

———◇ MONDAY, JULY 27 ◇———

Though official figures were not announced, Saturday's crowd broke the record for the Polo Grounds. That means that considerably more than 25,000 viewed the game—not counting the thousands who stood on the 155th street viaduct and on Coogan's Bluff, nor those on the free list.

On Oct. 10, 1905, the Giants and Athletics played the second game of the world's series before an immense crowd. The National Commission, which had charge of the box office, announced that 24,992 had paid to see this game. The word of Secretary Fred Knowles after Saturday's game is accepted as fact, and Mr. Knowles declared it was the biggest crowd ever.

In neither league do club owners give out actual attendance figures.

Some profess to, but the writer knows positively that there are always some "added starters" to these statements. The New York club has never announced attendance figures, and except for the big game in 1905, estimates are mere guesswork. —Sid Mercer, New York *Globe*

By his great hitting Friday and Saturday Hans Wagner passed Mike Donlin in the race for National League batting honors. The great Honus made seven hits in eight times at bat, while Michael Angelo failed to peel off even one safety in seven trips to the plate. Wagner's average is .340, and Donlin's is .328. —New York *Globe*

——— NATIONAL LEAGUE STANDINGS ———

	W	L	PCT.	GB		W	L	PCT.	GB
Pittsburgh ...	53	35	.602	—	Cincinnati .	46	42	.523	7
Chicago	49	35	.583	2	Boston	38	47	.447	13½
New York ...	50	36	.581	2	Brooklyn ..	31	54	.365	20½
Philadelphia .	42	38	.525	7	St. Louis ...	30	54	.357	21

———◇ **TUESDAY, JULY 28** ◇———

{On July 27, in New York, the Giants lost to Pittsburgh 4 to 3. Winning pitcher, Maddox; losing pitcher, Crandall. Giants' standing: 50 wins, 37 losses, in third place.}

Before the Pittsburgh Pirates got through bumping the ball to parts of the field where New York outfielders were not they had established a lead the Giants could never overcome. As usual Hans Wagner was the chief factor in the Giant downfall. The "Flying Dutchman" hit for two bases the first and second time he came to bat. The first time he tallied on Abbaticchio's sacrifice and Wilson's double. The next time Honus scored Clarke and came through himself on a sacrifice and Wilson's triple to right.

Crandall succeeded in checking the "Flying Dutchman's" great batting streak {seven straight hits} when he made him foul out to Bridwell.

Roger Bresnahan made a season's record recently with three sacrifice hits. Yesterday he made another with four consecutive bases on balls. The last gift to Roger came in the eighth and resulted in a merry-go-round that brought the Giants within a run of the Pirates. {Nick} Maddox had been very effective until then, when he walked Bresnahan and Donlin. Cy Seymour wouldn't wait and banged a fly on which Bresnahan took third. Donlin stole second and in doing so bumped Wagner. The "Flying Dutchman" limped around as though he was crippled for life. Nearly the whole Pirate crew gathered around to sympathize. Fred Clarke and Donlin had a few words about it and Umpire Bob Emslie had to interfere. Finally Maddox tried again and almost broke Devlin's arm with a wild pitch.

When Maddox was waved out of the box and Young Cy Young appeared to take his place, it dawned on the Giants and the fans that the wily Wagner had pulled off a trick. {Irving Young, mentioned in the entry of May 10, had recently been traded from Boston to Pittsburgh.} While he was apparently in agony Young had been warming up like a house afire back of the stand. When the pitchers changed places Honus ceased to limp. —New York *World*

Miss Neuralgia Nearsilk, in the stand, asked her escort: "Who is that peculiar-looking person out there where I am pointing?" "That," replied the provider, "is Hans Wagner. He is the greatest ball player that ever lived."

"Mercy to goodness!" exclaimed Neuralgia, "if he can play that well with his legs all bowed up, just think what a player he would be if his legs were straight!"

A funny thing happened in the third inning. With two men out Mike Donlin smashed what looked like a sure two-bagger down the line between Wagner and Leach. Honus started after the ball like the cute little fielder he is, and actually wrapped his big paw around it some thirty feet outside the diamond. Not content with this phenomenal stop he threw to first without even looking, but Michael had just crossed the bag. Mike and Hans are in a bitter struggle for batting supremacy, so you can't blame either of them for working overtime in cutting off the other's hits.
—William F. Kirk, New York *American*

By disregarding the custom of letting the first pitch go by, the Pirates won yesterday. Most young pitchers try to put their first offering to a batsman over the plate. A great many times it is safe to do this, for many good hitters scorn to move at the first offering. Crandall kept sticking the first one over yesterday. Fred Clarke passed the word to waste no time. The result was that of the Pirates' five extra-base hits in the second and fourth innings four were made off the first ball pitched. From these hits came all the Pittsburgh runs.

Members of the Pittsburgh team insist Umpire Klem was handed a gold brick by allowing Doyle to take his base in the ninth. It was a good "stall," however, for McGraw and Doyle got away with it. The ball Doyle dodged seemed to have missed him by a foot, but it hit something. Spectators thought it tipped Doyle's bat. Larry stood on his head, wriggled around on one ear, came down kerflop, and then arose with an expression of great pain. He limped around in a circle embracing his own right shoulder. After a minute of this performance he faced Klem with a "dying sheep" expression. The stony-hearted arbitrator told Larry to quit kidding and come back and bat. McGraw ran over to Doyle and began to massage the supposed wound. Tommy Leach ran up and when he observed McGraw's hand under Doyle's blouse and noticed a fresh look of agony on Larry's face, he yelled: "Look out for McGraw, he's pinching him." Klem ran down to the group and when Doyle bared his shoulder the umpire saw a black and blue spot. He motioned Doyle to first, and Leach informed the umpire he had been the victim of a "skin" game, and that McGraw's thumb and forefinger, not the ball, had produced the welt.

—Sid Mercer, New York *Globe*

In fielding Wagner's second hit, McCormick was about as fast as the progress of the erection of St. John's Cathedral. And it was that way throughout the game. There may be things McCormick does well, but in this list you can't include playing left field.

—W. W. Aulick, New York *Times*

Among those present at the Herald Square Theatre last night were Mr. and Mrs. Michael Donlin. They occupied a box, and Mr. Mike's new

$350 dress suit and diamond studs attracted almost as much favorable comment as Mrs. Mike's $500 bird-of-paradise hat.

—New York *Evening Mail*

CHICAGO, July 28—It is said here that the Chicago Cubs will protest against the action of the New York Giants in not playing a scheduled game in St. Louis last Wednesday {see July 22, second entry}. The *Tribune* has the following editorial on the subject:

"That the New York Giants club is a law unto itself long has been an axiom among those who have followed that organization. The latest illustration was furnished when the New York club omitted to play Wednesday's scheduled game in St. Louis for no known reason except to have an opportunity to reach New York the day before they would begin a crucial series with Pittsburgh. Presumably it was Manager McGraw's belief that his club would stand a better chance if his players had a good night's rest before the series instead of having to sleep in hot berths and then get out and play ball.

"In order to do this the Giants had to have collusion on the part of the St. Louis club. If the latter had refused to postpone Wednesday's game, the Giants would have had to stay and play. That would have meant reaching New York on Friday morning and playing Pittsburgh that afternoon. They would then have been on even terms with Pittsburgh, which had to play Brooklyn on Thursday while the Giants were resting, then travel all night on a sleeper and meet New York on its own grounds without a solid night's sleep.

"Unless checked sharply, such practices can evolve into great injury to the game. From postponing a game to help a club it is only a short step to laying down for the same purpose."

—New York *Evening Mail*

———◇ **WEDNESDAY, JULY 29** ◇———

{On July 28, in New York, the Giants and Pittsburgh played a 16-inning game ended by darkness with the teams tied 2 to 2. Since the game ended in a tie, there were no pitchers of record. Giants' standing remained 50 wins, 37 losses, third place.}

The most sensational game of the season was called at 7 o'clock last night to allow rooters to catch their breath. When the charming Mr. Klem took off his cap and announced that nothing more was to be expected in the way of amusement, the score was 2 to 2.

Sixteen innings with two runs per side is not a usual combination, and when the sixteen innings are as full of startling situations and splendid plays as in yesterday's struggle, it's something you can tell to your grandchildren, when they come.

A statistician could have secured some very interesting dope in connection with the great battle. It would be absorbing to know, for instance, how many cold chickens, steaks and chops were left on dinner tables last evening in various sections of Manhattan; how many wives greeted their frantic husbands with, "Well, I thought you were never going to come"; how many engagements for the theater were broken.

"I know what I'll catch when I get home," said one rooter. "My wife won't do a thing but lecture me." "Tell her it was an extra-inning game," suggested a friend. "I told her that last night when there wasn't an extra-inning game," was the disconsolate reply.
                                        —William F. Kirk, New York *American*

About 80,000 paid to see the Giant-Pirate series. The average price paid by fans is 65 cents, so altogether some $50,000 was taken in between Friday and Tuesday, or about as much as the Pittsburgh team takes in during a full month at home.   —New York *Evening Mail*

———◇ **THURSDAY, JULY 30** ◇———

{On July 29, in New York, the Giants defeated St. Louis 1 to 0. Winning pitcher, Mathewson; losing pitcher, Sallee. Giants' standing: 51 wins, 37 losses, in third place.}

Fast baseball at the Polo Grounds yesterday, and praise be that Mr. Shortstop Charles took it into his hand to fumble, and that a bit later there was a passed ball. Otherwise Tuesday's record of 16 innings would surely have looked like an ordinary game, and we'd all have had to stay in our seats until Umpire Johnstone called the session.

Neither Mathewson nor Sallee would yield the fraction of an inch, so the fourth-inning run was a large lump of luck. Doyle went out at first because Gilbert was alert. Bresnahan bowled over to Charles, who fumbled and became immediately as popular with the spectating 5,000 as he would have been in St. Louis if he'd scored a home run on the telegraph bulletin boards. After Charles has fumbled, and Bresnahan is safe on first, there's a passed ball, and Bresnahan scores, and that's all the scoring.　　　　　　　　　—W. W. Aulick, New York *Times*

———◇ **FRIDAY, JULY 31** ◇———

{On July 30, in New York, the Giants defeated St. Louis 11 to 0. Winning pitcher, McGinnity; losing pitcher, Karger. Giants' standing: 52 wins, 37 losses, in third place.}

What a merry time it was at the Polo Grounds yesterday! The crack of bats enlivened every inning, and when the sun was setting the tired scorers announced that New York had scored eleven runs on 16 hits, including four lusty singles in four times at bat by McGinnity, which, as Muggsy McGraw remarked, is "going some" for a pitcher.
　　　　　　　　　—New York *Tribune*

It got so bad in the eighth inning that Capt. Mike Donlin, losing all interest in the game and despairing of being relieved from duty by ordinary methods, must start a doings with Umpire Johnstone.

But where is the chance for a battle when the umpire tells Mike to walk on four balls? You, nor I, gentle reader, could figure out a possibility. But Mike could and did. "It was four balls, all right," agreed Mr. Donlin, "but doggone that pitcher's ornery skin, why didn't he give 'em to me sooner? He was more than twenty seconds in giving me that last one. Why, a Manhattan Beach waiter is a section of chain lightning compared to that can of cold molasses!"

Mr. Johnstone cautioned our Captain. "Have a care, Michael," he counseled, "or I will do you disciplinary mischief."

"As far as you like," decided Mr. Donlin, "a rebuff at your hands is equivalent to a Class A compliment."

And Mr. Johnstone said that just for that Donlin had to get out of the game. And Donlin made for the clubhouse and was in his store clothes in time that would have made the late Bysonby look like a loiterer.

You never heard of a man kicking himself out of a game because he got a base on balls, did you? You have to pay a lot of attention to the Polo Grounds these days. Things happen up there.

—W. W. Aulick, New York *Times*

———◇ SATURDAY, AUGUST 1 ◇———

{On July 31, in New York, the Giants defeated St. Louis 9 to 2. Winning pitcher, Taylor; losing pitcher, Lush. Giants' standing: 53 wins, 37 losses, in third place.}

Now, who would suspect that Fred Tenney had a vein of humor in his Down East makeup?

But Fred Tenney did really spring a new joke yesterday, a rich one too, for it was impromptu and coming from a man who always wears a Cotton Mather visage was the surprise of the season, an epoch, as it were.

Tenney's joke, which is bound to become famous, was sprung on the unsuspecting populace in the eighth inning. Whatever it was that struck the usually mobile Frederick, it hit him hard. He started to steal second while {St. Louis pitcher} "Bugs" Raymond held the ball, and Fred made the pilfer all right. "Bugs" threw the ball to third, thinking that Luther Taylor, the runner on third, would be foolish to walk off and be "ketched." But Luther, although his hearing is not the best, has a "wiseness" that does acrobating stunts, simply stood where he was.

Then, what do you think? Fred, the funny Puritan, just ran back to first and gave "Bugs" the cracked-lip smile. "Bugs" was dumbfounded. The joke coming from Tenney was as dense to "Bugs" as a glass of beer that is all froth. So "Bugs" looked at Tenney and Tenney looked at "Bugs" and probably said "bughouse."

But when "Bugs" pitched the next ball Tenney darted for second again, and blamed if he didn't do the second-story act again, and all in one inning.

The funniest thing about the joke was that Tenney would have been out if a St. Louis player had thrown the ball to first and Tenney had been touched, or if the ball had been thrown to second and that base touched, but this didn't dawn on the Cardinals.

Tenney made the mistake of touching second and thus made himself liable to being put out by any opposing player who had the wisdom to tag him on the second-base bag.

A base runner cannot run backward, but it was not in Umpire Johnstone's province to put the Cardinals wise.

But Tenney springing the "gag"! Anything can make me laugh now. Fred, you little rascal!

The Cardinals were toyed with yesterday, as on Thursday, and that brings up the question of whether it is good to "show up" an opposing team as the Giants did. It appears to me as a reflection on the league itself.

—Sam Crane, New York *Evening Journal*

Mike Donlin, one of the best ball players who ever graced a New York uniform, and without doubt the most popular player the city has ever had, will make his debut as an actor with his wife in vaudeville at a local theater in October a few days after the close of the season.

Donlin and his wife, known theatrically as Mabel Hite, the cleverest funny woman on the stage today, signed contracts yesterday with a firm of managers whereby they will get $20,000 for a ten weeks' engagement. They have several offers from other managers to continue the contract on the same terms, and an offer has been made to star them together in a musical comedy.

Donlin's theatrical career will mark the end of his baseball history. He wants to quit while at the height of his popularity, and will go out of the National League in a blaze of glory. His theatrical engagements will keep him busy through the Winter and until late in the Summer, so ball playing will be out of the question. Donlin is a high-salaried man on the diamond, but would never earn as much there as in vaudeville, and he knows the value of money.   —Nie, New York *Evening Mail*

——◇ SUNDAY, AUGUST 2 ◇——

{On August 1, in New York, the Giants beat St. Louis 6 to 1. Winning pitcher, Crandall; losing pitcher, Beebe. Giants' standing: 54 wins, 37 losses, in third place.}

Using {Cardinal president} Stanley Robison's St. Louis athletes as mops the Giants cleaned up on the series with the Missourians and humbled them in easy fashion. As the Cubs were beaten by the Doves, the McGrawites repose within easy striking distance of second place and not far from the top.

The doings of the fifth inning, when four runs were recorded, broke the hearts of President Robison and Manager McCloskey. Fred Beebe, the St. Louis twirler, lasted through this inning, but after he had been hit for two singles and a double in the next period was derricked. Beebe was provoked at his withdrawal and fired his glove in such fashion that Charles, the Cardinal third-sacker, received it in his face.

—New York *Press*

{From a signed article in the New York *World* by Richard "Rube" Marquard.}

When the report circulated that I had been sold to the Giants for $11,000 I was the most interested person in Indianapolis in hearing about it. But at the time you couldn't prove by me that there was $11,000 in the whole world. Funny, isn't it, that a man can be worth so much money to somebody else and maybe not have a solitary sou himself!

I was born in Cleveland, O., on Oct. 9, 1887. I hate to admit it, but you can see that I will not be old enough to vote until next October. Another thing the matter with me, besides my youth, is that I am 6 feet 3 inches tall. I weigh 182 pounds. Therefore I am a long, lank kid.

My parents, who were French, died when I was a kid and I've practically been my own boss ever since. I attended institutions of learning in Cleveland, but I got most of my education on ball fields. If a man keeps his eyes and ears open he can pick up a lot of knowledge on the diamond—knowledge that has nothing to do with playing baseball, too.

I began to grow when I was born and I've kept it up ever since. Unless I cease stretching out I guess they'll have to hoist the sky a little higher so that I can hobble along without bumping my head on it every time I step up the gutter. I'm now so tall my friends have nicknamed me the "human lighthouse" and the "animated steeple" and I have to stoop when I consult with the umpire.

I have not figured out whether my height is an advantage or a handicap. Sometimes I believe the short pitcher has the advantage because he can throw an upshoot easier than the tall pitcher, but then the tall fellow can shoot the ball downward in a straight slant that annoys batters.

I remember the first big game I ever pitched. It was in Cleveland, my home town, and a great crowd turned out. I struck out 24 men and allowed only one hit, and the next day I was famous in my town. I was heralded as a second Rube Waddell. {One of baseball's best left-handed pitchers, Rube Waddell, whose major league career began in 1897, was famed for striking out batters; his last winning season came in 1908. Marquard gained his nickname because of a supposed pitching resemblance to Waddell.}

About this time I had a big chicken farm 25 miles west of Cleveland, and when I wasn't playing ball I spent my time raising chickens for the Cleveland markets. Raising chickens paid me as well, if not a lot better, than playing baseball, but the game had a fascination for me, and I could not keep out of it.

Unlike most athletes, I have no fixed method of training. I eat anything I want, providing I think it will agree with me. My methods of living and of diet are simple in the extreme. In fact, I have always been an exponent of the simple life. Only once did I try "living high." That was after I had begun pitching professional ball. I got the idea I ought to tog myself out in gay raiment, so I took the money I got for pitching and bought a gorgeous suit of clothes. It was of a florid cast of countenance, and it made itself heard in the dark, it was so loud. To match it I had a pair of yellow shoes that sneezed like a man with hay fever when I walked. I thought I was the best dressed man in the country till my friends saw me, and then I heard so many things about my appearance that I shook the duds forever. Since then I've lived quietly.

When I report to New York, I will do my best to help McGraw win the pennant. I shall strive to show New Yorkers they were not "gold-bricked" when they got me.

—Richard "Rube" Marquard, New York *World*

————◇ **MONDAY, AUGUST 3** ◇————

Not in years has the National League had such a contest as is being waged at present. In the last two years the Cubs clinched their hold on the pennant by August 1, and it was merely a matter of speculation just how many games they would be in advance of other teams at the end of the season. The story is altogether different this season. The Pirates, Cubs and Giants are very evenly matched, and it is impossible to say which team will finish in front. —New York *Tribune*

Donlin, Seymour, Tenney and Devlin have taken part in all Giants' games, which speaks well for their physical condition and their behavior toward umpires. —New York *World*

CHICAGO, Aug. 3—Umpire Klem says the tendency of knights of the indicator is to call decisions too fast, before the play is really over, and thereby hangs nearly half the mistakes they make and the trouble they have with players and spectators.

"Naturally," he said, "we umpires want to make our decisions sharp, clear and decisive, so everyone may know we are not guessing. Lack of positiveness in giving close decisions is sure to bring on a heap of trouble with the players.

"Still, there is an immense amount of kicking because the umpire calls a ball or strike before the ball is actually over the plate and the 'break' is missed. That hurts the pitcher or the batter and a kick is sure to follow. The same holds true on close base decisions. A little less haste will result in a good deal more accuracy."

—New York *Evening Telegram*

——— NATIONAL LEAGUE STANDINGS ———

	W	L	PCT.	GB		W	L	PCT.	GB
Pittsburgh ...	57	36	.613	—	Cincinnati ...	48	47	.505	10
Chicago	55	37	.598	1½	Boston	41	52	.441	16
New York ...	54	37	.593	2	Brooklyn	33	57	.367	22½
Philadelphia .	48	40	.545	6½	St. Louis	31	61	.337	25½

——◇ **TUESDAY, AUGUST 4** ◇——

{On August 3, in New York, the Giants defeated Cincinnati 6 to 0. Winning pitcher, Wiltse; losing pitcher, Spade. Giants' standing: 55 wins, 37 losses, in third place.}

Covered with whitewash the Cincinnati Reds left the field after their first game of the series with the Giants. It was merely a fresh coat McGraw's men gave the Reds, who had been shut out 29 innings in succession before reaching town. Sharp fielding, in which Al Bridwell played the star part, kept them from home plate.

—New York *World*

Jack Barry, a good, reliable ball player, was grabbed by McGraw yesterday morning and got in the game toward the latter part of the afternoon. There are two stories as to how Barry became a Giant. The New Yorks claim to have purchased him from St. Louis, while the Cardinal management says they released him unconditionally. The latter sounds reasonable. Barry is a good player, and such men are not wanted on the St. Louis team. He knows more about the game than Manager McCloskey ever dreamed of and perhaps was trying to teach the rest of the squad how to take a game occasionally. That is the same as treason in the Cardinal camp, where last place and no work suits everyone down to the ground.

If you count Marquard and Jack Myers, who will join the team later this month, the Giants could put three full teams in the field. There are 25 men in New York uniform every day at the Polo Grounds, and

McGraw is not thinking of letting anyone go. He is not going to lose the pennant on account of accidents to his regulars.

—Nie, New York *Evening Mail*

If Bridwell keeps on stopping those seeming impossibilities and getting them over to first ten feet ahead of the runner, like he did yesterday, he'll be using the star's dressing room and getting his name featured on big type on the program. The more you watch his play the more firmly you are convinced that in order to be a proper shortstop a man doesn't have to do a kangaroo crouch and walk like a pretzel. Hello, Hans!

—W. W. Aulick, New York *Times*

It looks as if President Harry Pulliam, who never before allowed his emotions for the Giants to run away with him, realizes the advantage of having them "cop" the flag. The worthy executive is casting no stones in the runaway of McGraw. Indeed, he is even bringing pressure to further Giant interests, so it is hinted by those who know.

Evidently the umpires have caught the spirit of their boss. It must be acknowledged that umpiring will not beat the Giants out of anything in 1908. Without casting reflections on the integrity of the umpires, it is nevertheless noticeable that seldom is a visitor favored on a "hairline" decision.

—New York *American*

CHICAGO, Aug. 3—Bookmaking on baseball games in Chicago has not been profitable, and bookmakers announced they are going out of the business.

Among those who have made books and the amounts lost are: James O'Leary, $6,000; Barney Zacharias, $15,000; John Burns, $4,000; "Honey" Waixel, $2,500; Philip Wexler, $1,500; Samuel Tuckhorn, $3,500; Patrick O'Malley, $3,500; and Romey Held, $1,000.

Besides their losses, thousands of dollars have been lost by proprietors of cigar stores and saloons.

"The baseball 'fan' is too wise. He knows too much about the game," said one disgusted bookmaker.

—New York *American*

———◇ **WEDNESDAY, AUGUST 5** ◇———

{On August 4, in New York, the Giants defeated Cincinnati in a doubleheader, 4 to 3 (in 12 innings) and 4 to 1 (8 innings, called because of darkness). Winning pitcher, Mathewson (both games); losing pitcher, Coakley (both games). Giants' standing: 57 wins, 37 losses, in second place.}

By winning both games from Cincinnati the Giants bounded into second place, coming within five points of Pittsburgh.

It took the Giants twelve innings to win the first game because McGinnity weakened in the ninth and the visitors tied the score by making two runs. Mathewson, who sat in the clubhouse waiting to work the second game, was called upon to do the lifesaving. When he entered the box one run had tallied and the second came over on a long fly off his delivery, but after that the Reds never had much of a chance.

The second game, though, was the better of the two, and J. Bentley Seymour did most of the scintillating, for on one occasion he drove the leather down to the right-field gate for a home run and on another occasion he smashed it so hard it struck the slat fence over the right-field bleachers and never came back. About 16,000 spectators roared and shouted and yelled, and women in the grandstand screamed their delight. The affair took on the complexion of a testimonial to Seymour.

—New York *Herald*

Yesterday at Washington Park in Brooklyn's game with St. Louis only one ball was in play during the entire game. The sphere started at 4 o'clock and held out for nine rounds. The Cardinals and Dodgers slapped the horsehide all over, but it always came back for more. It was fouled around in the normal way, but always came back. It was whacked to the clubhouse gate for a home run, and after the umpire looked it over to see if it was damaged it went right back to the pitcher's mound. {Brooklyn first baseman} Tim Jordan also smashed it good and hard when he fouled it against the right-field bleachers, but it was still in good shape. "It looked as if I would have to take the ball out in the eighth inning," said Umpire Klem, "but I saw the ball was game and always coming back for more. In order that it might set a record I concluded it would be wise to let the ball play until it wept down and out. Since it will hardly happen again, I would like to find who has the ball just to keep it as a souvenir."

—Mark Roth, New York *Globe*

PHILADELPHIA, Aug. 5—Frank Chance, who is a member of the joint rules committee of the major leagues, is flatfooted against the "spit ball," and is instituting a campaign to have legislation passed next Winter abolishing it. The leader of the Cubs has never been an advocate of the "spit-ball" delivery, but until his recent visit to Buffalo to watch the work of Pitcher {George} McConnell, of the Bisons, he never actively opposed it.

Several reasons were advanced by Chance for prohibiting the use of this style of delivery. It is hard on catchers, injuring their hands; it causes fielders to make wild throws; it is repulsive both in name and to the view of spectators, and its abolition would do much to increase batting.

At Buffalo, Chance found three catchers injured through the use of this form of delivery. McConnell is entirely a "spit-baller," and during the game the fielders had to lose time in handling the ball by wiping it off every time before they threw it. Although McConnell pitched a good game, winning 2 to 0, Chance refused to negotiate for him solely because he relies on the "spit ball." {McConnell would pitch for three seasons with the New York Yankees and, after Chance had departed in 1912, for two years with the Cubs, winning 17 games while losing 41.}

—New York *Evening Telegram*

CHICAGO, Aug. 5—Efforts to stamp out gambling in baseball will immediately be made by the American League. President Johnson will issue a bulletin to every American League club, calling attention to the prevalence of betting and asking each club owner to enforce to the letter the section in the league constitution prohibiting betting.

President Johnson figures that it may be necessary to arrest everyone caught making bets at ball parks. If the city police cannot be trusted to enforce the order, he will recommend that club owners assign private detectives to ferret out bettors and those receiving bets.

—New York *Evening Telegram*

———◇ THURSDAY, AUGUST 6 ◇———

{On August 5, in New York, the Giants played a 4 to 4 tie with Cincinnati, the game called at the end of 9 innings because of rain.}

There was no change yesterday in the National League standing, for stupid play and a foolish attempt by the Giants to show they could be as funny against Cincinnati as against St. Louis robbed New York of a chance to climb into first place while the Cubs and Pirates were idle. The Giants led 3 to 0 at the end of the eighth, but the Reds got to Crandall in the ninth, and, helped by some horseplay, in which the idolized Donlin figured, they scored four runs. Only good batting by McCormick and Herzog, who are so young they still take baseball seriously, saved the Giants from an absolutely needless defeat, as the run they drove in tied the game.

Tenney was badly spiked in the fourth and gave way to Merkle, who played an excellent game, making one unassisted double play that was the most brilliant play of the afternoon. In the sixth inning Kane and Huggins had walked, and Lobert drove a screaming liner to right. Merkle leaped high, speared the hit with one hand and completed the double play by beating Huggins to the bag by ten feet. He got the ball to Bridwell at second base in time for a triple play, but Bridwell dropped a perfect throw. Merkle's catch was as pretty as any piece of fielding seen in New York this season.

Crandall had beautiful support for eight innings, and he and the Giant fielders kept out of hot water until that unhappy last period.

Lobert singled to right, and Donlin, after picking up the ball, played with it, tossing it from one hand to the other. Lobert made for second base, and, naturally, beat Donlin's leisurely throw. {George "Dode"} Paskert tapped through shortstop, and Mitchell walked. Crandall was taken out and Taylor took his place. {Larry} McLean forced Mitchell and Lobert scored. {George "Admiral"} Schlei's fly to Seymour scored Paskert, and {Bob} Coulson, who ran for McLean, scored on {Mike} Mowrey's single after {Rudy} Hulswitt had made a safe hit, and the latter got home when Arthur Devlin hit him in the back in an attempt to stop him at the plate.

The Giants' trouble had been that they were too sure of the game, and no team can go against the Reds with that spirit.

—New York *Tribune*

Mr. and Mrs. Mike Donlin yesterday signed an eight weeks' contract to appear in "vodevil." They open Oct. 26 at Hammerstein's, and this booking will not take them any further than Brooklyn. After that they may roam out to Chicago and other cities.

Mrs. Donlin, one of the cleverest comediennes on the stage today, says she will not order Mike to appear for rehearsal just now. At present she is "pulling" for him to lead the National League in batting, and she hasn't missed a game at the Polo Grounds since "The Merry-Go-Round" closed two weeks ago.

"It's not true that I intend to quit baseball," says Mike. "If I divide my time between the diamond and the stage, my baseball career will help me get money in vaudeville, and I might as well get all that is coming to me.

"I also wish to correct a few statements going the rounds," continued "der Captain." "I wish it distinctly understood that I am not going to try to play Hamlet, nor do I intend to do that Salome thing, for by the time I start the weather will be too cold for such costumes. Mrs. Donlin is whipping our act into shape. She will be the real scream in it and I am content to be a piece of scenery if she hands me the part."

—New York *Globe*

President Ban Johnson of the American League might well turn his anti-gambling crusade to New York. Since the "lid" was clamped on the gambling end of metropolitan horse racing, a number of new faces, unfamiliar to "dyed-in-the-wool" fans have made their appearance. {In July a bill passed by the legislature and signed by the governor had prohibited horse-race wagering within the state of New York.} These recruit enthusiasts are noticeable for the large sums of money they carry with them.

There is more gambling on baseball about local parks now than at any time in the history of the game. It hasn't become an open proposition yet, but it is drifting that way.

New York bettors are not educated to the game yet. Over in Chicago, St. Louis and Cincinnati, the gambling element has been well schooled. But it will not take New Yorkers long to get wise if the thing is permitted. —New York *Tribune*

———◇ FRIDAY, AUGUST 7 ◇———

{On August 6, in New York, the Giants lost to Cincinnati 5 to 0. Winning pitcher, Spade; losing pitcher, McGinnity. Giants' standing: 57 wins, 38 losses, in third place.}

There was plenty of German ginger up at the Polo Grounds yesterday. The poor old Zinzinnati boys won a game, and Manager Ganzel presented every member of the club, while said members were shower bathing, with his best regards. Manager McGraw handed his perspiring gladiators the best regards he could get out of his system, and there was enough paprika in his well-formed sentences to make a bunch of old cabbage look like a Mexican dinner.

A heavy rain came our way about 3 o'clock, and for one solid hour it came down like the first inning of the Deluge. Thousands of fans who might have attended in ordinary circumstances stayed downtown, and the gathering reminded us of an enthusiastic bunch of Highland {Yankees} rooters. Perhaps that is one reason why the Giants were not there with the old paper {refers to paper money, as used for tickets}. They have been going along at such a lively clip they are not used to small crowds, and the empty bleachers must have taken their ginger away.

Umpire Rigler was about the busiest cup of tea you ever saw. The grounds were so wet almost every ball pitched had to be taken to cover for a dry cleaning. It was up to Rigler to decide whether the ball was too wet to handle and to hit, and you can be sure he looked them over judiciously. Most umpires wouldn't know a dry ball from a highball, but Umpire Rigler never made one bad decision. Perhaps fifty balls were exchanged during the dismal affair, and he didn't miss one.

—William F. Kirk, New York *American*

Mr. John J. McGraw thought he was cutting into a fine, ripe can-teloupe this afternoon and was much surpised to find a lemon of the sourest variety. The Giant leader forced the Reds to play ball after a hard rain had soaked the yard and there was every legitimate reason for a postponement. Mr. McGraw acted in this inhospitable manner because he thought our boys would be easy picking, and he saw a chance of landing in first place. It never occurred to him that his pennant chasers would not win. But the red worm, having been stepped on six straight times, was due to turn. It not only turned; it stood up on its hind legs, reared, bucked, and tore around in the most scandalous manner. Therefore the long losing streak, beat by the tie game yesterday, was smashed today when our boys, sore at having to play on a soaked field, daubed the chesty Giants with whitewash.

—Jack Ryder, Cincinnati *Enquirer*

———◇ SATURDAY, AUGUST 8 ◇———

{On August 7, in New York, the Giants' scheduled game with the Cubs was postponed because of rain.}

When the Chicago Cubs won the National League pennant, a news-paper man out in Chicago {Charles Dryden of the *Tribune*} started to call Frank Chance the "peerless leader." Today the Cubs are battling to keep their heads above fourth place and one does not hear much of the peerless leader thing unless a laugh goes with it.

For the time being you've got to give the title to Johnny McGraw. Few people, even the most rabid fans, realize what a wonderful fight McGraw has made this season, and that the Giants are second is due far more to his wonderful generalship than to the playing of the team.

Everywhere McGraw is feared by opposing players, and there is not a fan in Pittsburgh or Chicago or St. Louis or Cincinnati or Boston or Philadelphia who down in his heart would not like to see McGraw lead-ing their team.   —Nie, New York *Evening Mail*

In my estimation, the New York club makes a big mistake in not giving out the numbers who attend games. If they did so it would set a record we want here in good old New York, the best baseball city on earth. Out in Chicago they say they cop the country on crowds, but in New York we know different. The money is here, anyhow. Most Chicago patrons are twenty-five-centers, but in New York baseball patrons do not think they are getting their money's worth unless they give up four bits.

In New York if 1,000 twenty-five-centers look at a game it is considered a big crowd. In Chicago the two-bit people run the game. That is the difference between New York and Chicago on everything.

—Sam Crane, New York *Evening Journal*

Baseball is only in its infancy, declare many able critics, and it looks as though ball parks now in existence would be all too small for the multitudes ten years from now. What is to be done? It is impossible to elongate present fields in most cases. On some grounds—like the Cub park, for instance—the limit has been reached in seating capacity. Mr. Murphy has double-decked his stands clear round the field, and put boxes on the grass till catchers and first basemen have little room to chase foul flies. Even then, people are turned away. The solution: Take a lesson from England. I have a photograph of the grandstand at Epsom, the great English race course. It has six decks, rising high in the air. Six decks—just think of it! A six-decked stand, running round the field, as is now the case at Cub park, would hold 60,000—and the day is not far distant when 60,000 people will be at baseball games. Yes.

—W. A. Phelon, *Sporting Life*

—————◇ **SUNDAY, AUGUST 9** ◇—————

{On August 8, in New York, the Giants defeated Chicago 4 to 1. Winning pitcher, Wiltse; losing pitcher, Brown. Giants' standing: 58 wins, 38 losses, in second place.}

That's how we like to win—with 30,000 folks sitting, standing, and hanging around saying "Ain't they grand!" when we make a hit or get a ball off the other pitcher. Victory is twice as sweet when witnessed. Remember when you got a stranglehold on your first cigarette and puffed proudly without getting sick as She came along? Remember the admiration, tinctured with awe, with which She regarded you? Ever so much more satisfactory than puffing back of the woodshed, eh?

That's the way it was yesterday. We beat the Chicagos, with as big a crowd as the Polo Grounds ever held on hand. And maybe the final score wasn't of the sort that you whistle as you go out! We're willing to bet none of the grand old masters of song ever put over a composition worthy of mention on the same staff as that score of yesterday.

And we all knew Chicago yesterday. We'd been getting a gradual line on Chicago since they started from the top of the chute some days ago, and we were unafraid even when they threatened us with Brown. "Brown? Brown?" we tried to remember where and how we had heard this word. Oh, yes, to be sure. Pitcher for Chicago, isn't he? Very well, Brown. Stand there on that little slab where we can see you, and we will change your color in about one consecutive inning. Hold fast, there, Brown, or you'll fade in this strong sunlight.

Even the best of teams couldn't have stopped us yesterday. We had our crowd with us.   —W. W. Aulick, New York *Times*

We have it on good authority that Mr. Francois Chance gave an interview Saturday in which he alleged that the Giants had shot their bolt. "We have their number now," said Mr. Chance, "and they are due for a cleaning. They do not class with us." Right you are, Francois. They do not.

The haughty Cubs, as they lined up yesterday against the gingery Giants, were another Falstaff's army. {See Shakespeare's *Henry IV, Part I*, Act IV, Scene 2.} They were so beaten up when the ninth inning was history they looked like so many Teddy bears in a second-hand store. {Named after President Theodore Roosevelt, the Teddy bear had first appeared in the summer of 1904.} Every time one of 'em got a wallop in the stomach he said "Ma-ma" just as cute. (Chicago papers please copy.)

George Wiltse pitched a splendid game and received brilliant support. This clever southpaw is working in a more masterful manner than ever in his career, and you can't hand him too many bouquets.

                    —William F. Kirk, New York *American*

Who is today's greatest baseball player? Most fans would probably give the accolade to Hans Wagner, but two players have come up to challenge Wagner for the title of "the greatest ball player," Mike Donlin, of the Giants, and Ty Cobb, the sensational young player of Detroit, who has made greater strides to the front in two years of major league service than any other player ever did in the same length of time.

Mike Donlin's admirers—and no man that ever wore the uniform of the Giants was more popular in this city than Turkey Donlin—claim he is handicapped by his position in right field. Otherwise nobody would dispute that he is Wagner's equal. His batting has been the most consistent and timely of any player in the National League. Few players know the game as well as Donlin. From his position he sizes up every play at once, and as captain of the team doesn't hesitate to "call" his men when they slip up or praise them when they do good work. Donlin infuses the Giants with the spirit that wins pennants.

—G. O. Tidden, New York *World*

I see but one team with a chance to beat us, Pittsburgh. Chicago I cannot see with smoked glasses. Frank Chance's braves are not possessed of the proper spirit, in my estimation. Everything was lovely while the Windy City lads were showing a stern chase to the rest of the company. But when collared the Cubs have proved quite docile.

Chicago had some tough luck, but no more than fell the way of New York. We have outgamed them and will continue so to do. But the Pirates! Ah, there's the dig. Pittsburgh may be a one-man team, but that man is a "dilly." The Pirates are every bit as aggressive as any member of baseball's select society. Where I figure to beat them out is in teamwork and all around generalship. Then, too, we have the advantage of finishing the season at home. The Pirates will wind up on the road.

—George Wiltse, New York *American*

Chicago, in my mind, is the one team we have to beat. I figure the Cubs stronger than the Pirates because of the experience of Frank Chance's men and the confidence that the successes of two consecutive years have engendered. Chicago boasts a crackerjack pitching staff, and has a hard-hitting, fast-fielding, heady, aggressive team. I believe the Giants outgame the Cubs, and I think this will win the pennant for us.

Pittsburgh, of course, must be reckoned with. But the Pirates are more or less a one-man aggregation. Without Hans Wagner Pittsburgh would have a hard time to get into the first division.

Our greatest chance, I believe, lies in the fact that we will finish the season at home. The encouragement of a friendly big city is no small factor in a team's success.

—Christy Mathewson, New York *American*

———◇ **MONDAY, AUGUST 10** ◇———

On Saturday, August 8, the sandwich man at the Polo Grounds announced officially that he had sold 92,687,463,106 sandwiches during the afternoon. He leaves for Europe on an early boat and will endeavor to cop a German nobleman for his daughter. The peanut man will probably follow suit. —Rube Goldberg, New York *Evening Mail*

Breezing along, Hans Wagner starts the week at the top of the National League swat artists, nine points ahead of Mike Donlin. Last week the big Dutchman added seven points to his average and now is batting .335. Donlin fell off one point to .326.

Donlin is New York's only representative in select society. Larry Doyle is batting .274, an improvement of eight points in a week, and Bresnahan and Bridwell are the next best regulars with .268 and .267.

—New York *Evening Mail*

——— NATIONAL LEAGUE STANDINGS ———

	W	L	PCT.	GB		W	L	PCT.	GB
Pittsburgh ...	60	37	.619	—	Cincinnati ...	51	51	.500	11½
New York ...	58	38	.604	1½	Boston	44	54	.449	16½
Chicago	56	41	.577	4	Brooklyn	36	60	.375	23½
Philadelphia .	51	42	.548	7	St. Louis	32	65	.330	28

———◇ TUESDAY, AUGUST 11 ◇———

{On August 10, in New York, the Giants defeated Chicago 3 to 2. Winning pitcher, Mathewson; losing pitcher, Overall. Giants' standing: 59 wins, 38 losses, in second place.}

Das German Cubs, Sheckard, Steinfeldt, Slagle and all the rest of 'em were taken over the hurdles yesterday before the largest Monday crowd that ever saw a baseball game in the United States. At least 20,000 people were there to see McGraw's men pound the stuffing out of the world's champs, and what they didn't do in the way of cheering and chuckling might as well be left undone.

Monday, as a rule, is a poor baseball day. People who spend Sunday batting around Coney Island and Fort George do not generally possess any pepper on washday. It is a blue day, is Monday, particularly for folks who draw salaries on Saturday. John T. Brush is not exactly an optimist, and he never dreamed that yesterday's game would pack the grounds.

The game was a magnificent pitchers' battle between Christy Mathewson and Jumbo Overall, and it would be hard to say which deserves more credit. Matty was found for more hits, but inasmuch as he held the Cubs to two runs and beat them, he must be accorded a slight shade.

Our trio of runs came in the opening chapter. Tenney lined to center, and Herzog, who played second base in place of Doyle, drew a base on balls. Doyle, by the way, hurt his ankle in practice before the game, and may be out for some time. Herzog showed steadiness and class, and looks like a dandy understudy for Laughing Larry. After he had reached first base, Bresnahan doubled to left, the ball rolling to the crowd.

An obliging special policeman, one of those efficient guardians of the peace we all respect so much, stopped the ball and chucked it back toward the plate. Nobody wanted this sleuth to break into the assist column, and perhaps, being a true policeman, that is why he did it. Herzog could have scored easily, but he was sent back to third base by Umpire O'Day, who ruled it a blocked ball.

McGraw walked out to the special policeman and said something. It was too far for us to determine what Gentle Jawn got off, but a sound came wafting along on the Summer zephyrs that made a noise like "cheese." That's right, Jawn. Give 'em the dickens. It didn't make much difference, the way things turned out, as Herzog scored by a splendid slide when Donlin sent a chopper down the groove.

Then Donlin and Bresnahan tried a little double stealing, and while Captain Mike was waltzing up and down the line between first and second base Roger made a bolt for the plate. Evers threw wild and Roger scored hands down, Captain Mike going to third base. Seymour's fly to centerfield scored Mike, and that is how we got 'em.

—William F. Kirk, New York *American*

We kept our 3 to 0 lead till the eighth, and then Tinker rounded his batting work with his third hit, a beautiful drive to left center good for three bases. Pay a little attention to Tinker, you batting statisticians, and figure out what sort of a percentage three hits out of three times at bat is, eh? When Overall was thrown out at first by Herzog, Tinker squeezed home, and just to show we appreciate Chicago endeavor we gave Tinker our kind applause and cautioned him not to do it again while he's in these parts. —W. W. Aulick, New York *Times*

INDIANAPOLIS, Aug. 10—That Pitcher Rube Marquard, of the Indianapolis team, has experienced a reversal of form cannot be denied. Rube has lost six and won only one game since the announcement of his sale to the New York Giants. —New York *American*

————◇ **WEDNESDAY, AUGUST 12** ◇————

{On August 11, in New York, the Giants lost to Chicago 4 to 0 in a game called after 6 innings because of rain. Winning pitcher, Pfiester; losing pitcher, Wiltse. The second game of a scheduled doubleheader was postponed. Giants' standing: 59 wins, 39 losses, in second place.}

Not only every midweek but every Saturday record went by the board yesterday. Fully 10,000 disappointed fans raged around the entrances after all had been closed.

The scene inside, after it began to rain hard, was really wonderful. Chicago was four runs ahead in the sixth inning when the Giants came to bat. It was raining so hard nine umpires out of ten would have called the game, giving Chicago a 2 to 0 victory. Perhaps O'Day thought of doing so, but scarcely a fan had made a move to bolt, although only a part of the grandstand offered protection from the driving rain, and once the inning started no umpire would have dared to stop play.

The ball was so wet Pfiester could do little with it, and a score of thousand straw hats leaped up in the rain as Wiltse walked to first on four balls. Tenney followed, and the crowd went crazy as he slammed a single over second, one of two hits by the Giants all afternoon. Every man was on his feet as Herzog came to bat.

The youngster stabbed valiantly at a straight ball, but it shot toward Evers, who made a wonderful stop and threw to Tinker in time to catch Tenney at second. Tinker hurled the ball to Chance, trying for a double play, and the fury of the fans was unrestrained as Rigler called Herzog out. There was reason for the roar of disapproval, for it looked as if Herzog had beaten the ball by at least a foot. McGraw, ordered off the field by O'Day a few minutes before, rushed out from his temporary retirement protesting vigorously, as did Donlin, but the protest was of no avail.

The cross timbers supporting the roof of the grandstand afforded a good view and a seat as well, and they were in demand from the start. In climbing up to one of them a man's foot turned the wheel that controls a fire hydrant, and five seconds later water spurted out of a two-inch nozzle and drenched a hundred persons sitting in the line of fire. The crowd in the aisle at the back was so dense it was nearly ten minutes before the source of the trouble could be found.

Bar one time—and we don't place too much faith in that Ark story at that—there never has been so much rain falling in one place as descended yesterday on the Polo Grounds. At the seventh-inning point Mr. O'Day called the game. Many gentlemen then spoke their mind to him. The mildest among them said Mr. O'Day was a "robber." But most of them were quite frank, and the consensus of opinion was that Mr. O'Day is the person who struck Billy Patterson, stole the remains of A. T. Stewart, sunk the *Maine*, and did his best to press the crown of thorns on the brow of the laboring man.　　　　　—W. W. Aulick, New York *Times*

Figures on the check carried away by the Chicago club were the largest ever paid a visiting club for three days of play. It took several money bags to cart the receipts away yesterday and a detail of police was provided to see that no strong-armed persons interfered with the circulation of this wad through the streets of Harlem.

—Sid Mercer, New York *Globe*

If the lady who parted with her slipper in the mud near second base about 3:45 yesterday, while doing 440 yards across the field in record time, will leave her name and address with Groundkeeper John Murphy, the article will be returned to her. Otherwise it may be put on the bargain counter. It's as good as new but slightly water stained. Those sprints across the field in the pelting rain were highly enjoyed by those under cover. Incidentally the latest styles in hosiery were duly noted and approved of with loud acclaim.

—New York *Globe*

——◇ THURSDAY, AUGUST 13 ◇——

{On August 12, in New York, Brooklyn beat the Giants 5 to 1. Winning pitcher, Rucker; losing pitcher, Crandall. Giants' standing: 59 wins, 40 losses, in second place.}

About the time William Jennings Bryan was accepting the Presidential nomination in quaint old Lincoln, Nebraska, the New York Giants were accepting a lemon in honor of the Brooklyn club's President Ebbets.

Brooklyn hasn't got a very good baseball club, but for some strange reason the Donovan men play their heads off to beat the McGraw men. No matter how many games they may drop to second-rate clubs like St. Louis, they invariably jump in and play like fiends incarnate when they reach the Polo Grounds. There isn't much brotherly love between the Dodgers and Polo Grounders. The relations between these bands of gladiators are very much Cain and Abel.

Our Giants played a listless game, but the main reason for our humiliation was a stocky southpaw named Rucker. He had everything and didn't forget to use everything. Before his speedy cannonading the Giants looked like a tame lot of children.

—William F. Kirk, New York *American*

Mike Donlin struck out twice, and the crowd hooted the Giant captain as he fanned the second time. It's hard to be an idol at the Polo Grounds.

—Brooklyn *Eagle*

——◇ **FRIDAY, AUGUST 14** ◇——

{On August 13, in New York, the Giants defeated Brooklyn 5 to 3. Winning pitcher, Mathewson; losing pitcher, Bell. Giants' standing: 60 wins, 40 losses, in second place.}

Leon Ames, who made his debut yesterday, didn't do so well, and Brooklyn got three runs before the second inning was finished. "Big Six" went in next inning, pitching out the game in his usual gilt-edged style.

The last of the fifth had plenty of action and brought victory to the Giants. Donlin started it with a stiff three-bagger to left. {George "Whitey"} Alperman had just taken {John} Hummell's place at second base and celebrated his arrival by laying for Captain Mike as he rounded second, giving him the shoulder in such a manner that Mike whirled several times and fell heavily on his back. It was as deliberate a piece of foul work as was ever seen on a baseball diamond, and when O'Day told Mike to go to third base, the crowd cheered the umpire and hissed Alperman roundly.

Alperman deserved all the roasting he got. Baseball is usually free from football tactics, and it should be kept so. If a lot of young rah! rah! boys want to kick the bridgework out of each other's mouths in a rugby game, let 'em do it. But when a professional baseball player tries a trick that may result in broken bones and perhaps ruin a man's earning capacity, he is not thoroughbred.

—William F. Kirk, New York *American*

The Giants are becoming so speedy they get "pinched" for speeding. After they walloped Brooklyn there was little time to catch the train for St. Louis. All but Mathewson, Merkle and Devlin got away to a good start. This trio, with Secretary Fred Knowles, hopped into a taxicab and ordered the "shofar" to go as fast as he liked.

Not many of these "demon drivers" get a chance to carry the mighty Mathewson, and this one certainly pried apart the zephyrs in the race to the ferry {from Manhattan to Jersey City, from where westward-bound trains then departed}.

The pinch came when the car was within hailing distance of the boat. When Matty promised to trim Chicago and Pittsburgh the man in blue and brass decided to lock up the "shofar" and his car and send the players on their way.

The "cop's" parting remark to Matty was: "If you shoot 'em over as fast as this car was traveling you'll win the pennant."

The "shofar" was fined, but the club will pay the freight.

—New York *Evening Mail*

——◇ **SATURDAY, AUGUST 15** ◇——

St. Louis, Aug. 15—It could hardly be called a team, the aggregation which rolled into town. It was more like a caravan or an army of invaders, the party of 37 people, for, besides the players, there is an enlarged collection of war correspondents, and, to add eclat to the outfit Mrs. Michael Donlin (nee Mabel Hite), Mrs. J. Bentley Seymour, and Mrs. William Malarkey are along, and in Chicago Mrs. Arthur Devlin will join them.

Such a pretentious crowd cannot travel without a physician, so Dr. James Creamer, surgeon extraordinary to the Giants at home, is making the journey. —Nie, New York *Globe*

St. Louis, Aug. 15—The Giants arrived shortly before 10 o'clock last night, hot, tired and dusty, but on time, and this was a godsend, for the heat throughout the journey had been fierce.

It was fortunate that Secretary Knowles arranged to take the flyer

Thursday at 6:30 P.M., for the boys were assured a good night's rest before today's game.

Mike Donlin's wife, Mabel Hite, has become a pronounced fan, and is "rooting terribly hard" for Mike to beat out Wagner for batting honors. When McGraw bought a paper last night at the Union Station, Mrs. Donlin rushed up and asked "How many hits did Wagner get?" McGraw replied, "Hans won the game as usual." Mrs. Donlin said plaintively, "Oh, pshaw!" with a pucker of her pretty lips.

—Sam Crane, New York *Evening Journal*

Ball players are very much worked up over the action of the National Commission in prohibiting club owners from making presents to players, and there is a strong probability of their forming a players' protective association to combat the act and to fight against further restrictions of their rights, as regards presents, bonuses and the salary question.

One prominent player of the Cardinals told me, "We have to get together, that's all, and join a labor organization as a body. We cannot be secure in our rights unless we are banded together under some such body that we know we must stick to or show ourselves lobsters if we don't stick. We don't want a ball player at the head of our organization, but someone out of baseball altogether who is a good executive and can enforce our rights with regular labor confederation methods.

"The club owners are making enough money to give us a fair show. The next thing we know they will spring a low salary limit on us, and then where will we be? I spoke to several of the Reds and they are all for a protective association, and several Giants also told me they are with me. I am going to talk to the Eastern players and get them to work for it among the players I can't see. We will get the thing going this Winter sure as you're a foot high."

—Sam Crane, New York *Evening Journal*

———◇ SUNDAY, AUGUST 16 ◇———

{On August 15, in St. Louis, the Giants won 5 to 1. Winning pitcher, Wiltse; losing pitcher, Sallee. Giants' standing: 61 wins, 40 losses, in second place.}

Sᴛ. Louɪs, Aug. 15—With Wiltse the Wonderful in the box, the Gotham athletes took the first game of the series from the St. Louis Cardinals, knocking {Harry Franklin} Sallee, who twice has beaten them this season, off the rubber. Captain Mike Donlin delivered the key blow in the fifth, with Bresnahan on second, a long fly to centerfield. Shaw came in on the ball, went out on it, and finally lost it, Bresnahan walking home ahead of the galloping Mike, credited with a four-bagger.

—New York *Press*

In the last inning Roger Bresnahan drew a base on balls, and was then picked off base. But Roger's wits were with him and he didn't make a futile attempt to get back. He just quietly walked to second base, claiming a balk, and Mr. Johnstone approved of it.

Also in the ninth, with Koney {first baseman Ed Konetchy} at bat and two strikes on him, Wiltse sailed one through close to the outside corner. Mr. Klem hesitated, and again Bresnahan used his wits and threw the ball to the third baseman instead of the pitcher.

"Strike three! You're out," cried Klem.

—James Crusinberry, St. Louis *Post-Dispatch*

{From a signed article in the New York *World* by Larry Doyle.}

L. L. Doyle, that's me. That stands for Lawrence Louis Doyle, the signboard they nailed onto me at the christening font in Breese, Ill., but my friends insist on calling me "Laughing Larry."

Breese was well named. I think it was the windiest place on earth. That's how I account for my early affection for the mines. I wanted to get off the earth without being blown off, so what was more natural than to burrow?

It is not surprising that I began to play baseball at an early age. It was about the only thing for me to do. I was never imbued with the idea of setting the world afire with my superior mentality, therefore I didn't make the town schoolteacher earn his salary. And so while the other kids were pretending to assimilate problems in elementary arithmetic I was building a foundation as a ball player. And I've never regretted it.

Swinging on the ball with a bat developed my arms and shoulders, and it was not long before I was physically qualified to work in the mines. My father was a miner, and he "broke me in" as a coal digger.

Working in a mine is like going up in a balloon, only in the opposite direction. You don't think anything of it if you are used to it, but when you first go down into the earth there comes a sudden realization of what might happen to you. Nowadays the mines can be lighted by electricity, and it's comparatively simple to go through a mine. But when you get caught without a light in some deep labyrinth in the bowels of the earth it's no picnic.

Of course, I kept up my ball playing. When I had time to myself I managed to get up a game. One day I was in a game when some strangers came along and watched. I landed on one ball for a homer, and three innings later I repeated the trick. After the game one of the men said I was wasting my time playing for fun. He said I could make money playing with semi-professional teams, and once I got the idea I couldn't get rid of it. I began to sell my services, and there was a big demand for them. I quit mining, and gave all my time to ball playing.

I joined the Mattoon team, in the Three-Eye League. I remained with the team when it was taken into the K.I.T. League. I played pretty good ball with these fellows, and then was traded to Springfield. I had a fair streak with this team, batted around .325 and had a good fielding average.

I noticed that Dan Brouthers {An outstanding major league first baseman in the 1880s and '90s, Brouthers became one of baseball's first scouts, acting in this capacity for John McGraw.} trailed the team a good deal, and last year when I heard that Manager McGraw had paid $4,500 for me I began to think I could really play the national game. I have played pretty hard since joining the Giants, but I have not been very lucky.

Nearly all ball players smoke, and I'm no exception. I don't drink intoxicating liquor, though, because I don't like it. I don't believe there is a man in the big league now who diets himself. A ball player is supposed to be tough enough to eat anything that doesn't eat him first, and we're all blessed with prodigious appetites, but I am inclined to believe I've got several other men's appetites in addition to my own. I eat enough for three ordinary men. I haven't any favorite article of food. I play them all without showing any partiality, and at that I'm only five feet nine inches in height and weigh 165 pounds.

I play baseball for the fun I get out of it, and the managers are foolish enough to pay me for having fun.

—Larry Doyle, New York *World*

———◇ **MONDAY, AUGUST 17** ◇———

{On August 16, in St. Louis, the Giants lost a doubleheader, 6 to 5 and 3 to 2. Winning pitchers, Lush and Karger; losing pitchers, McGinnity and Ames. Giants' standing: 61 wins, 42 losses, in second place.}

Muggsy McGraw and his Giants will have to settle into a steadier pace and exert more energy if they expect to win the pennant. By dropping a doubleheader to our lowly Cardinals the chances for the Gotham team were sadly crippled.

McGraw has not the class of the team that won the world's championship for him in 1905. He has a splendid club, with hitting and fielding strength, experienced in all tricks of the game and aggressive to the point of danger. But it is not a power like his champions of three years ago. If he sticks to second place to the end of the season he will be doing well.

Without Mathewson or Wiltse in the box, the Giants are a second-class team. Should one of these twirlers be rendered incapable, McGraw would probably fall to the second division in a hurry.

On the Polo Grounds in New York, where policemen dare not tread and visiting players and umpires are in danger of their lives, victories have been comparatively easy for the Giants. Their determination and reputations have undoubtedly struck many officials with fear.

The Giants try to carry this magnetic power over umpires on the road. But criticism parsed on the umpires Saturday seemed to have had a bracing effect yesterday. They turned about and on one or two occasions actually showed a will of their own and a power to speak out against the Giants.

McGraw, Bresnahan, Donlin and the others tried the same tactics as on Saturday and to the surprise of all Klem and Johnstone stood their ground. At one time Bresnahan tried the same trick of hurling the ball to the third baseman when a doubtful third strike came up, but little Klem called it a ball and stood his ground without apparent fear when Bresnahan whirled and faced him.

—James Crusinberry, St. Louis *Post-Dispatch*

St. Louis, Aug. 17—St. Louis fans yesterday got up on their hind legs and yelled gleefully as Cardinal after Cardinal glided over the gum of home plate. New York fans cannot imagine the hunger of Mound City rooters to beat the Giants, and of all rabid fans I have to give the medal to those in St. Louis. They want everything in sight and as much more as is hidden. They are all umpires, and how they clamor in their greedy hoggishness for all the best of it. I have the idea the name "rooter" originated in St. Louis on account of the insatiable desire of St. Louis fans to "hog" everything. There was not even a strike called that the decision was not greeted with a roar of disapproval, and the most insane objections were made by spectators a mile or so away who couldn't see whether the ball cut the plate or was a yard wide of it.

St. Louis fans do not appear able to see anything beyond what their own players do, but it was always so in Kerry Patch village. Sectional pride is proper and natural, but the Giants are surely entitled to the same courteous treatment that is accorded St. Louis players in the big city.

—Sam Crane, New York *Evening Journal*

They have fallen off slightly, but the leaders in the chase for National League batting honors stand about as they did a week ago. Hans Wagner still leads by a safe margin, with Mike Donlin runner-up. Against .338 a week ago Wagner now boasts of .334, and Donlin dropped to .321.

Outside of Wagner and Donlin the National League has but two .300 athletes, Zimmerman and Evers, of the Cubs, with .313 and .300. Bridwell now is McGraw's second batter, his .281 four points better than Larry Doyle's average. Roger Bresnahan is fourth with .262.

—New York *Evening Mail*

Ames and Bresnahan indulged in a bit of comedy quarreling in the sixth inning that brought down wrathy words from Captain Mike Donlin. Bresnahan signaled for one kind of curve and Ames refused to throw it. {Tom} Reilly was batting. Ames persisted and started to throw what he wished and Bresnahan deliberately stood to one side, refusing to catch the ball. It happened that Reilly tried to bunt and fouled it. Donlin came on the tear and order was restored.

—St. Louis *Post-Dispatch*

——— NATIONAL LEAGUE STANDINGS ———

	W	L	PCT.	GB		W	L	PCT.	GB
Pittsburgh ...	64	39	.622	—	Cincinnati ...	55	53	.509	11½
New York ...	61	42	.592	3	Boston	46	59	.438	19
Chicago	58	45	.563	6	Brooklyn	38	64	.372	25½
Philadelphia .	56	44	.560	6½	St. Louis	36	68	.346	28½

———◊ **TUESDAY, AUGUST 18** ◊———

{On August 17, in St. Louis, the Giants won 3 to 0, a game called after 6 innings because of rain. Winning pitcher, Mathewson; losing pitcher, Sallee. Giants' standing: 62 wins, 42 losses, in second place.}

Even the elements delight in kicking our lowly Cardinals. Yesterday a thunderstorm lingered on the outside of the park until enough innings had been played to declare a game, then the storm broke into the grounds and sent the players scampering, with the Giants the victors.

In the middle of the fifth the storm seemed to linger at the main entrance. The New Yorkers were at bat. They had to be retired and then put three Cardinals out or it would be no game. One Giant was out and one was on third base. A terrific thunder clap caused McGraw to leap from the bench. He ran to the third-base coaching line. Cy Seymour was there. "Steal home on the next play," yelled McGraw. Seymour dashed for home and ran into Catcher {John} Bliss with the ball in his hands. He was out. Jack Barry was at bat. "Strike out, Jack," yelled McGraw. Jack swung wildly and then scampered with the other New Yorkers to their fielding positions.

Three Cardinals had to be put out before a game could be completed. Again and again the storm cried its warning in thunderous calls. Bobby Byrne rolled a ground ball to Bridwell and was out. Reilly popped to Bridwell. Bliss delayed things by singling. Then Beebe hit to Herzog and was thrown out, completing enough play to allow a game.

The rain descended at once, though not heavy enough to call the game until after another inning had been played.

Christy Mathewson was on the mound for the Giants. He is the same great twirler as of old. His speed may not be so great as in the past, but his wits are greater. The team is filled with confidence as soon as he steps into the box. He is one of the greatest pitchers the game has ever seen and he seems good for several years to come.

—James Crusinberry, St. Louis *Post-Dispatch*

SPRINGFIELD, Ill., Aug. 18—The Giants left St. Louis with an even break, much less success than they anticipated. Mathewson does not play Sunday ball, although there is no clause in his contract to that effect. When he first joined the Giants {late in 1900} he expressed the wish not to work on Sundays, and his desire has been granted ever since. {Mathewson's mother wanted her son to become a minister, and she was not pleased when he entered professional baseball; to appease her, he agreed not to play on Sundays.} But if he had been on the field Sunday chances are the Giants would have won both games.

In these pinch times when every victory counts an awful lot, if Matty could be induced to throw aside his "scruples" the Giants would have a much rosier show to win the pennant. Matty is loyal to his club, but I and all of his fellow-players wish he would step into the breach and help out on Sundays. Rival clubs take advantage of Matty's refusal to play on the first day of the week and crowd in doubleheaders at every opportunity. It places McGraw at a disadvantage and also his team.

I think Matty is the only player now who does not play on Sunday. If he is thoroughly conscientious he deserves credit. But is he?

—Sam Crane, New York *Evening Journal*

⸻◇ WEDNESDAY, AUGUST 19 ◇⸻

CINCINNATI, Aug. 19—It was a delightful trip the Giants took to Spring-field yesterday {for an exhibition game}, making a pleasant break in the hard grind. The boys were entertained with a whole-souled heartiness that, coming after the hoodlumish treatment in St. Louis, was like an oasis of pleasure in a desert of disgust.

The game was distinguished by the appearance of John J. McGraw, who took Doyle's place at second base in the last two innings. Unfortunately, the new utility man didn't have a chance, but he cavorted around like a young fellow. Mac had no opportunity to hit, as he didn't go to bat.

{One would scarcely surmise from Sam Crane's account of this "pleasant break in the hard grind" that on the day the Giants visited Springfield the city was in fact an armed camp. On the preceding week-end, seven blacks had been killed by a white mob, and so the governor declared martial law and sent National Guard troops to patrol the streets of this "oasis of pleasure."}

—Sam Crane, New York *Evening Journal*

⸻◇ THURSDAY, AUGUST 20 ◇⸻

{On August 19, in Cincinnati, the Giants won, in 10 innings, 3 to 1. Winning pitcher, Wiltse; losing pitcher, Spade. Giants' standing: 63 wins, 42 losses, in second place.}

The Giants are one notch nearer to those awful Pirates by taking a fierce ten-round battle at League Park. Fighting every inch of the way, the teams came to the ninth round with McGraw's outfit a run to the good. The Reds got their lone tally in the ninth and had a wonderful opportunity to win, but George Wiltse was too tough. The enemy closed the deal by some fancy slugging in the tenth.

The game was a delightful struggle, with Bob Spade lined up against George Wiltse, presently the league's greatest southpaw. The left-hander had much the better of the argument. The cadaverous but skillful Mr. Wiltse pitched a remarkably clever game against a team which usually drives southpaws to the tall and uncut. Mr. Wiltse allowed four singles, only one of which was a clean drive.

—Jack Ryder, Cincinnati *Enquirer*

Pittsburgh and Chicago will puncture New York's pennant prospects on the present trip and send the Giants home fighting to keep out of fourth place. The Pirates are going at so fast a gait it is doubtful if they will be displaced. —*The Sporting News*

It has leaked out that McGraw had nothing to do with the purchase of Rube Marquard. The Giants' pitching staff looked a bit wabbly a while back, and John T. Brush thought he would surprise McGraw by digging up a new box artist. Accordingly, Mr. Brush did sneak away to look over minor leaguers. Through the Indianapolis officials Mr. Brush learned that two or three teams were bidding for Marquard, and that was enough for him. He plunked down $11,000, then told McGraw what he had done. There is no record of McGraw being tremendously enthused over the purchase. —Nie, New York *Globe*

◇ FRIDAY, AUGUST 21 ◇

{On August 20, in Cincinnati, New York won 2 to 0. Winning pitcher, Mathewson; losing pitcher, Coakley. Giants' standing: 64 wins, 42 losses, tied with Pittsburgh for first place.}

With a tie for first place in sight, Manager McGraw sent the great Mathewson against the Reds, and the dope worked out right, although our boys pounded Matty for eight solid bingles, while the Giants got just four off Dr. A. J. Coakley. The Reds' work on the green also was more consistent than that of McGraw's men, but the lone Red foozle cost a Giant tally, while New York erred thrice without losing anything.

Matty was hit hard enough to cause a lot of anxiety in Giant bosoms, but his own steadiness, with much-needed assistance from Doyle and Bridwell, pulled him through.

—Jack Ryder, *Cincinnati Enquirer*

In the sixth yesterday things got tangled up dangerously, and I could feel the carmine perspiration oozing from every pore. With one out, Lobert lambasted a double to right, and Paskert followed with a solid single going fast and over second. It looked a cinch that Lobert would score, but the wise Mr. Bridwell, after making a robbery stop, seeing he had no chance to nail the batter at first, whipped the ball like a shot to Devlin, and Lobert, who had overrun third, was nipped by an eyelash, and then only because Devlin had his foot between the bag and Lobert's "kangaroos."

Umpire Klem was fortunately right where the play was made and called the runner out. The crowd yelled blue thunder, but after the game Ganzel acknowledged the decision was right, but he made an awful belch at the time, possibly for effect. It was a narrow squeak, and Klem deserves all kinds of credit for following the play so closely.

It was superb headwork on Bridwell's part—quick thought and quick action. It possibly saved the game.

—Sam Crane, New York *Evening Journal*

———◇ **SATURDAY, AUGUST 22** ◇———

WASHINGTON, Aug. 21—Catcher Charley Street, of the Washington team, this morning accomplished the unparalleled feat of catching a baseball thrown from one of the small windows near the top of the Washington monument, 505 feet from the ground.

Street made the attempt at the instigation of the *Washington Post* to settle the question long under dispute as to whether the catch could be made. Before Street made the catch 12 balls had been dropped, most being deflected by the stiff breeze which made it impossible to reach them. On the thirteenth ball Street made the catch. The ball struck his mitt with terrific force and jarred him considerably.

Street caught against Detroit in the afternoon and did not display ill effects from his experience. —Cincinnati *Enquirer*

CINCINNATI, Aug. 22—Mathewson has cut out checker playing on this visit to Cincinnati and for the entire trip. Several noted checker players, including the champion of Ohio, have called on Matty and invited him to the checker club, but Matty refused. It is strictly business on this trip.
—Sam Crane, New York *Evening Journal*

"McGraw, Knowles & Mathewson"—that's how the sign over the door will read on the Marbridge Building at 34th street and Broadway soon after the Giants play off the world's series. The manager, star pitcher, and secretary of the New York club will have the largest billiard hall in America, and a nice little cafe will be run on the side.

Ball players, as a rule, do not make good businessmen. That was why Mr. Knowles was taken into the company. The man who beats the cash register when the Giants' secretary is counting up the house will have to go some and in addition McGraw will make his employees wear tights so that there will be no pockets in which to carry loose change.
—Nie, New York *Globe*

——◇ SUNDAY, AUGUST 23 ◇——

{On August 22, in Cincinnati, the Giants won 5 to 1. Winning pitcher, McGinnity; losing pitcher, Ewing. Giants' standing: 65 wins, 42 losses, in second place.}

After offering old Joe McGinnity to the Cincinnati club for almost nothing yesterday morning, Manager McGraw was forced to send the veteran in against the Reds at League Park in the afternoon, and the Iron Man performed in his 1903 style. Isn't baseball a funny proposition? Here is a pitcher the Giants are trying to give away. Necessity forces his use a few hours after the gift proposition is made, and the old boy works like a Mathewson.

McGinnity would not have been used if the Red management had cared to take him at their own terms, as McGraw had requested in the morning. But the offer was spurned, and the Iron Man remained a Giant. So he was available when Ames blew up at the getaway.

Ames was wild and utterly unable to locate the plate. He passed the first two men, and McGraw, with characteristic promptness, yanked him out, and called on old Joe to show why he should not be allowed to seek salary elsewhere. The Iron Man proceeded to pitch rings around the Reds, making our boys look like a lot of bloomer girls.

McGinnity has nerve, control and a dinky curve ball, and he gets by on the first two. A Red batter steps to the plate. Old Joe slips the first one right over. According to immemorial custom, the batter never hits at the first one, so old Joe has him in the hole right off the reel. Then a little nerve, perfect control and the queer little curve, calculated to an inch, causes a pop-up or a small-sized fanning bee.

—Jack Ryder, Cincinnati Enquirer

CINCINNATI, Aug. 22—There was one drawback to the complete happiness of the Giants when they left town tonight—the fact that Catcher Snodgrass had his thumb so badly lacerated when hit by a foul in practice he will not be able to play again this season, and perhaps never, as amputation may be necessary. {Snodgrass would in fact be an outfielder on three Giant pennant-winning teams, 1911–13.}

—New York World

——◇ MONDAY, AUGUST 24 ◇——

"A doubleheader may not be played between Pittsburgh and New York this afternoon. I was not notified that two games were to be played 24 hours in advance in accordance with league rules and consequently we are not compelled to do so."

Thus spoke John McGraw, manager of the New York Giants, yesterday at 3 P.M. The team arrived in the morning from Cincinnati, having an open date.

McGraw did not say he would refuse to play two games, but pointed out his right to do so. "Pittsburgh cannot force us to play," he continued. "League rules plainly say that the president of the league or the home club shall notify the other club at least 24 hours before time for calling the first game. This the management of the Pittsburgh team did not do and so it is up to me whether the Pirates and Giants shall play two games tomorrow."   —E. M. Thierry, Pittsburgh *Dispatch*

PITTSBURGH, Aug. 24—Manager McGraw decided early this morning he would agree to play a doubleheader. McGraw at first thought his players would be too tired after their trip from Cincinnati to do themselves justice, but after calling roll this morning he found everyone in prime fettle and eager to play. The Giants' manager then called Barney Dreyfuss on the phone and told him two games would be played.

—Sam Crane, New York *Evening Journal*

Local fans will have the opportunity of seeing the championship struggle at Pittsburgh today between the Pirates and Giants. A monster electric diamond, known as Campton's baseball bulletin, has been erected at Madison Square Garden and another at the Gotham theater on 125th street. All remaining games this season will be shown at both places.

—New York *Evening Mail*

———— NATIONAL LEAGUE STANDINGS ————

	W	L	PCT.	GB		W	L	PCT.	GB
Pittsburgh ...	66	42	.611	—	Cincinnati ...	56	56	.500	12
New York ...	65	42	.607	½	Boston	49	63	.438	19
Chicago	64	47	.577	3½	Brooklyn	40	68	.370	26
Philadelphia .	57	49	.538	8	St. Louis	40	70	.364	27

————◇ TUESDAY, AUGUST 25 ◇————

{On August 24, in Pittsburgh, the Giants won a doubleheader, 4 to 1 and 5 to 1. Winning pitchers, Wiltse and Mathewson; losing pitchers, Willis and Leifield. Giants' standing: 67 wins, 42 losses, in first place.}

In the presence of 16,440 sorely depressed human megaphones the hateful New York Giants on Exposition Park field pushed our beloved Pirates out of first place in the race for the happy emblem of baseball superiority.

It was one of the largest gatherings of baseball fans and bugs in the history of Pittsburgh, and it was a representative one, composed largely of well-groomed men and fashionably dressed women.

So great was the outpouring hundreds sat on the grass, forming a human frame two-thirds of the way around the yard.

—C. B. Power, Pittsburgh *Dispatch*

PITTSBURGH, Aug. 25—Perhaps the hundreds of New York rooters did not "gloat a few" last evening. New Yorkers owned the town last night and as I fumbled around for my downy couch at 11 o'clock I could still hear Joe Humphreys's foggy voice reiterating that Mike Donlin would beat out Hans Wagner by several "gas house" (N.Y.) blocks.

For the first time this season the Giants have an undisputed hold on first place, and I don't know how they can be "ketched."

It took the Giants a while before they could get a correct and proper line on Willis in the first game, but they "sure did" at last, and my! oh my! what a stinging of the bulb there was! Wiltse started the eighth with a safe Texas-leaguer to short center. Tenney's little dump, intended for a suicide splash, went a little too fast to Willis, and Wiltse was smothered at second. Then Doyle, king slugger of the day, singled to center. Bresnahan was on pins and needles. It was up to him to do things, for in the first inning he had failed to lean against the ball when he had a chance to send in runs, and dear old Roger had his teeth set and his head up. He lined a beauty over second that {Roy} Thomas tried to make a circus catch of and pitched forward onto his face in a vain attempt to clutch the sphere. Roy plowed up the ground for yards with his nose, but the ball scooted under him and netted Roger three bases. Tenney and Doyle cavorted over the bases, while Pittsburgh fans made music with their mouths that sounded like a banshee's wail.

At this stage our old friend Mike Donlin essayed to do a Donlin stunt. His wife looked down from her private box and shouted: "Mike, dear, if you don't make a hit I will never speak to you again, and you can take back your old bracelet."

These were her exact words, for I heard them. Mike must have, too, for he certainly tickled the ball. He shot it on a dead line to left like a bullet, and Fred Clarke might as well have tried to stop a twelve-inch shell. The ball went shooting to the low fence in deep left, and another home run was down to Mike's credit, as well as smiles and return to favor of his pretty better half. That clinched the game there and then. All the pepper the Pirates had shown went up in the smoke of their brunette burg.

With the first game tucked away, and Mathewson in the box, it looked very sweet for both games. And so it resulted. After Doyle banged a safe hit in the first inning and took third on Thomas's error and scored on Donlin's sacrifice bunt, the game looked lead-pipe to a certainty. But when Doyle drove in two more in another inning by a double and Donlin shoved over a pair by a drive over second later on, it was all over for fair.

Mathewson's pitching was simply up to his class, which is the top notch of them all. He lighted up when forced to do so and showed how he is the peer of any twirler in the business. You can't beat him—that's all, and the game never saw his equal.

—Sam Crane, New York *Evening Journal*

Sam Crane, who played second base in fast company long before many present-day fans dreamed of baseball, is with the Giants. {Crane played for eight teams during seven seasons from 1880 until 1890.}

—Pittsburgh *Dispatch*

When McGraw put through his deal with Boston the big cheer of the fans was that Fred Tenney would be their first baseman. A young catcher named Needham and an infielder called Bridwell were thrown in to make weight. That was the dope.

Nobody here knew anything about Bridwell then, but now thousands of New York fans can recognize him by his shoelaces. He is the little god of the bleachers, idol of the infield, pinch-hitter of the coming champions. Three months ago fans yawned and wondered when "McGraw would brace up the short field." Now they wonder what Bridwell's contract next year will call for.

Bridwell goes after everything. Always a weak hitter, he has developed a knack of going to the plate and pasting one out when it is up to him to get runs across. From a mild, graceful player he changed into a brilliant, aggressive one. A constitutionally weak batter, he has become the prize game hitter of the team. He deserves his cheers, and every time you give one for Bridwell give one for the manager that made him find himself. —J. W. McConaughy, New York *Evening Journal*

———◇ WEDNESDAY, AUGUST 26 ◇———

{On August 25, in Pittsburgh, the Giants won 5 to 3. Winning pitcher, Crandall; losing pitcher, Maddox. Giants' standing: 68 wins, 42 losses, in first place.}

PITTSBURGH, Aug. 25—It was Crandall's turn to beat the Pirates, and the best new pitcher the Giants have unearthed since the discovery of Mathewson was up to his task. He pitched a cool, heady game, and although hit as hard as Maddox, the Pirate boxman, he showed better judgment and was almost always in full control of the situation with men on base.

—New York *Tribune*

PITTSBURGH, Aug. 25—Today, in murky Pittsburgh, home of the smokestack and the stogie, our Gingery Giants proved beyond all doubt they are the class of the league.

The Pirates do not look so terrible now. One week ago it was the general impression around the circuit that if the Giants were to win the pennant they would have to beat Pittsburgh. But McGraw, crafty little gent that he is, gave out an interview and said: "I do not fear Pittsburgh in the least. It is Chicago we must beat to win the flag." This surprising statement, coming just when the Pirates were soaring and the Cubs losing, astounded and unnerved the Pittsburghers. The supreme contempt shown by Manager Mac for the club on top evidently got the "goat" of Mr. Frederick Clarke. McGraw does not know a thing. He goes to the races too much.

The Pirates seem to have lost their nerve. In practice today they roamed around like tramps moving up a pace in the bread line. They didn't make many slips because they didn't go after much of anything. Their heads are down. Three weeks ago it was generally conceded that one of the three clubs would break under the terribly grueling strain of the three-cornered fight that has thrilled the baseball world. The Pirates have broken.

Thousands of dollars have been wagered in this city on the exciting race. The bets are not generally made at the park, and they are not made by real lovers of the game. The gambling element in Pittsburgh, always notorious plungers on the national game, confine their operations to cafes and poolrooms. The money certainly goes down, and tonight there is many a lantern jaw in the homes of the millionaires.

—William F. Kirk, New York *American*

PITTSBURGH, Aug. 25—A feature which gave much amusement to fans yesterday occurred in the third. Doyle had made a nice triple, but later permitted Tommy Leach to engage him in conversation, and Doyle, forgetting himself, stepped off the bag. Catcher Gibson, taking the sign from Leach, whipped the ball down and poor Doyle was caught by an inch, though he made a noble try to knock Leach to bits getting back to the bag. —New York *Herald*

PITTSBURGH, Aug. 26—The Giants have begun to spend that world's championship money. Arthur Devlin will buy Mrs. Devlin a Persian lamb coat, Roger Bresnahan will have his home in Toledo repainted. Mabel Hite will get another diamond bracelet with Donlin's share, and Larry Doyle is thinking of buying an interest in the Breese (Ill.) *Weekly Clarion* and becoming an editor.

All around the hotel this morning one could stumble over a Giant busy with paper and pencil figuring out what he wants most.

—Nie, New York *Globe*

Malarkey will be sent to Buffalo in the Eastern League. McGraw thinks he may develop into a winning pitcher with more work and experience than he can get with the Giants. Malarkey lacks confidence, as a remark he made when McGraw told him to warm up one day during a game shows: "Why, Mr. McGraw," he said, "I don't think I have got a thing." Anyone who knows McGraw can imagine what a hit that made with him. {This marked the end of Malarkey's one-season major league career, which included a single victory, gained in relief over Boston on April 28.}

—Sam Crane, New York *Evening Journal*

Every great championship team has owed much success to a great catcher. Boston {the Red Sox} had {Lou} Criger. Billy Sullivan was a mainspring of the White Sox, and Johnny Kling has been a power for the Cubs. The Giants have Bresnahan.

The Big Toledo detective is one of the small group of backstops who stands 'way out from the ordinary run of receivers. {During the off-season Bresnahan was employed as a private detective in his home town.} Bresnahan knows baseball as few men know it, and he has the build and force to put his knowledge into action.

In a hot game when things begin to go wrong he is a composite of ginger and bad language. In his clumsy shinguards and wind-pad, his head in a wire cage, through which at intervals comes a stream of reproof and comment as he fusses around the plate, he suggests a grotesque overgrown hen trying to get the family in out of the rain. And generally he succeeds.

Bresnahan does not have a delightful personality. He once made a speech to Arthur Devlin which brought in return a punch on the nose. But Bresnahan isn't there to be loved.

In the batting box he is almost as valuable as he is behind. He is a game, vicious hitter and when it takes one to bring in needed runs fans would as soon see Roger at the plate as some men who are ahead of him in percentage. But his great specialty is "waiting." He gets more bases on balls than any man in either league. {By the end of the season he would lead the league in bases on balls with 83.} His patience makes Job look like a petulant party.

—J. W. McConaughy, New York *Evening Journal*

——◇ THURSDAY, AUGUST 27 ◇——

{On August 26, in Pittsburgh, the Giants won 4 to 3. Winning pitcher, McGinnity; losing pitcher, Young. Giants' standing: 69 wins, 42 losses, in first place.}

PITTSBURGH, Aug. 26—The Gingery Giants made it four straight, doing more than their closest friends expected. The town is in mourning. Barney Dreyfuss refuses to be interviewed. Fred Clarke is confined to bed. Honus Wagner has mental "charley horse." All Pittsburgh weeps.

The game today, the best of the series, was won in the eleventh hour. In the ninth inning, with the score 3 to 2, the long-suffering fans began to perk up. But Jawn McGraw never stopped. Out near the third-base line he crouched, and you should have heard the things he told "Young Cy," Young. Even as the Giant leader spoke, it came to pass and Young was chased to the bench.

Like other games of late, it was not that we won, it was the way we came from behind. It was like 1905. Many a game was won then by pluck and strategy and, unless the writer is greatly mistaken, many another game is going to be ours. The Giants are now invincible.

Luther Taylor pitched until taken out in the eighth to allow Needham to bat. The deaf mute pitched one of his old-time games, mowing Pirates down with ease and grace. McGinnity pitched the eighth, and when the Giants assumed the lead, McGraw took no chances. Although Joe was working smoothly, Mac sent in "Big Six" to retire the last three men.　　　　—William F. Kirk, New York *American*

The Giants have been the surprise of the year. I admire them for their pugnacity and earnestness. McGraw has the laugh on all of us who tried to show he erred in his trade with Boston. McGraw made a fine deal, and the results prove it. Tenney never played better, while Bridwell has developed into a good hitter and a brilliant shortstop. Doyle, too, is improving all the time and is a star with the stick. Donlin, Bresnahan, Devlin, Seymour, Mathewson, and Wiltse deserve all the credit due to men who have played grand ball.　　　　—Joe Vila, *The Sporting News*

If there is one Giant who deserves a bigger share of glory for New York's position at the top of the ladder, it's Frederick "Cambridge" Tenney. He is like wine—he improves with age.

He is not only playing a grand game, but his coaching is making the youngsters, Bridwell and Doyle, the spiciest pair ever to cavort around the keystone corner of an infield. And his great ability to "stretch" has given Arthur Devlin the greatest fielding season he has had since joining the Giants.

With his swatstick, too, Tenney has a record to be proud of. Best of all, he is a pinch-hitter of the first water. Game after game he has won with a timely clout. In the tightest pinch he is as cool as a five-cent piece of ice to a Houston street dweller on a midsummer day.

Tenney follows the Comiskey school of fielding his position, going in fast for bunts, and being a quick and clever left-handed thrower, he often catches the runner at second on what was considered simply an out at first. His plays made in this way were a great innovation back in the '90's and resulted in the play later being made a double play.

Yes, John McGraw was as crazy as a fox when he secured Tenney.

—W. S. Farnsworth, New York *Evening Journal*

{From a signed article in the New York *American* by Christy Mathewson.}

To the casual fan there may seem very little difference in the shoots and curves that fly past the batsman. But the man at the plate knows differently. To him the various kinds of curves are numbered by the hundreds, and when he faces a first-class twirler with perfect control they all look equally hard to bat.

A pitcher's value is almost invariably measured by his ability to change his pace or mix up the style of ball he is delivering. Unless he mixes them up pretty well he is of little use against a clever team.

Of various balls used by latter-day pitchers the fast ball, which may end with an inward shoot, outward shoot or upward shoot, comes first. All pitchers must be able to use this ball with more or less success. Then comes the slow ball, which does not curve or revolve; the drop curve, one of the most popular curves; the out-curve, which is seldom used in the big leagues; the raise ball, an underhand curve, used with very little success by anyone except McGinnity; the fall-away, which I have used, if I may be pardoned for saying so, with greater effectiveness than any other pitcher (it is my favorite); and the spit ball, a style of delivery the science of which cannot be explained and one very difficult to control.

During the past few years I have relied almost entirely on the drop curve, fast ball and fall-away, and I believe they are the most useful to pitchers today.

It takes a good physical specimen to be a successful twirler. Knotted muscles, however, are not essential, as the ball is propelled mainly by a body swing and the bulk of the power is derived from the back and shoulders, the arm acting as a whipcord to snap the ball. The more a pitcher learns to get the power from his body, the more he will save his arm and the longer he will be able to do himself justice in the box.

I attribute much of my success to my ability to get most of the pro-pelling force from the swing of the body.

When mastered there is no more successful ball than the drop curve. It can be made to break very abruptly or a gradual break can be put to it. When it breaks quickly the batter invariably hits over it and misses it entirely. It is what I usually rely on when there is a man on third base and no one out. —Christy Mathewson, New York *American*

———◇ **FRIDAY, AUGUST 28** ◇———

{On August 27, in Chicago, the Giants lost 5 to 1. Winning pitcher, Pfiester; losing pitcher, Wiltse. Giants' standing: 69 wins, 43 losses, in first place.}

When two stellar athletic bodies, traveling through space in the same orbit and with equal velocity, meet in the middle of a baseball diamond, something will smash. There was no exception to the law of the universe when the New York Giants crashed head on into the world's champions on the West Side yesterday. The impact was terrific, both projectiles were jarred severely, but Chicago came out of the wreck an easy victor.

By a wide margin the largest crowd that has squeezed into the park this year saw the triumph and rooted themselves into a compact jam of yelping humanity. From noon until time to start the game long lines of eager patrons besieged every ticket window, and an hour before the battle was scheduled to start not another inch of space was left in the enlarged stands. Under this tremendous pressure President Murphy's resolution to keep the field clear melted like wax in a candle flame. First an effort was made to keep the overflow on foul ground. The old lady who tried to keep back the ocean with her broom would have been an odds-on favorite in comparison. Soon the dammed up stream burst its barrier and flowed around the entire field.

Groomed and tuned up for the great occasion George Wiltse was pitted against his long-time southpaw opponent, Jack Pfiester, the man with the nine-lived hoodoo, and all the glory was Pfiester's.

The Cubs' support of Pfiester was brilliant. Tinker was a chief factor and once prevented a probable tally by a dashing one-handed pinch of a hit from Seymour. Once Evers not only cut off a clean hit for which he had to dive headlong, but actually sat up in time to throw the runner out at first without getting to his feet.

For three innings it was an even break, with the issue oscillating first one way and then the other. A double play from Tinker to Evers to Chance snuffed out a budding Giant run in the first, and in the next three rounds the one hit an inning was nullified by clever defense.

In the fourth Chance's men solved Wiltse's delivery for a cluster of four hard drives. Evers led with a double into the crowd, and Steinfeldt pounded a liner into right. Cap Donlin tore in like a race horse and tried for the hit but muffed it close to the ground, and Evers scored. A foul fly put Howard down, but Tinker responded to the mad yelling with a single. When Kling followed with that wallop over Bridwell's head it seemed as if the fans would tear the plant and themselves into pieces in the delirium of their joy. Far out past the last outpost the ball traveled into a scattered line of rooters, and as Steinfeldt, Tinker, and Kling scampered across the plate the joy knew no bounds. But only one of the three tallies would stand on account of the ground rules, for an ever-curious daughter of Eve had picked up the ball, perhaps thinking it was another apple from the garden of Eden, and her act left no doubt that the hit had gone into the crowd. If she can be identified that woman will be barred from the park forever, as relentlessly as her primeval ancestress was shut out from that other paradise.   —I. E. Sanborn, Chicago *Tribune*

To McGraw and his men the disappointment of the day was Wiltse, for the Cubs are supposedly weak in front of a portwheeler.

McGraw was annoyed but not frightened. "I didn't expect Wiltse to get such a beating," he said, "and I thought we could hit more effectively against Pfiester. Still, we were pretty tired from our ride, and the strain of taking four games from Pittsburgh evidently had a reaction. Tomorrow is a rest day. We will rest and get back all our steam. On Saturday Matty will pitch, and we will win sure as fate. The flag is as good as cinched for the Polo Grounds."

Chance and his tribe are wildly exuberant and think they will stop Mathewson cold. "We are hitting," said the Chicago manager, "and that is what gets the games. If we can hit a left-hander as hard as we did Wiltse, we will hit Matty or any other right-hander."   —New York *Sun*

CHICAGO, Aug. 27—Chicago presents the spectacle of a great city positively raving over baseball. Everything else is forgotten—politics, business, home and family. At downtown bulletin boards, where the game was reproduced in miniature, crowds were estimated at 50,000.

In offices tickers bringing bulletins absorbed all the attention. Grocers' boys and telephones conveyed the news of the great game to thousands of residences, for in Chicago women understand baseball and are as deeply interested as men. Hundreds of buildings in the vicinity of the ball park were black with spectators, while telegraph and telephone poles looked as though immense swarms of giant bugs had settled at their tops.

—New York *Herald*

A girl with a white dress and immense purple hat got behind the catcher, and over 900 fans lost all sight of the game. She stuck for seven innings, amid cries of "A dollar for a foul tip into the purple lid," and then left with a contemptuous glare at the wild myriads.

—Chicago *Journal*

——◇ SATURDAY, AUGUST 29 ◇——

The tribe of speculators, which has had poor picking in Cub tickets since the plant was enlarged, started to dip its hands into pockets of local fans again. The club has used every effort to keep tickets out of speculators' hands, but it is impossible to do so altogether. Refusing to sell tickets to scalpers only compels them to send helpers in relays to buy two or three seats at a time. The public cannot be protected altogether without serious inconvenience to themselves.

—I. E. Sanborn, Chicago *Tribune*

CHICAGO, Aug. 29—The Giants' spirit was amply illustrated by Mathewson last night. It looked like it might rain today and make a doubleheader necessary on Sunday. Matty hunted up McGraw and volunteered to pitch Sunday. "Big Six," it must be recalled, has a clause in his contract saying he shall not be called on to pitch Sunday ball—and he never has pitched on the Sabbath—but so much depends on these games Christy was willing to lay aside his principles for one afternoon.

—Nie, New York *Globe*

Today's and tomorrow's games at Chicago will be reproduced at Madison Square Garden on the electric diamond commencing promptly at 4 o'clock New York time. It will be the first time in many years that New York fans will have the opportunity to witness a Sunday game.

—New York *Evening Mail*

CINCINNATI, August 24—Herewith is an announcement that may foretell a revolution in baseball. It is an assured fact that in the major leagues games will be played at night if plans of President Herrmann, of the Cincinnati club, and George P. Cahill, a Philadelphia inventor, prove feasible. Herrmann, Cahill and several Cincinnati men organized the Night Baseball Development Co., incorporated at Columbus with a capital stock of $50,000. Five steel towers, 100 feet high, will be erected at League Park at once, and powerful searchlights will be mounted on the towers. Cahill has been working on the lighting part of the scheme for more than four years and believes he has solved the problem.

President Herrmann has great faith in the practicability of the Cahill system. If it works successfully every fan who has ever been docked a half day's pay for sneaking out to the ball park will worship Mr. Herrmann. Think of it! Baseball every afternoon and evening. Great double bill. Two frolics daily. Take the children in the afternoon and come back yourself for the night show. Pitchers for today: Ewing and Mathewson at 3:30; Spade and Wiltse at 8 P.M. No tie games. Play never stopped on account of darkness. Stay and see the finish. —*Sporting Life*

{From a signed article in the New York *American* by Christy Mathewson.}

The fall-away or fadeaway ball is the most effective style of pitching I have yet discovered.

So far as I know, I am the only pitcher that habitually uses this method. I have tried to teach it to several players, but none ever suceeded in getting it down well enough to make use of it.

I use the fadeaway in every game and it has never failed me when my control was in working order. It is the ball that has won for me all my baseball honors.

It is an exceptionally slow ball and relieves the strain on the pitcher as well as puzzling batsmen. A simple definition for the fall-away is a ball that curves out from a left-handed batter when pitched by a right-handed pitcher.

The ball sails through the air at a deceptive gait until it is about six feet from the batsman, where it begins to curve outward and downward. The rotary motion of hand just before the ball is let go imparts the outward curve to the ball. As it passes the batsman it is revolving at a great rate.

Such a ball is calculated to deceive the greatest batter. He is deceived at the start as to the speed of the ball. As it rushes toward him it looks like a fast high ball; six feet from him, when it begins to drop, it has the appearance of a slow drop ball, and then as he swings it is traveling in two directions at once.

I invariably use the ball when two men are on base, and the opposing batsmen know it. The knowledge, however, does them little good.

There would doubtless be many pitchers besides myself using the ball today but for the difficulty in acquiring the peculiar twists of the hand which are necessary when delivering the fadeaway.

{Carl Hubbell, the great left-handed pitcher who won 253 games for the Giants between 1928 and 1943, told the author of this book that his screwball pitch and Matty's fadeaway were identical. Among all the pitchers in baseball's Hall of Fame, only Mathewson and Hubbell had mastered this pitch.}

—Christy Mathewson, New York *American*

————◇ **SUNDAY, AUGUST 30** ◇————

{On August 29, in Chicago, the Giants lost 3 to 2. Winning pitcher, Brown; losing pitcher, Mathewson. Giants' standing: 69 wins, 44 losses, in first place.}

Concentrating their attack into one brilliant, irresistible rush in a single wildly delirious inning, Chicago's world's champions won the second game of their epoch-making series with the New York Giants, climbed one notch higher in their uphill scramble for the pennant, and sent next to the largest mob that ever jammed the Cub plant into the seventy-seventh level of terrestrial paradise.

By that well-timed assault, Chance's men battered the great Christy Mathewson until he actually was groggy for a few minutes, and turned what started out as a Giant victory into defeat in the short space of time required for making five solid hits.

Before that sensational period rooters were dreading the possibility that their own hero of three-fingered fame, Mordecai Brown, was doomed to defeat. Starting off with a whirlwind attack McGraw's tribe tore off three rattling hits and scored a run with only one out. Chicago's army of fans was aghast. Then, with a sudden turn of the kaleidoscope, fate shifted the tide.

Brown's famous opponent began as if he was going to pitch the battle of his life. For three innings the tall, fair-haired Giant was as invincible as a stone wall, as puzzling as the whispering of a Sphinx. Then in the fourth inning came the furious Cub attack, and for ten minutes there was more joy to the square inch in Chicago than there ever were microbes in its atmosphere. Hofman started with a line soak into the left-field crowd for a ground-rule double. Sheckard's careful bunt advanced the runner a notch nearer the goal. Chance then pushed a little fly just out of Bridwell's reach. Hofman was across the plate tying the score while thousands of hats went sailing into the air. But this demonstration was a whisper by comparison with what was coming.

Evers, Steinfeldt, and Howard in quick succession socked the ball squarely on the nose and the hits were like rapid-fire shots from a magazine gun in the hands of a sharpshooter. The earth trembled with the tremendous roaring, and when Evers crossed the plate with the third and what proved to be the winning run, nothing was left in the throats of the rooters but a consistent succession of gleeful yelps.

With the lead of two runs there was little chance that Brown would fail to hold the Giants back the rest of the way.

Only once before in the history of the West Side park have as many people been accommodated within these historic precincts, at the first game of the world's series with Detroit last October.

—I. E. Sanborn, Chicago *Tribune*

The most remarkable thing about the scoreboards which the *Tribune* used to show about 10,000 enthusiasts the progress of the game was the way in which the crowd endowed the lights with personalities. The incandescent bulbs were joshed and hissed every bit as heartily as were the players miles away.

Four hours men stood on the sidewalks and sat on the curb with their feet in the gutters to have good places from which to view the reproduction of the conflict. From the top windows of the Hartford building to the lower ones where bankers sat in easy chairs and watched the flashing lights with closer interest and for a longer time than they ever watched a stock ticker, from every inch of ground at the intersection of Madison and Dearborn where a human body could be squeezed cheers and jeers arose. At the second scoreboard displayed from the Illinois Central station at Randolph street was a similar scene.

The intense interest and direct personal way in which the lights were considered was shown when at a particularly thrilling point Mr. Brown was about to pitch and a streetcar blocked the view of many on the west side of the street. Fearful that they might miss something hundreds shouted:

"Hold the ball a minute, Brownie! Hold it."

—Chicago *Tribune*

During the past week thousands of businessmen temporarily gave up business to devote themselves to baseball. From 2 o'clock until 6 each afternoon crowds besieged scoreboards, bulletins, and tickers to secure the latest results of Giants' games.

Steady processions departed from offices to hunt the nearest source of information and obtain the latest news. Department stores and factories organized relays and sent boys to get the score. In some places regular forces of messengers were established by which hungry fans could obtain information from the West. Wherever there was a ticker in a hotel or other public place a throng packed so closely around it that the nearest man to the instrument was informally chosen spokesman for the crowd and yelled the result inning after inning.

Drivers of trucks and cabs drove blocks out of their way to scan bulletin boards. Streetcars were halted in front of scoreboards, and even in hospitals the baseball tidings were carried to patients. Everything was sidetracked for the latest news from the seat of the baseball war.

—New York *Times*

The ground rules yesterday were such as perhaps were never made before. So dense was the crowd back of first and so close to the base line it was agreed to make a hit among those fans good for only one base.

—New York *Sun*

Mathewson started so splendidly it seemed for a time that "Big Six" would destroy the hoodoo that attaches itself to him every time he hooks up with Brown. Since 1905 Matty has not beaten Brown. {Mathewson had last defeated Brown on June 13, 1905, when the Giants won 1 to 0.}

—New York *Press*

──────◇ **MONDAY, AUGUST 31** ◇──────

{On August 30, in Chicago, the Giants lost 2 to 1. Winning pitcher, Pfiester; losing pitcher, Crandall. Giants' standing: 69 wins, 45 losses, in first place.}

Jack Pfiester came into his own yesterday by winning his third straight game from the skyrockety Giants, triumphing over Crandall in the final battle of the series, which gave Chicago's Cubs a clean sweep, a clear title to second place, and closed all but half a game of the gap that was separating them from first place only four days ago.

No longer will Chicago's fans struggle with the pretzel curves of the great southpaw's patronymic; no longer will it be mispronounced by seven out of every eight bugs and bugettes. Pfiester, the spelling of which has been the occasion of as many wagers as its mispronunciation, will be dropped as meaningless and inappropriate, and for the rest of time and part of eternity Mr. Pfiester of private life will be known to the public and the historians as Jack the Giant Killer.

Pitching brilliantly before absolutely faultless support, Jack held the Giants to a single run, which came from a pass. Five times they hit him for safeties, but two were infield scratches. Chance's warriors touched Crandall for only five hits, but every one was of the cleancut variety, and three counted in the run column, leaving only two for the waste basket.

Manager McGraw's choice of Crandall, instead of sending Wiltse back to the slab, was a confession of desperation. After the trimming the Cubs gave the Giants' willowy southpaw on Thursday the Gotham leader knew that Wiltse could not stop the Cubs yesterday. Gambler by nature, McGraw took the gambler's chance and sent a youngster against the veteran world beaters, knowing it would not cost the Giants anything and might mean a lucky break and victory.

Right well young Crandall performed. He was harder to beat than either of the stars who had taken their beating in the series. But he was no match in the pinches for his rival, the Killer, and he had no such perfect team behind him.   —I. E. Sanborn, Chicago *Tribune*

CHICAGO, Aug. 30—On a warm, sunny Sunday afternoon near the end of August a close observer might have seen 17 or 18 men in automobiles rushing madly for the Union Station in Chicago. The foam of battle still lingered on their lips, à la asparagus, and the bumps of their saturnine features indicated they had been running for Sweeney {a slang expression meaning to run away from something threatening or dangerous}. They were the Giants, going away from here. They were leaving the city by Lake Michigan more in sorrow than anger, victims of a series as disastrous as some of the 1906 and 1907 campaigns.

Singularly enough, the crowd today was not nearly so large as the Thursday or Saturday gatherings. The total count today could not have been over 17,000—and on a bright Sunday afternoon. Charley Murphy stood as near the turnstile as he could get. His ear is so finely trained that when the turnstile is not clicking over .300 he knows it in a jiffy, and he began to fidget when time for the game was almost called and the gates began to look comfortably wide instead of being crammed.

"It was the newspapers that scared 'em away," declared the magnate. "They had altogether too much dope this morning about the terrible crush yesterday. Thousands of baseball fans read the statements and decided to stay at home, on the front porch. It was thoughtless of them, to say the least." With this diatribe, the friend of Big Bill Taft reached into his pocket and gave a scribe a good ten-cent cigar. {William Howard Taft had lately become the Republican Party's nominee for president.} Hard luck, Charley. The papers ought to be ashamed of themselves.

The solitary run gained by McGraw's men yesterday came in the second inning. Donlin walked and Cy Seymour singled clean to right field, Captain Mike going to third. Devlin hit into a fast double play, Evers to Tinker to Chance. Those double plays have done much damage to our boys here in Chicago. {Franklin P. Adams's poem "Tinker to Evers to Chance" would be published in the New York *Evening Mail* in July 1910.}   —William F. Kirk, New York *American*

SOUTH BEND, Ind., Aug. 30 {en route to Boston}—The Giants might have changed their luck if they hadn't lost so many runs by weird base running. The limit of foolish work on the bases was when Barry allowed himself to be forced out at second yesterday on Bridwell's single to right. It was as clean a hit as was ever made, and Barry was guilty of a most serious error of judgment in not running. He was looking right at the ball, too, and ran back to first, thinking Evers, with the ball going ten feet over his head, would catch it. As Crandall walloped a long fly to Hofman, on whose catch Barry could have easily reached third, with only one out, the seriousness of his mistake can be appreciated. It may have lost the game.   —Sam Crane, New York *Evening Journal*

After the game a cushion battle between 3,000 in the stands and 5,000 in the field raged for 15 minutes, during which many women were injured and their hats demolished. The police were powerless. In this way the crowd expressed its joy over the victory.   —New York *World*

Mike Donlin and Hans Wagner are still battling for National League batting honors. The Turkey didn't gain on the Teuton last week even if the Giants did trounce the Pirates four straight. Wagner has an average of .337 while Donlin is batting .322. Among Giant regulars, Doyle and Bridwell have the second and third highest batting averages, .296 and .281.
                                        —New York *World*

Sacrificing a runner on first or second is almost never done by the Giants, the hit-and-run play being used almost exclusively. Once in a while a Giant will attempt to catch the enemy unawares by laying down a sacrifice bunt, but the general rule of play, as stated by Manager McGraw himself, is to eliminate the sacrifice play as much as possible and stick to "hitting it out."

"What's the use of having hitters if they can't advance the base runner in that way?" queried McGraw.   —Chicago *News*

——— NATIONAL LEAGUE STANDINGS ———

	W	L	PCT.	GB		W	L	PCT.	GB
New York ...	69	45	.605	—	Cincinnati ...	58	59	.498	12½
Chicago	70	47	.599	½	Boston	50	67	.427	20½
Pittsburgh ...	69	47	.595	1	Brooklyn	43	71	.377	26
Philadelphia .	60	52	.536	8	St. Louis	42	73	.365	27½

———◇ TUESDAY, SEPTEMBER 1 ◇———

BOSTON, Sept. 1—By taking the Lake Shore "flyer" out of Chicago at 5:30 Sunday afternoon the Giants got here last night and obtained a good night's rest before tackling Boston in a doubleheader today. It took some tall hustling to make the train, but through Secretary Knowles' thoughtfulness auto cars were on hand outside the ball park, and the players were whirled to the Lake Shore station with time to spare.

The players spent the long day on the train playing various games of cards, McGraw even allowing the great American game of "Hanky Pank" {any of several games, popular in carnivals, usually costing five or ten cents to play} to be played for a small limit, to take the attention and minds of the boys off baseball and the strenuous pennant race.

—Sam Crane, New York *Evening Journal*

Just how hard a road the Giants still have to travel is illustrated by looking over their schedule. McGraw's men have 40 games to play in 29 playing days. This means a number of doubleheaders, a majority with strong teams. It surely is a hard schedule, but it is, in a measure, offset by the fact that two-thirds of the games will be played on the Polo Grounds.

—New York *Evening Mail*

John J. McGraw, Jekyll and Hyde.

That is how the little manager looks to folks who really know him. Outside New York so few fans know anything about J. Muggs off the field that he has come to be regarded as the incarnation of rowdyism, the personification of meanness and howling blatancy.

That's what J. Muggs is, all right, when it comes to the arena. But off the field McGraw is the kindliest, most generous and most sympathetic of men. The supporter of a herd of pensioners—a long list of poor creatures, who, if McGraw should die or be reduced to sudden poverty, would at once fall into utter destitution. The most loyal of friends, the most steadfast of good fellows.

John J. McGraw spends his big salary, it is said, in horse racing. He does—a few dollars of it. Fifty percent of John McGraw's money goes direct to the support of sick, crippled, helpless dependents, mostly people who have no claim on him but were brought to his notice by sympathetic friends. The little manager has a charity list that would make most millionaires look like pikers. He has charity toward all, malice toward none, and will go miles out of his way to help an invalid woman or crippled child.

John McGraw's great heart contracts to the dimensions of a bean when he gets on a ball field. The gentle sympathy and eager kindliness narrow down to the shape of a spike, with rust on the same. The generous giver becomes the howling wolf. The prince of nature's noblemen becomes so fierce, so vicious, so unendurable, his own men ever and anon take a punch at his chops in the dressing room.

How do you figure it all out?   —Chicago *Journal*

———◇ **WEDNESDAY, SEPTEMBER 2** ◇———

{On September 1, in Boston, the Giants won a doubleheader, 4 to 1 and 8 to 0. Winning pitchers, Wiltse and Mathewson; losing pitchers, Tuckey and Flaherty. Giants' standing: 71 wins, 45 losses, in first place.}

The New York Giants made the most of their doubleheader yesterday and won both games. They needed them, for Pittsburgh put Cincinnati away twice and jumped to second place. The Cubs were surprised by the Cardinals, who downed them in a ten-inning game, and now Chicago isn't quite as sure of the pennant as it was 24 hours ago.

—New York *Sun*

BOSTON, Sept. 1—Getting back into their rapid stride which carried them to the top of the league heap, John J. McGraw's Glittering Giants, ambitious to recover ground lost in Chicago, twice feasted on Joe Kelley's Doves.

The Manhattan Marvels played wonderfully in all departments of the game, making only one error behind Wiltse and according Mathewson perfect support. The star whaler of the day was Arthur Devlin, who could not make a hit in Chicago. McGraw's classy third-sacker got in six screaming, slashing slaps, one a homer over the left-field fence and another a triple to deep center.   —New York *Press*

Yesterday was Mike Donlin's birthday, not the anniversary of his birth but of his regeneration. It was just one year ago yesterday since Mike looked on wine when it was red and boarded the water wagon, and, accordingly, Mrs. Donlin and a few friends surprised him last night with a little banquet. Water, watermelon, water ices, and finger bowls formed the principal features of the affair, and miniature little sprinkling wagons were the souvenirs. A large cake graced the center of the table, and in it was stuck one lighted candle. The cake bore a card which read, "From the Retail Liquor Dealers' Association."

The whole team contributed something to the celebration, and Mike made a little speech and said he would stick to the water wagon until there were twenty candles on the cake.   —Nie, New York *Globe*

When work shuts up its dusty shop, and world-worn millionaires
Trail in behind their office boys on "L" and Subway stairs,
When brain-spent boss and nerve-spent clerk and brawn-spent workingman
Fight greedily in swarming trains to get what space they can,
Some urchin on a platform seat cries out in screaming glee
Behind a page of two-foot type, "The Giants wins, b'Gee!"
And furrowed scowls are smoothed in smiles, and everything the day
Has brought of trial, defeat and grief is cast, the while, away.

"The Giants Wins!" That triumph makes our own defeats no less.
It eases not the rugged road to what we call success.

It neither lifts the load we bear, nor vanquishes a foe
Of all the eager enemies along the way we go.
And yet it wakes the same old thrill we used to know of old
Before the red, warm blood of youth ran sluggishly and cold.
And through that throng of wan-faced boys and jaded, faded men,
There runs a rumbling undertone: "We've won! We've won again!"

Who says the world is growing old; that all men used to know
Of simple, honest happiness has vanished long ago?
Who says that city graft and greed, and city craft and guile
Have robbed all city human kind of everything worth while?
When men still feel a boy's delight, and in a boy's own way
Cheer on the valiant victors in the Game they used to play.
No pessimism need appal; forgive them for their sins,
But bet on them as long as they will shout "The Giants wins!"
    —James J. Montague, editorial page, New York *American*

——◇ THURSDAY, SEPTEMBER 3 ◇——

Yesterday's game at the South End grounds was called off on account of wet grounds, and Manager John McGraw was in good humor as he sat and fanned with a few friends. He is extra sweet on Doyle.

"I hung on to Doyle," McGraw said, "when the New York fans and critics were calling for his scalp and even furnished me with a hand-painted tin can. I stuck to Doyle, and today I would not trade him for any man playing baseball. Think of it, in the last series at Pittsburgh and Chicago Doyle got in no less than 18 safe hits. Every time he went to bat he hit the ball clean and hard. There is nothing like having confidence in one's own judgment."   —T. H. Murnane, Boston *Globe*

——◇ FRIDAY, SEPTEMBER 4 ◇——

{On September 3, in Boston, the Giants won a doubleheader, 3 to 0 and 8 to 5. Winning pitchers: McGinnity and Ames; losing pitchers, Lindaman and Dorner. Giants' standing: 73 wins, 45 losses, in first place.}

The old South End battlefield saw another slaughter of innocents yesterday. After "Iron Man" McGinnity pitched a shut-out, Ames twirled a strong game until the seventh, when Boston scored three runs. Then the great Mathewson came to the rescue and held Boston hitless for one inning, and he in turn was relieved by Taylor.

The Giants were on their toes every minute while the home team went through the game as a matter of form. The crowd seemed to show a preference for the visitors, several young fellows singing between innings, "Cherries Will Soon Be Ripe."　　　　　—Boston *Globe*

Most Boston fans want to see the Giants win, now that their own team is out of the race, but local pride pushes them along in the desire to witness a victory by their own. If Western fans would only forget their rabid soreness against New York and anything and everything hailing from the big city, baseball would be better off and the danger of a war between this country and Japan would be reduced to a minimum.

If an issue does arise between the two countries, just have them put two representative ball teams on the diamond and any question between them, even of the gravest nature, would be settled then and there. In my humble opinion, when baseball becomes the all national sport, as it is bound to be, the game will do more to subdue war talk than the big navies.　　　　　—Sam Crane, New York *Evening Journal*

———◇ SATURDAY, SEPTEMBER 5 ◇———

{On September 4, in Philadelphia, the Giants won 8 to 1. Winning pitcher, Wiltse; losing pitcher, Sparks. Giants' standing: 74 wins, 45 losses, in first place.}

There is no balm in Gilead or any other Pennsylvania flag station for the Phillies. From the time Frederick Tenney, the boisterous Brunonian {referring to Brown University}, hit the first ball of the game for a double, it was a long joy ride for New York.

The Giants constructed 15 safe hits, and every man who had a bat made a hit except Bresnahan. Larry Doyle made four hits and might have had five had he not been intentionally passed on his last trip to the plate.

Wiltse, the Giant boxman, got results. He curled his cross-fire around the pates of Quaker clubbers with deadly effect, holding them to four hits. —Philadelphia *North American*

PHILADELPHIA, Sept. 5—Without the leadership of Manager McGraw the Giants go into battle today and twice Monday. It may be for a longer time, but let's hope it's for three days only. Mac was suspended indefinitely by President Pulliam for yelling "Fifteen minutes late" at Umpire Klem in Boston Thursday, when as a matter of fact, Klem was nearly 20 minutes behind a play at first base which caused the trouble. McGraw's suspension, however, is purely technical. He can keep out of sight of umpires here and still be where he can put his hand on any player on the Giants' bench. That and the language of Luther Taylor will do the rest. Where Mac will be missed most will be in the coaching box, and the way the Giants got caught napping at first and second yesterday because no one looked out for them was something marvelous to behold.

—Nie, New York *Globe*

CINCINNATI, Sept. 5—For the world's series games there will be hereafter four umpires, the National Commission announced today. Two shall come from the National and two from the American League staff of umpires. A recommendation to this effect, made some weeks ago by the commission, has been approved by both leagues. {Only two umpires, one from each league, had been assigned to world series games played before 1908.}

—Chicago *Journal*

ST. LOUIS, Sept. 4—Ball players of the future may form a part of the American Federation of Labor. President Samuel Gompers approves it, seeing no reason why, like other labor, it should not organize and tote union cards and work on a union schedule.

"I can see no reason why they should not organize if they wish to," he said. "Baseball playing has become a skilled profession, and many thousands who assemble to see games prove it has become a utility. As skill is required to play I see no objection to those of the craft joining for mutual advantage."

If ball players decide to form a union fans may be furnished the delightful spectacle of a "strike" different from those common to baseball parks. And there may be "walkouts" when a southpaw shows up for work without a card. The question of the future for members of major league teams may be "Do you belong to the union?" rather than "What is your batting average?"
—Chicago *Tribune*

SPECIAL REPORT:
CONTROVERSY IN PITTSBURGH

{While in Philadelphia the Giants were winning easily, in Pittsburgh the Pirates and Cubs played one of the most crucial games in the history of baseball. New York fans recognized that since it involved the Giants' two rivals for the pennant, the contest was important, but few of them could have comprehended the true significance of what took place at Exposition Park. With one slight exception, no New York newspaper reported anything remarkable about the game except that it had been an extraordinary pitchers' battle. One sentence in the final edition of the *Globe* reported that Chicago would protest the outcome but did not mention the grounds for the protest. Fans in Chicago and Pittsburgh, however, were not unmindful of what underlaid this action.}

PITTSBURGH, Sept. 4—In a magnificently pitched battle the Cubs received the short end of a 1 to 0 verdict in ten innings.

But there is an outside chance that the defeat will be wiped out and the Cubs and Pirates ordered to do it all over again on the strength of a protest which the Cub management will file with President Pulliam.

To get wise to the preceding remark it is necessary to acquire a few details of what happened to terminate that grand struggle between Brown and Willis. Manager Clarke opened the Pittsburgh tenth with a single. Leach sacrificed him to second. Wagner then bounded a fast one toward right field. Evers almost made a brilliant stop but could only check the force of the ball enough to hold Clarke at third. {Warren} Gill, a late recruit from the minors, was next and Brown soaked him in the slats with a curve, filling the bases with one out. Abby was then struck out.

Wilson, never a fearsome batsman, was next and what did this recent graduate from the minors do but soak the first ball Brown pitched on the nose. It went like a shot past Evers, landing safely in short center, and Clarke scored the winning run.

Everybody thought it was over and started for the clubhouse. That everybody included First Baseman Gill and O'Day, and thereby hangs the protest. Gill ran halfway to second base and as soon as he saw the hit fall safely he returned to the Pirates' bench. He did not go within 30 feet of second base at any time.

Evers, seeing Gill's break for the bench, yelled for Slagle to throw the ball. Jimmy did and Evers touched second base with it, then wheeled to claim a force out, only to see Umpire O'Day making fast tracks for an exit with his back turned completely to what had been pulled off. Evers made his claim for the out, which retired the side and consequently wiped out Clarke's run, but the veteran umpire remarked: "Clarke was over the plate, so his run counted anyway."

If O'Day had watched the finish of that base hit and had seen what really came off, he could not have decided otherwise than in Chicago's favor, ruling out Clarke's run and leaving the score tied at 0 to 0. Everyone knows no run can count if the third out is made before the batsman reaches first, or if the third man out is forced out. Gill hadn't touched second base yet, and so Clarke's run could not have scored but for the fact O'Day took it for granted the game was over when Wilson's hit landed safe.   —I. E. Sanborn, Chicago *Tribune*

President Charles W. Murphy, of Chicago, in a telegram to Harry C. Pulliam says:

"Chicago protests today's game. . . . Chicago claims Gill should have touched second base before he ran to the clubhouse, and will prove by affidavits of a number of persons that he failed to do so."

As soon as Clarke crossed the plate, Umpire Hank O'Day turned to the players' bench to get a drink of water. Evers yelled at Slagle, who threw the ball to Evers, who called, "O'Day, O'Day." Hank failed to hear him owing to the noise made by the crowd leaving the park. Tinker, however, ran to the hydrant and called the thirsty umpire's attention to what happened, but Hank merely remarked: "Clarke has crossed the plate."

"I do not expect the protest will be allowed," said Mr. Murphy, "but it is certainly just, and should prove a strong argument in favor of the double-umpire system." —Pittsburgh *Post*

{At this point I call attention to the "letter to the editor" reproduced from the July 19 issue of the Chicago *Tribune*. This letter, published when the Cubs were at home, may have provided the idea for the play that brought on Charles Murphy's protest. This game against Pittsburgh marked the Cubs' first opportunity since the appearance of the letter to put into effect this play, which they had never tried before. It should be noted that after Wilson had presumably driven home the winning run, not only Evers but other members of the Chicago team, including Slagle and Tinker, did not immediately head for the clubhouse but held their ground as if they were anticipating Gill's infraction. This play, incidentally, provided a brief moment of notoriety for Warren Gill, whose major league career was confined to 27 games in 1908.}

◇ SUNDAY, SEPTEMBER 6 ◇

{On September 5, in Philadelphia, the Giants won 5 to 1. Winning pitcher, Mathewson; losing pitcher, McQuillan. Giants' standing: 75 wins, 45 losses, in first place.}

The Phillies failed again to lower New York's percentage in the chase for the pennant, and the Giants, with Pittsburgh's defeat by Chicago, now top the procession by 15 points.

After the first inning McQuillan, who started for the Phillies, was easy for the Giants. McGraw's hirelings catered to anything "Big Mac" shot up to the plate, finally hitting him so hard in the sixth Foxen finished the game.

In the face of the Giants' hitting, Mathewson pitched a game hard to beat. The efforts of the Phillies to dent the whirling horsehide were painful to behold. They got seven hits, but with men on base Mathewson held the batters in the hollow of his hand.　　　—Philadelphia *Inquirer*

That final play of Friday's game between the Cubs and Pirates is one that does not come often, but next time it happens it is safe to predict that none who took part in the game will overlook the importance of touching the next base. Mr. Murphy's protest, backed up with a batch of affidavits, will not likely result in throwing out this game—in fact Murphy himself does not expect it. He does hope, however, that the incident will add emphasis to the demand for the double-umpire system. O'Day is one of the best officials who ever umpired, but he certainly should have had an assistant in a game in which two of the fastest teams in the major leagues were engaged in a bitter struggle for the upper hand in one of the hottest three-cornered fights for the pennant ever waged in the National League.　　　—Pittsburgh *Post*

◇ MONDAY, SEPTEMBER 7 ◇

PHILADELPHIA, Sept. 7—Can a man play ball and think at the same time? Can a player run bases, watch opposing players, tell when to start and when not to?

I think not. When he can he is above the ordinary and soon becomes a manager. Of course there is an exception every now and then—occasionally the game produces a man like Wagner, but not often.

For the last two days the Giants have been left to think for themselves. McGraw has been under suspension and off the coaching lines, and what the players have done, when they tried to figure out in their own noodles the right plays, has been something weird.

In two days here Donlin has been caught off base four times. Bresnahan tried twice to steal second when there was no chance in the world to make the play, and McCormick has been nailed far off first base. Others, too, have been put out the same way and have tried the hit and run at the most inopportune moments.

If he never earned the title before McGraw has certainly stamped himself this year the world's greatest manager. He has plugged along with hardly more than two pitchers. He has had a long uphill fight. He has seen his team throw away game after game and yet he has pulled them through by quick thinking and by judiciously nursing along his two great box artists.

McGraw has his own systems of play which have been tremendously successful, and yet they are directly opposite to the way most players like to go after a game.

And that is what causes the trouble when the team is left to itself. The men persist in trying the moves which are directly opposite to what McGraw calls the "Giants' system," but which is in reality "McGraw's system." And when they do—well, they tried it here Friday and Saturday.

—Nie, New York *Globe*

NATIONAL LEAGUE STANDINGS

	W	L	PCT.	GB		W	L	PCT.	GB
New York ...	75	45	.625	—	Cincinnati ...	60	64	.484	17
Pittsburgh ...	76	49	.608	1½	Boston	52	73	.416	25½
Chicago	76	50	.603	2	Brooklyn	44	78	.361	32
Philadelphia .	65	54	.546	9½	St. Louis	44	79	.358	32½

◇ TUESDAY, SEPTEMBER 8 ◇

{On September 7, in Philadelphia, the Giants split a doubleheader, winning 5 to 0 and losing 2 to 1. Winning pitchers: Wiltse and Richie; losing pitchers, Foxen and Crandall. Giants' standing: 76 wins, 46 losses, in first place.}

The Phillies secured some balm by snatching the afternoon battle yesterday right out of the hands of the New Yorks after one of the most exciting finishes made at Broad and Huntingdon streets this year.

The morning game went to New York by 5 to 0, the Phillies giving a dopey exhibition of how not to hit when men were on base, besides doing several foolish stunts. And during the first eight innings of the afternoon game it looked as if New York would get another shut-out victory. Up to the ninth the Giants had a 1 to 0 margin, and it looked a foregone conclusion what the outcome was to be.

That last inning will not be forgotten for a long time. After Titus had been retired, {Sherwood} Magee smashed a sizzling liner to right for a base, and then {Kitty} Bransfield plastered the horsehide against the fence of the left-field bleachers, scoring Magee and sending the crowd wild. {Fred} Osborne sent a wicked-looking grounder to Bridwell, who fumbled the ball, Kitty reaching third and Osborne first. Captain Mike Doolan then earned all sorts of praise by shooting one between Devlin and Bridwell sending in Bransfield with the winning run.

—Philadelphia *Inquirer*

Roger Bresnahan's the boy to get on base. Did you ever notice him when he comes to bat and see him pull his shirt out all around his waistline? Do you know why he does that? He widens his girth so that the pitcher may hit him. Roger has often got his base with a howl that makes you think his ribs are caved in, and the ball only rapped the flowing folds of that shirt.

And that's on the level.

—Gym Bagley, New York *Evening Mail*

So much had the surroundings of the Polo Grounds been changed this afternoon six score "old fans" who had occupied seats since the days of the Brotherhood in 1890 were ousted from their positions and wandered aimlessly around the grandstand and bleachers looking for available sites to preempt for another 20 years. This field was opened to the public in 1890 and has not been changed since then.

In the "Roost," as it was called, in the right corner of the field bleachers, something like 50 patrons have sat year after year, and they were turned out today simply because baseball has become so popular that the Polo Grounds could not accommodate the spectators.

To take the place of 1,000 bleacher seats which have been withdrawn, there is a new stand that will accommodate 3,000 fans.

It has been built with a sweeping curve, and when the other improvements are finished there will be a stand on the right-field side of the diamond that will practically mean a complete circuit of the diamond.

—New York *Evening Telegram*

The Pittsburgh baseball club blames the closing of the Cosmopolitan National Bank for the loss to Chicago last Saturday. Half a dozen of the club's leading players had money in this bank, and when they heard of its closure they became nervous and could not play their game, so it is said, and Chicago won 2 to 0.　　　　　　　　　　—Chicago *Tribune*

——◇ WEDNESDAY, SEPTEMBER 9 ◇——

{On September 8, in New York, the Giants defeated Brooklyn in 11 innings, 1 to 0. Winning pitcher, Mathewson; losing pitcher, Rucker. Giants' standing: 77 wins, 46 losses, in first place.}

In the last inning of one of the most bitterly contested pitchers' battles ever fought at the Polo Grounds, with 15,000 fans praying that the game would not be called on account of darkness, young Al Bridwell (may his tribe increase) cuffed a clean single to left and chased Cy Seymour across the plate with the winning run.

When all you fans are old, and have your grandchildren around your knees, and are talking about great baseball games, don't forget to allude to a little game played at the Polo Grounds yesterday. Seldom have two twirlers fought such a grueling fight. Young Nap Rucker kept his various offerings coming over the plate with bewildering versatility, and while he allowed many more hits than his brilliant rival, Mathewson, he pitched a masterly game and only caved in the eleventh hour because he was pitted against the greatest twirler that ever threw a ball.

With its new seating capacity, the Polo Grounds will accommodate about 25,000 before the "S.R.O." sign is flaunted. As the park stands today, it has the largest seating capacity of any ball park in the country.

—William F. Kirk, New York *American*

Larry Doyle, the phenomenal young second baseman, was badly spiked by Hummell and will not play again for at least ten days. The accident may prove to be a very serious handicap to the Giants, for Larry has been stinging the ball better than perhaps any other player on the team and was the sensation of the Western jaunt. There was never a Giant batting rally that Larry didn't figure in, and his fielding was such that he was considered the prize package kid of the season.

There was no excuse for Hummell cutting Doyle down. Hummell was out so far on a force play that he hadn't a show to make the bag. So why was Doyle spiked so high up on his leg? I don't want to accuse Hummell of deliberately spiking Doyle, but it was surely an accident that could have been avoided.

The Brooklyns are almost as well satisfied to beat the Giants as to win the pennant, and considering the old-time inter-city feeling between the two burgs, that is possibly commendable, but crippling of players should not enter into a strife, no matter how bitter.

—Sam Crane, New York *Evening Journal*

{The following item was the most detailed reference to Chicago's protest of the September 4 game in the only New York newspaper that mentioned the incident.}

President Pulliam has thrown out the Chicago club's protest of last Friday's game in Pittsburgh, and the 1 to 0 victory of Pittsburgh will stand. Pulliam had affidavits of all kinds submitted by the Chicago club, but he and Hank O'Day held that the game was fairly won, and that Chicago's kick was far-fetched. The Cubs couldn't prove their contention, so Mr. Pulliam backed up his umpire.

"I think the baseball public prefers to see games settled on the field and not in this office," said Pulliam.   —New York *Globe*

The usual pell-mell rush through the press box resulted in an accident yesterday. After each game there is a helter-skelter scramble through that part of the stand. {At this time the press box in the Polo Grounds was located in the lower grandstand, close to the field.} The fans step on the

necks and hands of the poor scribes who are forced to linger a few moments after the game and then take a six-foot jump into the diamond.
Yesterday a big, heavy fan missed his footing and fell heavily on his side,
with his leg doubled under him. He sustained a fractured knee and had to
be assisted from the field by the surgeon who was called to attend him.
After this rush every day the wreckage of seats is strewn all over the press
box. Someday there will be a bad accident.

—Sid Mercer, New York *Globe*

———◇ THURSDAY, SEPTEMBER 10 ◇———

{On September 9, in New York, the Giants beat Brooklyn 7 to 3.
Winning pitcher, Ames; losing pitcher, Bell. Giants' standing: 78 wins, 46
losses, in first place.}

Leon Ames pitched a winning game yesterday. He had speed and control. Once upon a time Ames was very liberal with passes. Yesterday he
was as stingy as a passenger agent under the Interstate Commerce law.
That the big fellow once more can take his turn on the rubber brought
smiles to the face of John McGraw. It means the Giants are fortified in
the pitcher's box to stand off the Pirates and Cubs, who simply refuse
to lose.

The Giants didn't have to work so hard for victory as on Tuesday.
The absence of {catcher} Billy Bergen made a chapter in the game that
could be headed "Base Running Made Easy." Billy Maloney, who is now
very rusty as a backstop, caught for Brooklyn. {A major league outfielder
since 1901, Maloney had not caught in a game since 1902.} To be charita-
ble, he did his best, but that best was something awful when it came to
throwing to bases. Herzog, subbing for Doyle, added four steals to his
record.

—New York *World*

Had it not been for an accident, one of those unlucky and unexpected
gags that butt in at the wrong moment to thwart a well-laid and daring
plot, the Giants would have pulled off a stunt never before even attempted in big league society.

Occasionally, very occasionally, a runner steals home while the pitcher is making love to the ball. But for two men to work this, and in succession—that's going some.

Herzog pulled it on Bell yesterday and got away with it. Donlin followed him and made it, too, even cleaner than his brother thief. But Devlin, who knew it was coming and stood pat, had his bat in the way of the ball. He fouled it off unintentionally, and Mike's joke on the pitcher didn't take.

And, outside of that, how the Giants did steal bases—only nine of them. It was a constant procession around the corners, and most of them standing. They didn't even take the trouble to hit the dirt.

—Gym Bagley, New York *Evening Mail*

The Giants will play all the rest of their games at home, except those of September 10, scheduled for Brooklyn, and of October 1, 2 and 3, in Philadelphia. This advantage is fully appreciated by those acquainted with McGraw's methods and the extreme partisanship of Polo Grounds patrons. President Pulliam's best umpires will be assigned to the metropolis, but even the assurance of a square deal on decisions will not remove the handicap visiting players are under on the Giants' grounds. Because of the great advantage McGraw's team gains by its long stretch of games at home, it may be that the best team in the National League will not represent it in the world series of 1908.   —*The Sporting News*

——◇ FRIDAY, SEPTEMBER 11 ◇——

{On September 10, in Brooklyn, the Giants won 6 to 5. Winning pitcher, Taylor; losing pitcher, Rucker. Giants' standing: 79 wins, 46 losses, in first place.}

We beat the Brooklyns yesterday, but we knew we had been to the races. Pretty close, public, pretty close. Too close for comfort. However, it was a win, and as Pittsburgh suffered a lapse {losing to Cincinnati}, you may increase your ticket on the Giants.

Twelve thousand human persons, men and women, gathered together in peace and unity, and the management of the Brooklyn club indulged in the first smile of the season. That is to say when you use the word smile in its restricted sense. And an outturning of fair femininity such as makes us look upon ourselves as the only matinee idol worth specifying. Now, all this is very grateful, and moves to a sort of permissible gratulation, until the rude native next to us blurts out: "It's like this every Thursday—this is Ladies' Day."

Ladies' Day in Brooklyn means that ladies don't pay to get in. Oh, gallant Brooklyn! Oh, wise Brooklyn! Make a few notes of that, McGraw. {Since the 1890s women had been admitted free to Thursday games in Brooklyn. Several other cities also held "Ladies' Day," but the practice had not yet been sanctioned by the Giants or Yankees.}

—W. W. Aulick, New York *Times*

For some reason that has not been explained, the Patsies who look like dog meat when arrayed against other clubs seem to give us more trouble and distress to the square inch than any aggregation in the league. When they are playing Joe Kelley's Oslers, or Ganzel's Goats, or McCloskey's Misfits, they give up the ghost without even squawking—peacefully, prayerfully, like little Nell taking the count in "The Old Curiosity Shop." When they fling their spears against our brawny demons, they are beautiful in their Battling Nelson aggressiveness and mighty hard propositions all the way. They certainly made the gooseflesh come yesterday.

Joe McGinnity did the heaving for us until the seventh, when Dummy Taylor put on the pitching spangles. Up to that time in the seventh that they began to land on Joseph {and scored three runs}, he had been pitching a clean, consistent game, but suddenly the bingles began to jingle, and McGraw acted with his usual speed, calling the Iron Man to shelter before it was too late. The deaf mute let in the tying tally with a wild pitch, but after that the Brooklynites stopped their trouble-making, and it ended well.   —William F. Kirk, New York *American*

McGraw need not worry about Doyle being out. Charley Herzog is playing a great game at second, just as he had done at short and at third when the occasion demanded and is, without doubt, the best young player of the year. Yesterday he batted .500, stole a base, scored a run, and batted in another, and did great work in the field.

Donlin, however, was the Giants' best hitting bet of the day, getting four hits in four trips to the plate, three of them bunts placed just exactly right.

Umpire Johnstone made a ruling yesterday which will establish a precedent. When it came time for {Jim} Holmes {Brooklyn's second pitcher} to bat in the seventh Patsy Donovan sent Alperman from the bench with a bat in his hand. McGraw promptly jerked McGinnity from the box and then Donovan called Alperman and trotted Holmes up. Alperman had never reached the plate, but Johnstone said he was the batter and ruled Holmes out of the game.   —Nie, New York *Globe*

It is difficult to pick out one man on McGraw's. team and prove that he has done more than any other player toward lifting the team into first place. And therein lies the secret of the Giants' success. It is not a one-man team. The absence of any one star will not demoralize it. Larry Doyle, for example, has been a big factor in the victories of the last few weeks, but the Giants are winning without Doyle.

—Sid Mercer, New York *Globe*

It is high time baseball games were started at 3:30 instead of 4. There wouldn't be much chance of an extra-inning game unless an earlier start were made.   —New York *Sun*

───◇ **SATURDAY, SEPTEMBER 12** ◇───

{On September 11, in New York, the Giants beat Brooklyn 6 to 1. Winning pitcher, Crandall; losing pitcher, Wilhelm. Giants' standing: 80 wins, 46 losses, in first place.}

If the Pittsburgh and Chicago diamond athletes could see the brand of baseball the Giants are putting up now they certainly would feel like changing their routes when they depart from their reservations a few days hence. Those Brooklyn boys suffered another deep dent yesterday.

Well, sir! you ought to have seen that young fellow Herzog and that other young fellow McCormick, and also the young fellow Crandall, working at their trade! They did some joyous jolting, you may be sure.

Truly, each succeeding day makes the Giants look more and more like pennant winners. —New York *Herald*

Fred Tenney was full of pepper yesterday and radiated so much ginger he was almost a crab. He scolded Bresnahan, Crandall, Herzog, and the whole family. Tenney has bolstered up the infield of the Gingery Giants more than anybody except McGraw realizes.

Tenney had a repartee duel with Gentle Roger Bresnahan in the seventh inning that is worthy of more than passing mention. While {Tommy} McMillan was at bat Fred imagined there was a lack of speed in the battery work of Crandall and Bresnahan, so he shouted, "Wake up, Roger, wake up!" Roger resented this deeply. He looked at Tenney more in sorrow than anger. But there was an air of "Don't try to repeat!" about the stocky backstop that made Frederick close his trap. A moment later Tenney went after a hard, low foul ball that nobody could have captured. When he started back for the initial sack Gentle Roger shouted "What's the matter, Fred? Did you think it would bite you?" If we had two more crabs on the team like Bresnahan and Tenney we would never lose a game. —William F. Kirk, New York *American*

———◇ SUNDAY, SEPTEMBER 13 ◇———

{On September 12, in New York, the Giants beat Brooklyn 6 to 3. Winning pitcher, Mathewson; losing pitcher, McIntire. Giants' standing: 81 wins, 46 losses, in first place.}

There may on exceptional occasions have been more people at the Polo Grounds than yesterday, but never more noise. And at that the attendance was around 20,000, but a crowd of this size doesn't make us think in headlines any longer. We accepted the first-time filling of the new left-

field bleachers just as in former times we accepted the Brooklyn Bridge,
the Jersey Tunnel, the cocktail with an olive instead of a cherry, the
Times Building, and other evidences of advance.

—W. W. Aulick, New York *Times*

What mightily pleased the Brooklyn end of the big crowd was the
exceptional debut made by Jim Dunn, the raw recruit from Evansville of
the Three-Eye League, who arrived after an all-night train ride to become
Brooklyn's catcher. Things looked mighty bad for the Superbas before
Dunn's arrival. Billy Bergen {the regular catcher, who had been injured}
had gone home for the season. Al Farmer {second-string catcher} had sent
in his resignation, and Billy Maloney {outfielder turned catcher} had been
indefinitely suspended for his little argument with Johnstone the day
before.

Maloney's notification came while the team was practicing. A mes-
senger boy, in full regalia, appeared on the field, and after interviewing
Manager Donovan, took the envelope to Maloney, working behind the
bat. Billy signed for it in proper form and, after involuntarily digging
into his pocket for the tip that wasn't there, opened the missive and read
its contents. He then went on practicing, for be it known, a player is not
officially in eclipse until the game starts. Then he is compelled to obliter-
ate himself.

Dunn's advent into fast company was about as sensational as Heinie
Batch {a Brooklyn infielder-outfielder} a season or two ago {actually on
June 20, 1904}. On that occasion Batch made two home runs off Mathewson. Dunn, batting against the same pitcher, came up for his introduction
to the vast populace in the second inning and with two men on base
slammed out a double to right that hit the fence with a bang. The two
runners scored and Dunn tallied himself soon after, thus being instrumen-
tal in all the runs scored by the Superbas.

The next time up, Dunn drove a clean single to left and was immediately voted a "find" by the populace. On his fourth trip to the plate, with
two men on base, Dunn made good by caroming a hot one off Herzog's
shoe, filling the bases.

Dunn held McIntire nicely and won respect as a thrower by nailing
Tenney, the first man to attempt a steal. Only two bases were stolen on

him, quite a change from the recent wholesale robbery of New York runners. {Despite this auspicious start, Dunn's major league career ended after he had competed in only 30 games in 1908 and 1909, compiling a composite batting average of .169.}   —Brooklyn *Eagle*

Headed this way are the Pesky Pirates, the Chesty Cubs, the down-trodden Cardinals, and the Remarkable Reds. The third and last invasion of the East by Western clubs starts on Tuesday.

Among the games to be played by the Giants will be four doubleheaders, two with the Reds and one each with the Cubs and Pirates, making it necessary to squeeze into eight playing days 12 games. If McGraw's pitchers can stand up under this strain it looks like New York for a certainty to represent the National League in the world's series.

—New York *Press*

———◇ MONDAY, SEPTEMBER 14 ◇———

Mike Donlin will have to do some mighty slugging during the remainder of the season to take the batting lead away from Hans Wagner. Wagner's current average is .350, while Donlin is batting .327.

—New York *World*

——— NATIONAL LEAGUE STANDINGS ———

	W	L	PCT.	GB		W	L	PCT.	GB
New York ...	81	46	.638	—	Cincinnati ...	63	70	.474	21
Chicago	83	51	.620	1½	Boston	55	77	.417	28½
Pittsburgh ...	82	51	.617	2	Brooklyn	44	85	.341	38
Philadelphia .	71	56	.555	10	St. Louis	44	87	.336	39

———◇ TUESDAY, SEPTEMBER 15 ◇———

{On September 14, in New York, the Giants beat Brooklyn 4 to 3. Winning pitcher, Wiltse; losing pitcher, Pastorius. Giants' standing: 82 wins, 46 losses, in first place.}

Mr. J. Bentley Seymour, master mechanic at the baseball business, while in the performance of his duty at the Polo property yesterday had five opportunities at bat. He didn't miss any of them. First time up he slapped the leather into right field for two bases. Second time up he hit it into the middle of the lot for three bases. Third time up he hit it into right for two bases. Fourth time up he drove it into the middle for a fine single, and the fifth time up he hit it for a still finer single into right.

Fair day's labor? Well, rather!　　　　　—New York *Herald*

In the ninth Bridwell was badly spiked by Jordan, but no one knew it and Brid played out the inning. When he came to the bench, McGraw saw a big rip in his pants and blood stains on the cloth.

"What's that?" asked Mac.

"Oh, I got a scratch," replied Bridwell. "That's all."

But McGraw sent for Dr. Creamer and had the wound, an ugly one, patched up, before he would let Brid go to bat.

That is an example of the grit that obtains among this bunch, a grit that will land the old rag.

See if it doesn't.　　　　　—Gym Bagley, New York *Evening Mail*

——◇ WEDNESDAY, SEPTEMBER 16 ◇——

{On September 15, in New York, the Giants beat St. Louis, 5 to 4. Winning pitcher, Mathewson; losing pitcher, Higginbotham. Giants' standing: 83 wins, 46 losses, in first place.}

Leon Ames pitched great ball until the bingles began to collect in the eighth. He had control, and he had speed and curves thrown in. In the inning which brought on his downfall, he seemed to have as much as any twirler could expect, and yet the Miserable Missourians hit everything he had.

It was up to Matty, and "Big Six" responded nobly. Perhaps the Democratic Party can get along without McCarren {Patrick Henry McCarren, a well-known Brooklyn politician who had been a state senator since 1888} and it is a cinch that Republicans can get along without Hirsute Hughes {Governor Charles Evans Hughes of New York, who had lost out to Taft in a battle for the 1908 Republican presidential nomination} but the Giants cannot get along without Matty, and you can lay your last dime that way. Long live King Christy!

—William F. Kirk, New York *American*

────◇ **THURSDAY, SEPTEMBER 17** ◇────

{On September 16, in New York, the Giants beat St. Louis 6 to 2. Winning pitcher, Crandall; losing pitcher, Baldwin. Giants' standing: 84 wins, 46 losses, in first place.}

New York's pennant outlook took on additional improvement yesterday. The Poloists won from the Cardinals and the Pittsburghs broke even in a doubleheader with Philadelphia. The Chicagos beat Boston and tied Pittsburgh for second place. The first three teams have each won 84 games, but the Giants have lost six less than either of the other two.

—New York *Sun*

Yesterday's game between the Giants and Cardinals was New York's at all stages. It was not creditable baseball to either side, but the Giants were properly doing only enough playing to win, sparing their better efforts for future, more important occasions.

Donlin was ordered off the field in the seventh for disputing a decision by O'Day, in which Donlin was called out at first base, and a happy remark by McGraw, relating to Donlin's dispute, resulted in the manager being sent to the bench.   —New York *Tribune*

The great question now in local fandom is, Will Mike Donlin be sequestered for three days on account of his run-in with Umpire Hank O'Day yesterday?

I can say, officially, that Captain Donlin said nothing that will cause Sir Michael's retirement for the three days. I want to say, too, that Donlin was a wee bit lacking in good judgment by making such a holler, inasmuch as the Giants need his services at this stage of the game and the loss of his services would be a very serious handicap.

Thanks to the good sense with which Hank O'Day is blessed, he has taken a correct and proper view of the situation and instead of making a Donnybrook affair of the little "difficoolty," will handle the little clash himself, and the fiery but too irascible Michael will be on the job this afternoon.

Hank O'Day is one of the very few real umpires, and as such he should be appreciated by Mike Donlin, Roger Bresnahan and the other fiery Giants, who can be just as "crabby" and unreasonable as the worst umpire that ever lived. Umpire O'Day should be nursed, not trampled upon.

O'Day makes mistakes, of course, but when one thinks of all that an umpire must go through during a baseball season one feels like giving a medal to good old Hank O'Day. And I would be the first to "produce" for a medal for Hank. I have played ball with him and against him, and I can say that no squarer man ever lived. {O'Day had been a major league pitcher from 1884 through 1890 and won 70 games while losing 110. For part of 1889 he was a Giant, winning 9 and losing only 1. Among the other National League umpires, only Emslie, a pitcher for three years in the 1880s, had played major league baseball.}

　　　　　　　　　　　　　　　　—Sam Crane, New York *Evening Journal*

That the country at large is conceding the banner to New York was evidenced by the presence in the Brush stadium yesterday of experts from Detroit, sent here to get a line on the Giants. {In the American League, the Detroit Tigers were battling for the pennant and the right to play in the World Series.} The Michigan scouts, after witnessing the battle, reported that for ability to find weak points in an adversary there was nothing to compare with McGraw's aggregation.　　　—New York *Press*

The conduct of McGraw recently has been most reprehensible, and has excited editorial comment from critics all over the circuit. The opinion is general among baseball writers that the sooner the National League decides that it can get along without McGraw and his hoodlumism, the sooner will the ideal state of affairs be realized. McGraw was barred from the American League, he is persona non grata at most race tracks in the country, but he has for several years found a haven in the National

League, which has boasted ever since the inauguration of the Pulliam administration of a policy of advancement. One big step needs still to be taken, and when it comes to pass, McGraw will be beyond the pale of major league balldom. {McGraw was never "barred from the American League." In July 1902, after prolonged feuding with American League President Ban Johnson, McGraw resigned as manager of Baltimore, and left the American League for good, to go to the Giants. His departure led some American Leaguers for a while to compare McGraw to Benedict Arnold.}   —Ralph Davis, *The Sporting News*

The long-nosed rooters are crazy whenever young Herzog does anything noteworthy. Cries of "Herzog! Herzog! Goot poy, Herzog!" go up regularly, and there would be no let-up even if a million ham sandwiches suddenly fell among these believers in percentages and bargains.
                              —Joe Vila, *The Sporting News*

President Pulliam's decision on the protest filed by the Chicago club, in re its game of September 4, is in effect a dismissal for lack of proof to sustain the claim. When Wilson batted the ball that sent a runner home, the overflow crowd invaded the field and thereafter it would have been practically impossible for two umpires to have kept the four runners and the ball under supervision. The official in charge does not know that Gill proceeded to second and acquired legal right to that base, but the presumption that he did cannot be removed by the claim of members of the Chicago team. The umpire may not accept testimony of a player as a basis for a ruling. It is a baseball axiom that only that which the umpire sees occurs on a ball field. If the force-out did occur—Gill and five of his teammates say it did not—the umpire missed it and by implication officially ruled there was none by allowing the run that terminated the game. Chicago's protest was ill-advised and served only to afford the carping class of patrons an opportunity to question the integrity of the game.
                              —*The Sporting News*

It's all right!

John T. Brush says so.

"Florry" Ziegfeld's pretty show girls from the "Follies of 1908," 25 in number—count 'em—will, by permission of Mr. Brush, invade the Polo Grounds tomorrow and collect ten-cent subscriptions from the fans for the trophy to be presented by the *American* to the Giants at the end of the season. {The first of Ziegfeld's famous "Follies" had been produced in 1907.}

And some more good news!

The girls will go to the Polo Grounds from the New York Theatre in one of those rubberneck automobiles, a Knickerbocker five-seater, accommodating 25 people. The auto is contributed by Mrs. Frank B. Walker, president of the Knickerbocker Automobile Company, at 41st street and Broadway. The trophy committee {whose membership included Sam H. Harris, Florenz Ziegfeld, Victor Moore, De Wolf Hopper, George M. Cohan, and James J. Corbett} went to engage the machine from the Knickerbocker Company and stated the purpose to which it is to be put.

"Why," said Mrs. Walker, a businesswoman from head to heels, "I'm as enthusiastic a fan as any of you. You cannot pay me for the machine if it is to be used to gather money for a trophy. I'll donate its use for nothing."   —J. W. Hamer, New York *American*

———◇ **FRIDAY, SEPTEMBER 18** ◇———

{On September 17, in New York, the Giants beat St. Louis 10 to 5. Winning pitcher, Taylor; losing pitcher, Raymond. Giants' standing: 85 wins, 46 losses, in first place.}

After yesterday's culmination of Missouri courtesies we are not going to take much more stock in those magazine muck-rakings aimed at St. Louis sinfulness. If you ask us, the Westerners are represented, in a baseball way of speaking, by nine as perfect gents as ever left a series behind them. They left yesterday, accompanied by our best wishes. Would that they might have remained always.

There was some hitting yesterday. Five pitchers trotted out before the crowd, and four were used. Mr. Marquard's pitching appearance was purely Pickwickian. He didn't face a St. Louis batter. You see, McGinnity had started the game and had pitched four innings, at the end of which time the score was 3 to 1 in our favor. But to get at this result McGinnity had been let out of the batting procession, Barry hitting for him.

So McGinnity is out of the game, and across the lawn lopes something about 18 feet high, or so it seems, and the aidful umpire says: "Ladiesgmn, this is Mr. Marquard come to pitch for you. Grant him a little greet." Mr. Marquard, who arrived in town a couple of days ago, comes high—if we win the pennant we won't have to buy a flagpole, that is, if we can get Marky to stand still long enough. But after Marquard has thrown a few practice balls to Bresnahan, along comes Taylor, and the skyscraper retires to the bench.

—W. W. Aulick, New York *Times*

The main feature of the afternoon was the appearance of Mr. Marquard, the $11,000 peach. History tells us that once in the dim and distant past $10,000 was paid for Mike Kelley {a first baseman, Kelley played for Louisville's National League team in 1899, his sole major league season, and batted .241.}, and such later stars as Theodore Breitenstein and Spike Shannon also came under the head of "ten-thousand-dollar beauties." {Breitenstein pitched for St. Louis and Cincinnati in the 1890s, and in one five-year stretch, 1892–1896, lost 122 games.} But Mr. Marquard raised 'em a thousand, and he seemed to know it when McGraw sent him to the box to warm up and stall while Dummy Taylor was getting his more experienced wing in trim. Mr. Marquard may or may not prove to be a big league star, but if he falls a bit short, it won't be because he is lacking in genuine nerve and boyish self-confidence. He was in the pitcher's box only long enough to give the yearning fans one peek at him, but they were impressed by his pitching manners, and so was McGraw.

—William F. Kirk, New York *American*

Bingham—you may have heard of Bingham, he's got an office in the Police Commissioner's Department at 300 Mulberry Street—has at last woke up to the fact that when 20,000 or 30,000 citizens gather in a public place they are entitled to some sort of police protection.

So the regular bulls will be scattered around the Polo Grounds when the Giants and Pirates grapple. John T. Brush handed Brother Bingham a line of conversation regarding the necessity of policing the grounds during the stay of Pirates and Cubs that Bingham fell for, and he will send a couple of hundred blue-boys to hang around and make themselves useful should they be needed.   —Gym Bagley, New York *Evening Mail*

I tell you the Giants can't lose out unless they all drop dead. That looks cinchy enough, doesn't it? The McGraw bunch is going altogether too fast to allow any team coming from behind and beating them to the nearby wire.   —Sam Crane, New York *Evening Journal*

The old man called his son aside,
*   And kissed him on the brow.*
"Remember, my boy," the parent said,
*   "You're a full-fledged voter now.*
Look out, my son, for the country's good,
*   Let truth be your guiding star;*
Always live up to the golden rule,
*   No matter where you are.*
If you think Bill Taft is the better man,
*   Then let him be your choice;*
Or vote for William Jennings Bryan,
*   The man with the silvery voice.*
If Governor Hughes looks good to you
*   As head of this beautiful state,*
Then vote for him; if not, then vote
*   For the other candidate."*

But here the son broke in and said,
*   "These guys are new to me.*
I never heard of Taft or Hughes
*   Or Bryan, honestly.*
I never saw those queer old names
*   When looking through the score.*
I'd understand you better, pa,
*   If you mentioned John McGraw."*
*   —R. L. "Rube" Goldberg, New York *Evening Mail**

———◇ SATURDAY, SEPTEMBER 19 ◇———

{On September 18, in New York, the Giants defeated Pittsburgh in a doubleheader, 7 to 0 and 12 to 7. Winning pitchers, Mathewson and Wiltse; losing pitchers, Maddox and Leever. Giants' standing: 87 wins, 46 losses, in first place.}

The greatest throng of humanity ever attracted to a baseball game saw the Giants in a vicious, terrific five hours' battle defeat the Pirates twice and drive them out of the pennant race.

The event was national. It is doubtful if during the war so many people throughout the entire nation watched bulletins so anxiously. Then they waited to hear if Chancellorsville, Gettysburg or Antietam had been lost or won, whether a father, brother or son had died on the field of battle.

Yesterday the nation quivered and shook while 18 young men, most of whom will soon be quietly farming or running a cafe, played two games of baseball.

At the scene of combat the tension was evidenced in various ways. Men talked, or rather gibbered, to themselves. Forgetting all feminine reserve, women leaped up to cry as tears dotted their cheeks: "Hit the ball! Kill it! Run, oh, for heaven's sake, run!"

When Mike Donlin lifted the white horsehide sphere into the right bleachers, clinching the first game, this heart-deadening tension in the merest fragment of time changed to a roar that sounded like the swish of a planet, the crack of doom. "Matty" was pitching. The game was safe.

When little Herzog clipped the ball, with the score tied in the second game, and brought Bridwell home, giving New York a one-tally advantage, 40,000 mortals joined in a Olympian wake. If any one of these spectators had received an unexpected legacy of $30,000,000 he might have been dazed or delighted. He could not have done what he did yesterday. Herzog had hit the ball. America was getting something off its chest.

The common, garden variety of citizens of this nation is generally cool, collected and has to be "shown." Maybe that comes from Yankee blood. Give him a fight, a real soul-stirring sensation and he'll make a "jumping Frenchman look like a cigar store Indian." What the Giants did yesterday made a man forget grocer, butcher and undertaker bills.

The Giants fought with the desperation of the Bunker Hill warriors and the precision of Dewey's men at Manila. Of mixed Irish and German descent, they seemed to mix the pugnacity and persistence of both races.

There was no cheering, no demonstration in the first game when the mighty Mathewson strode to the box. While the fans regarded him safe as the Bank of England, they were uncertain. There was the brawny Wagner, with arms like a gorilla and elliptical legs, who leads the league in hitting. Wagner's face is drawn and ascetic. He seems about as happy as the Ancient Mariner when the spigot ran dry. You could feel, hear, see nothing but an awful tension.

In the second inning Mike Donlin began the scoring. He hit clean to short left. There was no effort. He chopped the ball downward. In sharp contrast was Cy Seymour, who hit under and flied out. This may account for Donlin's excellence in hitting. He keeps the ball on terra firma.

Arthur Devlin, a quiet, well-mannered young man, who took the H. O. {home economics, notoriously easy} course at Georgetown, set his teeth and lashed the ball for two bases inside the left foul line. He also hit down. Harry McCormick, a great hulking lad, who, like an elephant, which is said to be awful fast on its pins, swashed a drive to center and Donlin galloped home.

Still the awful hush, dreadful tension.

Fred Tenney, an ancient person, who went Ponce de Leon a couple better and discovered the fountain of youth, started the third inning with a two-base clout to left field. Out on the third-base coaching corner McGraw made some deaf and dumb signals with a broken forefinger. Thanks to Dummy Taylor all the Giants understand this lingo. Maybe that's why the Dummy is kept on the salary roll.

Herzog sacrificed Tenney according to orders and Mike Donlin brought him home. Donlin was speedily becoming the whole show.

Still the awful hush, dreadful tension. What were two runs lead with that gorilla person, "The Flying Dutchman," waiting to hit the ball to Kansas City!

In the fifth Mathewson gazed hard at Pitcher Maddox, a well-formed youth with a face like a dried apple. When one pitcher gets a hit off another it makes the "one" grin. Mathewson nearly laughed when he splashed a two-bagger to left. Maddox accumulated six more stresses in his neck.

It seemed to distract him and he passed Herzog. Bresnahan, the catcher, who suggests a Crusader in his complete suit of armor, leaned against the "pill" for two bases, scoring Mathewson.

Still the awful hush, dreadful tension.

It just didn't seem possible that Pittsburgh would lose. Or was it that everybody was so fearfully anxious they hesitated to yell?

With a lead of three runs and two out, Mike Donlin came to bat. His wife, Mabel Hite, leaned from an upper box exhorting him to "Kill it; bring them home; win the game!"

Eliminating all romance it cannot be said that Mike looked aloft with the love light in his eyes. No, he merely said to that unfortunate pitcher: "Put one over."

The foolish pitcher did, and a lad from Amsterdam avenue and 145th street finally got the ball in the right-field bleachers. It sailed upward and onward. Even as it sailed the creases in Maddox's face deepened, while Fred Clarke said part of what you say when starting a telephone conversation.

And now the deluge. The scene was more spectacular, more spontaneous than any before at the Polo Grounds.

The second game was more convulsive. George Wiltse had small control and not much speed and looked like a tired man in the box. With two out in the first Tommy Leach, who is a wealthy automobile dealer in the winter, clipped a two-bagger, the "Flying Dutchman" followed with another, and Abbaticchio laced a home run into the bleachers.

Now came an entirely new set of sensations. It would be small advantage for the Giants to win one game. It must be for them to annihilate Pittsburgh and perhaps cinch the pennant with double victory. The multitude was horribly nervous, shaky, almost sick. A three-run lead!

McGraw, Donlin, Herzog and Wiltse did not seem to think the case serious. They would hang on.

"Coming from behind" is the Giants' specialty this year. The championship team of 1905 was a more perfect team. It usually started off in the first inning by scoring and dismaying its opponents. This team is more spectacular and likes to fight with the enemy ahead. Thus yesterday in the seventh inning of the second game the Giants slaughtered their rivals by scoring six runs, and after that it was no contest.

—New York *World*

One thing is sure—the fair femininity part of yesterday's layout was very much front row, and most of the gazelles had their dear little score cards, too, keeping close track of hits and errors. Truth to say, they called most of the errors hits and most of the hits errors, but that didn't detract from their charms. It was announced in the *American* that the Ziegfeld showgirls would be on assignment, and thousands craned their necks in vain to pick out "the dozen prettiest girls in town." There were so many pretty girls the fair solicitors were lost in the sugary swarm. Oh, you Betties!   —William F. Kirk, New York *American*

The speculator pest was upon the Polo Grounds yesterday. The vendors must have reaped a harvest, for ordinary admissions were going at $1.50 each, seats in uncovered stands at $2, grandstand reserved seats from $3 to $5, and box seats from $5 up, according to the gullibility and wealth of the purchaser.

Yesterday a canvas was made before the game of regular ticket agencies in a dozen hotels along Broadway and 42nd street, but only one reply was received:

"We can't do anything for you; go to the speculators, they have all the tickets."   —New York *Times*

Two fans were perched on an advertising sign about 45 feet above the level of the diamond. Puzzle—tell how they got there and earn a season pass to the Yankee grounds.   —New York *Evening Mail*

CHICAGO, Sept. 12—Chicago's baseball romance ran into headwinds last Saturday when Frank Chance, manager of the world's champions, forbade the marriage of Artie Hofman and beautiful Rae Looker until after the baseball season is over. The wedding was to have taken place on September 7, the minister engaged, the invitations were about to be mailed, everything was in readiness. Mr. Hofman protested energetically when informed that a postponement of the nuptials would be necessary—"for the good of the team." But his protest went for naught. "I guess Miss

Looker and I can wait," said Mr. Hofman tonight. "She's as anxious to have the Cubs win as I am."   —Charles H. Zuber, *Sporting Life*

CINCINNATI, Sept. 15—The "spit ball" delivery has another powerful opponent in National League President Pulliam. "It's unclean; it prevents good fielding; it handicaps scientific batting; it's a freak, and so has no place in a straight sport." These are some of the arguments Pulliam advances against use of the "spit ball," which is being agitated almost as much these days as the political situation and the proper pronunciation of the word "lallapaloosa." "While I have not decided on a crusade against the 'spit ball,' " said Pulliam here, "I am strongly opposed to the use of that style of delivery. It is possible that between now and the time of the next meeting of the National League, there will be framed legislation to which both leagues will agree, and will do away with this offensive style of pitching. The 'spit ball' is no more essential to baseball than is the dog-faced boy to the three-ringed circus. Both are freaks, without which the big show would be much better off." {No restrictions were placed by the major leagues on the use of the spit-ball pitch until 1921, when seventeen men became designated spitballers, and they alone could thereafter employ the pitch. Spitballing in the big leagues ended when Burleigh Grimes retired after the 1934 season.}

—Charles H. Zuber, *Sporting Life*

———◇ SUNDAY, SEPTEMBER 20 ◇———

{On September 19, in New York, the Giants lost to Pittsburgh 6 to 2, in 10 innings. Winning pitcher, Leifield; losing pitcher, Crandall. Giants' standing: 87 wins, 47 losses, in first place.}

Smoke beat 'em. Wagner had his shoes full of it, and their gross tonnage is some. Leach concealed it under his cap; Leifield, the pitcher, had it up his sleeve, and Abbaticchio, the son of Caesar, had a bat loaded with it.

Sometimes the thick greasy vapor lay over the arena soppy as molasses on the bread you used to eat at home. Occasionally it lifted enough to glimpse the unholy grin on the face of Fred Clarke, and he does have an unholy grin. Again it settled down so you couldn't see whether Hans

Wagner had on a sheath gown or an ulster. {The latest creation of Parisian dress designers, the sheath gown was a current sensation on both sides of the Atlantic. It was so tight-fitting a woman could not walk in one but for a slit in its side, and in August, Anthony Comstock, head of the Society for the Suppression of Vice, had threatened to arrest and prosecute any woman who publicly appeared in New York City in a sheath gown.}

A lot of people said it was smoke wafted in from Minnesota, Dakota or some other distant place where there are forest fires. But the wise fans know differently. It was smoke from the "Smoky City." The "smoke-town" players were at home, as a clam in high water. They didn't give a whoop who pitched, what McGraw said on the coaching line, or whether a fair matron keeled over with nose bleed when an excited clergyman made the figure eight with his right elbow. They can beat the Giants in smoke, and they did.

The elbow catastrophe happened in the ninth, with the score 2 to 2, three on base and Mike Donlin at bat. He was a young parson, of weak countenance and there was Jersey mud on his heels. He stood with 1,000 others back of the seats on the grandstand and hadn't uttered a word until this supreme moment.

"Bang it, Mike! Slam it, Mike! Give 'em blazes, Mike!" were some of the things he yelled. A saloonkeeper nearby said the parson made it stronger than "blazes." He told Dr. Creamer, the Giants' physician, who was hustled up from the press box, that the "guy ought to be locked up."

By the time Dr. Creamer had stopped the nose bleed Mike Donlin had fouled out to Tommy Leach and the game was lost. The tenth inning saw Pittsburgh lace Pitcher Crandall all over the farm, bump in four runs and win 6 to 2. Chicago also won against Philadelphia, so while the Giants dropped a few points their two rivals crept up, but—wait till Monday.   —New York *World*

"Bet a million" John W. Gates was one of the 30,000 who saw the Giants go down to defeat yesterday. {A legendary figure on Wall Street, Gates was famed for his spectacular stock market transactions.}

John W. reached New York at noon today {Saturday} on the belated *Mauretania* from Liverpool with gloom plastered all over his countenance because he missed the doubleheader on Friday.

A week ago Saturday he boarded the *Mauretania*, believing he could reach New York in time to take in all of the Pittsburgh series. His son, Charley Gates, had made all the arrangements and had a box hired for Friday's games. All day Friday Charley was on board the revenue cutter off quarantine waiting for the big Cunarder to come up the bay.

As soon as he got back to Manhattan on Friday night he sent a wireless message to his father with the baseball scores, which made the financier more impatient than ever. When the *Mauretania* neared her pier Gates was willing to bet all kinds of the long green stuff that he would see the game that afternoon, and as soon as he set foot on solid ground he jumped into his auto and started for the Polo Grounds.

—C. B. Power, Pittsburgh *Dispatch*

DETROIT, Sept. 19—Now listen to the yell. The diamond athletes will not be handed a package of money for winning world championships after this. The National Commission has decided to put a ban on the offering of all bonus money.

Last year the Detroit owners gave their entire receipts to the champions, even after they had lost four straight in the world's series. Charley Murphy, of the Cubs, who won the games, didn't like it. He didn't want to shell out and raised a kick against such tactics.

Other league magnates had no great love for the scheme, and so the commission has forbidden the offering of special inducements or rewards. The players get 60 percent of the proceeds, anyway, and they figure this is enough.

This isn't the viewpoint of the player. He argues that he ought not to get 60 percent of the money, but all of it.   —New York *American*

◇ MONDAY, SEPTEMBER 21 ◇

Don't let the dull, deadening thought sear your untutored soul that because the Pirates laid us aboard Saturday and made a sieve of First Mate Ames and Quartermaster Crandall that Capt. McGraw isn't going to nail the champion bunting to the Polo Grounds mast.

I saw him myself buy the nails Saturday after the game. They were coffin size, the size that fits Pittsburgh and Chicago.

You don't begrudge the Pirates one game, do you? And that's all they're going to get. And the same goes for the Cubs when they hit town.

On Saturday Merkle got a chance at first when Tenney went to the clubhouse to rest his bad leg. And this boy is some first baseman. He's not as brilliant as Frederick, but it isn't always the most highly polished button on the soldier's coat that stops the bullet. Sometimes the soldier ducks.

Only once did Merkle show fog in his top hamper. There was a man on the bag, and, taking plenty of room, Bresnahan shot the signal across. Crandall pitched wide, but Merkle came in just as Roger was making ready to throw the Pirate out, and the move was wasted. Then Roger sprung a few sarcastic remarks in Merkle's direction because he didn't get the sign. Merkle didn't reply. He returned meekly to the base, with, no doubt, a mental resolve not be caught dozing again.

—Gym Bagley, New York *Evening Mail*

Complaints of regular patrons of the Polo Grounds that the best reserved seats on big days are to be secured only by purchasing from speculators at exorbitant prices is responsible for a new system of ticket distribution which goes into effect today.

Hereafter no reserved or box seats will be sold until the day of the game, and reservations can then be purchased only inside the park after admission has been paid. Purchasers of grandstand tickets can buy reserved seats at the box office in the rear of the stand. It will be a case of first come, first served.

There has been a demand for tickets for this week's games that is unprecedented in the experience of New York club officials. But Secretary Knowles has remailed checks for thousands of dollars to those who wished to purchase by mail, and his office force will be busy all week returning money to persons who wish to purchase in advance. This is an inconvenience and a hardship to regular patrons, and ticket speculators are to blame.   —Sid Mercer, New York *Globe*

The secret of the Giants' success lies in the strength of the reserve force. McGraw saw this some months ago and immediately imparted the idea to John T. Brush. Mr. Brush threw open the bankroll and told

McGraw to go as far as he liked. What did McGraw do? He went out and grabbed Merkle and Herzog. He already had Doyle. A little later he got McCormick and Dave Brain, and still later he took Jack Barry from St. Louis. He wanted Barry for his experience.

McGraw is prepared for any emergency. Now do you wonder why New York is up in the lead?

—Bozeman Bulger, Chicago *Journal*

More improvements are to be made at the Polo Grounds before the end of the season. John T. Brush is satisfied that the Giants will win the pennant, and is preparing for the record crowds that will attend the world's series games. Contracts have been let to add a seating capacity of about 7,000.

When the improvements are completed New York will have the largest baseball park in the country. The seating capacity will be close to 30,000, and will be second only to the athletic fields at Yale and Harvard.

—New York *Evening Mail*

——— NATIONAL LEAGUE STANDINGS ———

	W	L	PCT.	GB		W	L	PCT.	GB
New York ...	87	47	.649	—	Cincinnati ...	66	72	.478	23
Chicago	86	53	.619	3½	Boston	57	81	.413	32
Pittsburgh ...	86	54	.614	4	Brooklyn	47	90	.343	41½
Philadelphia .	73	61	.544	14	St. Louis	47	91	.341	42

———◇ **TUESDAY, SEPTEMBER 22** ◇———

{On September 21, in New York, the Giants lost to Pittsburgh 2 to 1. Winning pitcher, Willis; losing pitcher, Mathewson. Giants' standing: 87 wins, 48 losses, in first place.}

Why did Pittsburgh win the game,
Hank O'Day?
Don't you think it was a shame,
Hank O'Day?

When you made that rank decision,
When the thousands voiced derision,
Where in hades was your vision,
    Hank O'Day?

Pittsburgh left the island with an even break for the series, but the victory yesterday should never have been posted on the old blackboard. Granting that Pittsburgh might have shoved one tally across the plate, the worst we were entitled to was a draw.

In the third inning Umpire O'Day made an inexcusably bad decision when he called Wilson safe on first base. Umpires are human, and when they miss a "close one" now and then they should not be put on the pan, but the ruling made by O'Day, which practically put the Giants out of the running for the day, was absolutely weird.

Wilson led off the third with a grounder toward right field that looked like the sweetest kind of a single. Young Mr. Herzog dug after it like lightning, made a marvelous stop well out of the diamond, wheeled like a shot and sent the ball to Tenney in time to catch Wilson by at least a full yard. Perhaps O'Day didn't dream that Herzog could stop the ball, because he waved his arm majestically before the play was quite completed. Christy Mathewson, who seldom registers a kick, rushed over to O'Day in frantic protest and nearly swooned when he saw the Czar of the day wasn't kidding.

The decision, one of the worst ever seen on the grounds, robbed Herzog of the credit due to making a phenomenal play, and, far more important, cost the Giants the game. Gibson followed with a two-base hit, sending Wilson to third, and after Willis and Thomas had popped out, Fred Clarke got in a single down the left-field line—a hit that barely grazed Devlin's paws. On this slap Wilson and Gibson scored and the harm was done.

Manager Jawn got in bad with the twin umpires in the last of the third. Mac is trying to be a good boy these days, but he had witnessed that piece of arbitration in the first half of the same act, and the iron had entered his soul. So, naturally, he just couldn't help "alludin'" to certain judges of certain plays, and Umpire Klem, flying madly to the rescue of his brother in crime, called Manager Jawn in from the coaching lines. As the little corporal hoofed it for the bench he paused the tiniest part of a second and says to Klem, says he, "Herzog threw Wilson out three feet," he says. "Get off the field," Umpire Klem says, says he. "Throughout this long September afternoon I do not wish to see your face again!"

"All right," said Manager Jawn, and with these words he ducked into the little coop behind the players' bench and was swallowed up in the darkness for the time being.

But not for long. Chancing to gaze in the direction of the coop, Umpire Klem saw a tiny chink, and behind the chink two bright black eyes were shining, like the black eyes of an alert mouse peering from a hole in the wall.

"Murphy!" bellowed Umpire Klem, "shut that gate!"

The sturdy groundkeeper looked first at the gate and then at the umpire. For a moment he wavered between love and duty, and love won. He walked away and left the door open. If a German umpire wanted that door shut, reasoned the worthy groundkeeper, the German umpire would have to shut it himself. All honor to Murphy! In years to come children of present-day fans will tell in low whispers how Groundkeeper Murphy defied the umpire and refused to shut the coop door in the face of Manager Jawn McGraw.

—William F. Kirk, New York *American*

"They've got to show us. We are in the fight for the flag until the last inning of the last game of the season," declared Manager Fred Clarke after the Pirates had won the closing game of the series. The victory filled the Pirates with fresh hopes, and the smiles floating around the lobby of the Hotel Somerset were brighter than so many electric lights in a coal mine.

And the game—whew, it was a torrid affair! The best part of it was that Matty, he of the inflated chest and enlarged dome, a tall individual who has repeatedly done things to our beloved swatters, is charged with the defeat. —C. B. Power, Pittsburgh *Dispatch*

Yesterday's game was played in hurry-up style, only an hour and nineteen minutes being consumed in running it off.

—New York *Press*

———◇ WEDNESDAY, SEPTEMBER 23 ◇———

{On September 22, in New York, the Giants lost a doubleheader to Chicago 4 to 3 and 2 to 1. Winning pitchers, Overall and Brown; losing pitchers, Ames and Crandall. Giants' standing: 87 wins, 50 losses, in first place.}

In two fierce, grueling games which took the stamina out of players and spectators alike, Frank Chance's Chicago Cubs beat John McGraw's New York Giants twice yesterday. If the Giants lose today the Cubs will lead the pennant race.

The Cubs played better ball all the way, but they had some luck, and Lajoie says that luck is half the game of baseball. In addition, the Giants turned in some stupid work, made a couple of errors and failed to hit the ball at critical moments.

McGraw sent in "Red" Ames to pitch the first game. First inning Schulte got a single and that ended the attack. Second inning it was one, two, three and out. Third inning, Overall, a huge person, lifted a fly into the left-field crowd. Anything that hits the crowd in these games goes for a two-bagger. And it might be observed that a New York crowd is most complacent.

It shifted twice for Chicago's right-fielder to catch line drives in the second and materially helped Chicago to win. But when McCormick tried to get one in the left field the rooters clung to the turf. In any other city the crowd would have helped the home team, which is as it should be, for loyalty is part of the game.

McCormick could have seized Overall's drive if he had the nerve of Billy Sunday, who leaped over several rows of rooters at the moment of his conversion to evangelism. {The famous evangelist Billy Sunday had been a major league outfielder from 1883 to 1890.} The crowd didn't open for McCormick; he had no aspirations to be an evangelist, and Overall got a two-bagger. He took third on Haydon's out, on which Bridwell made a wretched mistake. He had the grounder and could have thrown Overall out. Instead he let the big pitcher lumber to third base, where Devlin was waiting for the ball. Following this, Bridwell tried to field a grounder from Schulte, booted the ball, and Overall scored.

Encouraged by this, Chicago cut loose in the next inning and won the game. Steinfeldt hit a beautiful single to center. He was nailed at second by Devlin, who captured Hofman's intended sacrifice. Tinker pasted a single past Bridwell, sending Hofman to second, and that long-legged youth then stole third. He did it cleverly with a Chicago slide, throwing his body one way, his hand toward the base.

The whole Chicago team is clever, machine-like, and game. They have Pittsburgh beaten at every point of the game, and the only way New York can win is to out-hit them.

Kling then grounded to Tenney, who fired the ball to Ames, covering first, and Ames dropped it. Overall came to bat again and whaled a long fly to centerfield. Seymour caught the ball, but he could not get it home in time to head off Tinker.

Chicago's success appeared to "rattle" the Giants. Herzog did not try to get a high fly from Haydon, which fell fair while Donlin, Seymour, Bridwell and Herzog gazed hard at the hole it made in the soft green turf. As these gentlemen bent their eyes earthward, Johnny Kling, who receives a matter of $7,000 for six months' work, cantered over the plate.

New York was baffled by Overall until the lucky seventh, when Capt. Mike Donlin jammed a two-bagger in right field. Seymour singled to right. Then Devlin doubled to right, scoring Donlin. Chance was scared now. He yanked Overall and put in "Three-Fingered" Brown. McCormick doubled to right, scoring Seymour and Devlin.

The Polo Grounds were now in bedlam. Perhaps the fans were never before so insane. "Dummy" Taylor sprained three fingers trying to say something and women unpinned their hats, chucking them into the diamond. This, at least, was novel.

For some reason McGraw ordered Bridwell to bunt, and to an outsider this seemed bad judgment. Said bunt resulted in McCormick being thrown out at third and after which Barry, who batted for Ames, flied out and likewise Tenney. The men were hitting hard and why not let Bridwell hit the ball? After that New York had no chance.

Otis Crandall pitched the second game and held the Cubs to five hits. But he gave two bases on balls in the sixth, thus enabling Chicago to score a brace of runs. Previous to this New York in the fourth inning had made one tally. Herzog, who made two marvelous stops during the day, led off with a double. Bresnahan brought him home with another double.

McGinnity relieved Ames in the eighth inning of the first game and did the same for Crandall in the eighth inning. The "Iron Man," Crandall, and Ames all pitched good ball. It was not their fault the Giants lost. The team was overcome by "Three-Fingered" Brown, who finished the first game for Overall and pitched the whole second game. The only thing for McGraw to do to beat Chicago is to dig up a pitcher with only two fingers. —New York *World*

In the second game yesterday we almost get a run several times. Read about what happened in the seventh.

Everybody up, of course {for the seventh-inning stretch}. Loud loyalty and deep rooting. If Master Donlin makes a single we will forgive the past. We will be among those present on his opening night to give him a hand. We will—Master Mike makes good. Thank you, Sir. Now, if we can persuade honest Seymour to do likewise. We cannot. Honest Seymour flies out. But look here—Devlin is walking, and Donlin is still on the diamond. Hope lives. But McCormick dies ten thousand deaths, as the horrible Haydon gathers in his high fly. Now it is Bridwell, and Bridwell waits patiently as Brown deals off the bad ones. Four of a kind fills the bases, and the roar is so loud you can touch it.

Three men on bases. Come on, Crandall, and bang your way into a million hearts. Three men on bases, and a single will tie the score. {Merkle was sent in to bat for Crandall.} Come on, Merkle, if they won't let Crandall bat. We trust in you, Merkle darlin'. You'd never let us down, would you, Merkle, with three men on base, a single to tie, and a chance to win? Step up, good man, and play baseball. Pshaw! Why did you hit at that first one? Why did you not wait? It wasn't worth your effort. Pick out a bonny one, Merkle, and then strike for the freedom of your sires, and a little bit more. Not that one, not that, Merkle. Didn't we give you waiting orders? Never mind, there is one chance left. Use it wisely. Get a firm hold on your bat, and slash away along the third-base line. If you are not in position, make it the right field, up as near the grandstand as you can get without fouling. Or, if you think you can pull it off, a Texas-leaguer will demoralize them. Or you might—Mr. Merkle has just struck out, gentlemen. Donlin, Devlin, and Bridwell, what of them? Were you ever at a reception where the lion of the hour and day came over to your corner, shook hands with the neighbor on your right, and the neighbor on your left, and then—looked coldly past you and walked on, leaving you with your dexter fork extended in the air and feeling foolish all over? That's how Messrs. Donlin, Devlin, and Bridwell felt when Mr. Merkle passed them up. Let's all go home. And they call themselves Cubs!   —W. W. Aulick, New York *Times*

There is no joy in Manhattan. Even so—it is well not to become too hilarious. A glance at the remainder of the schedule reveals some cold and chillsome facts.

While the Cubs are right at the heels of New York and in position to pull the Giants down, the rest of the tab shows that the Bears play only 11 more games, while New York plays 17. Of the 17, 8 are with Philadelphia, and it is a cinch that the Quakers will meekly heave up the sponge. With that big margin—17 games as compared to 11—the ultimate pennant chance seems more than feeble.

If the Cubs win 10 of the 11 games left—a most prodigious feat—they will finish with 100 won and 54 lost. To beat that New York would have to win 14 and lose 3. Take a more reasonable view. If the Cubs win 8 and lose 3, New York must win 12 and lose 5. It is tough going for the Cubs, but it is well to hope for the best—especially to hope that Philadelphia will play real ball.

The Pirates are not yet done for. They are only a game and a half back of the Cubs, and have 12 to go. In short, the race is still of the closest, fiercest pattern, and no prophet ever prophed who could foretell the finish.   —W. A. Phelon, Chicago *Journal*

"Muggsy" McGraw, the "Napoleon of baseball," was outgeneraled all the way yesterday, and to his bad judgment may be charged the loss of the second game.

To begin with, "Muggsy" tried to be foxy and "put something over" on Chance, with disastrous results. Before the first game he had Marquard, his $11,000 beauty, warm up as though intending to work him. He even went so far as to let Marquard walk out on the diamond just as the game was about to start, then suddenly called him back and out came Ames, who had been warming up secretly behind the grandstand. McGraw tried this trick again in the second game, Marquard and McGinnity warming up, and at the last minute Crandall showing from behind the stand. McGraw hoped to catch Chance napping and get some other pitcher than Overall and Brown. Instead he got two beatings.

—Chicago *News*

Hank O'Day won't allow "Dummy" Taylor on the coaching lines. He chased "Dummy" every time he got up. It's a pity the Giants can't use an orator when they carry him on the payroll.

—Chicago *Tribune*

Al Bridwell's batting slump hurts now, and Larry Doyle, the man the Cubs fear most, is a victim of his own carelessness. Bridwell has not made a timely hit for a long time, and his fielding is not as true as it was. Yesterday Bridwell had several chances to tie the score, but he didn't have a hit in his system. Neither did Tenney. Had Doyle been on the job yesterday one of the games might have been bagged. But Larry came up to the Polo Grounds the other day, got frisky, slipped, and fell down and now he is on the shelf again, as his fall reopened the wound in his ankle.

—Sid Mercer, New York *Globe*

———◇ THURSDAY, SEPTEMBER 24 ◇———

{On September 23, in New York, the Giants and Cubs played the most celebrated, most widely discussed, most controversial contest in the history of American sports. The game was declared a 1 to 1 tie.}

Rioting and wild disorder, in which spectators and players joined, causing a scene never witnessed in New York before, marked the conclusion at the Polo Grounds yesterday of the game between the Giants and Cubs. By cleverness in seeing an opportunity to deprive the Giants of their final and deciding run and quickness in seizing it, the Cubs had forced the umpire, Henry O'Day, to declare the game a tie, after half of the spectators had gone home in the belief that New York had won 2 to 1, and many of the New York players had left the field.

Through what appeared to be the carelessness of a single player, Merkle, in leaving first base after Bridwell's winning run had been scored and retiring from the field without touching second base and with the ball still in play, the final score as it stood last night was 1 to 1 instead of a victory for the home team.

In the fight between members of the opposing nines for the possession of the ball and the efforts of spectators, who rushed upon the field, to prevent the Chicago players from enjoying the fruits of their quick-wittedness, several players and the umpire were roughly handled and more or less severely hurt. Efforts of special policemen to clear the grounds were unavailing, and it took the regular policemen, called in from the outside, half an hour or more to quell the disturbance.

No similar situation had ever been seen in the history of baseball in New York. When the eighth inning came to a close the score was 1 to 1, and the 20,000 enthusiasts that filled the grandstand and bleachers to overflowing were "rooting" for the Giants with desperate hope. Chicago failed to score in the first half of the ninth, and in the last half Bridwell went to bat with McCormick on third base and Merkle, who had replaced Tenney, on first.

Bridwell made a clean hit over second base. McCormick raced home, making the score 2 to 1 in favor of the Giants, and there seemed nothing else to do but go home cheering. That is what most of the players did, and that, according to the decision rendered later by O'Day, is what young Mr. Merkle, the runner on first base, did. That little oversight of Merkle's gave Chicago their chance.

The runner had been forced off first by Bridwell's hit. The ball was in centerfield. Hofman, covering that position, saw Merkle leave first base and saunter toward the clubhouse. He threw the ball to Evers, on second, but it went wild and McGinnity caught it. He had seen the opening left by Merkle's mistake as quickly as the Chicagoans, and had rushed out from the coaching lines to take a hand in the proceedings. {Hofman's role in this incident has generally been underestimated, and yet because of his quickness in going after the ball instead of heading for the clubhouse, as most players would have done under similar circumstances, no one contributed more than he to the success of the play. One wonders if he would have been less alert if Frank Chance had not prevented him from marrying two weeks earlier. See the relevant entry for September 19.}

With the ball in his hand, McGinnity also started for the clubhouse.

Frank Chance got into action at this point and succeeded in holding McGinnity until other Chicago players could join in the effort to recover the ball. McGinnity, overpowered, threw the ball as far as he could into the crowd behind third base, the spectators having already begun to pile into the field. Steinfeldt and Tinker followed the ball into the crowd. Tinker seized it and threw to Evers, who stood proudly on second base holding the ball aloft, while O'Day, who had run down to second to see the play, was immediately surrounded by Chicago players.

Chance ran to O'Day, claiming the run did not count because Merkle had been forced at second. A riotous mob at once surrounded the couple, and although most did not know what it was all about everyone evidently recognized a good opportunity to get a shot at the umpire. Those within reach began pounding him on all available exposed parts not covered by the protector, while the unfortunate attackers on the outskirts began sending messages by way of cushions, newspapers, and other missiles.

A flying squadron of real police, reinforced by the special men, rushed O'Day to McGraw's coop under the grandstand and Chance was escorted off the field. Then the mob ran about the grounds throwing cushions and generally preparing for O'Day's reappearance, when it was made known that the game might not be given to the Giants. The police cleared the grounds and order was restored.

O'Day, under the press of circumstances, did not render a decision on the field, but after he had dressed he told a reporter of the *Herald* that Merkle had not gone to second and the run did not count. He said a run could not be tallied on the third out if the man was forced and put out at second.

Merkle said after the game that he had touched second en route for the clubhouse, and McGraw refused to say any more than that the game had been won fairly.

O'Day seemed very uncertain as to what he should do and was a long time coming to a decision, and when he did he seemed uncertain as to its justification. Should he report the game to President Pulliam as a tie the New York club will protest, for there was ample police protection on the grounds to clear the field and continue the contest.

The decision was really Emslie's, who was officiating on the bases, but he says he did not see the play, as he was watching first base, and O'Day had run out into the pitcher's box prepared to watch it.

The same situation arose in Pittsburgh on September 4, when Gill, on first base, ran for the clubhouse instead of going to second. As O'Day was officiating alone, he did not see the play, and the Cubs protested the Pirates' victory to President Pulliam, who upheld the umpire. O'Day saw all that happened yesterday, for he ran out, prepared for the occurrence.

Mr. Pulliam could not be seen last night up to a late hour, and he made no decision in the matter, but he gave out the following statement: "I made no decision in the matter, and I will not do so until it is presented to me in proper form."

The fact that Mr. Pulliam recognizes in his statement that there was some irregularity at the grounds intimates that he intends making a decision. Last night he was closeted at the New York Athletic Club with O'Day and Emslie, and until he renders a decision the game stands on the umpires' decision that Merkle was forced at second.

As for the game itself, Mathewson allowed the Cubs only five measly hits. Only one did any damage, and that was Tinker's home run in the fifth, and that only did about $3.50 worth to a certain shoe store.

Players to whom the Chicago club pays all sorts of fancy prices to knock the delivery of most pitchers where the fielders cannot get the ball looked like thirty cents when "Matty" got through. He struck out nine Cubs, usually with men on base. Pfiester shot up the slants from the port side for Chance's men and was effective in all but two innings.

The game was pregnant with thrilling plays and surprises. The first surprise was a revised batting order by McGraw, who placed Merkle in Tenney's place and shifted his other men around. {This was the only time during the entire season that Tenney failed to appear in the Giant starting line-up.} The youngster played like a fiend and came through with a single in the ninth that helped win the game. If he would only remember to run to second base when it is required—which reminds us of a man who had a thousand-dollar back and a ten-cent head.

Nobody made any progress toward home plate until Tinker hit for the circuit in the fifth. The ball went over second like a cannon shot and went skating through the grass in right center. Mike Donlin went over to stop it and tried to place his foot in its course, but failed, and the ball rolled to the ropes. Two or three ardent fans in a perfectly polite manner suggested to Mike that if he had stretched his anatomy on the greensward he might have stopped the ball and ended Tinker's wanderings on second base.

In the sixth the Giants came back and scored a run. Herzog reached first on a single to Steinfeldt, who threw too late to get the runner and wild as well, so the little second baseman drew up at second. Bresnahan sacrificed, and Herzog tied the score on Donlin's hit over second. Seymour scratched out a hit in front of second base when Emslie got in Evers' way and spoiled the play. Devlin flied out, however, and McCormick grounded to Evers.

Things went along until the ninth with the score a tie. Seymour, the first Giant up, burned a brown streak in the grass with a hot one down to Evers and found the ball waiting for him at first. Devlin, the only man to get two hits in the afternoon, singled but was forced at second by McCormick's grass cutter to Evers. Merkle came along with a timely single, moving McCormick to third.

Then Bridwell pinched one over second, which was followed by the main play of the afternoon—a squeeze play executed by the fans and O'Day, the latter squeezing in his coop.

The game was a baseball cocktail and "Matty" was the cherry in the ante-dinner drink. In fact, all our boys did rather well if Fred Merkle could gather the idea into his noodle that baseball custom does not permit a runner to take a shower and some light lunch in the clubhouse on the way to second.

Then again, taking it on the whole, an enormous baseball custom has had it from time immemorial that as soon as the winning run has crossed the plate everyone adjourns as hastily and yet nicely as possible to the clubhouse and exits.

—New York *Herald*

Frank Chance tried to take from John McGraw yesterday a well-earned victory. Unless Mr. Pulliam decides against New York, the game goes to her credit, for Umpires O'Day and Emslie admitted to newspaper men that they had not seen the play. O'Day was back of the catcher when the riot started and endeavored to reach first base, where Chance was struggling in the clutch of a mob. Emslie was trying to save himself and his wig from being trampled.

The crowd, following them, jammed into the home bench, upsetting Murphy, the groundkeeper, and stepping on McGraw's bulldog. They broke through the little door McGraw uses as exit when banished and groped their way in the darkness over barrels, boxes and trap holes. The umpires finally reached their dressing room, but the riot outside continued.

Chance was the target, and though he is a pugilist the crowd would have treated him harshly but for two fat policemen. Surrounded by them and some of his players, the Chicago manager "flying wedged" himself to the clubhouse. He was still bawling that he would protest the game and calling for O'Day.

When the umpires emerged in their citizen clothes O'Day was rattled and evasive; Emslie was rattled and frank. He said: "The crowd got to me so quick that I didn't see the play. I tried to reach O'Day to find out whether he got it, but you know what happened. I don't know what to say. I didn't see the play."

O'Day shouted back over his shoulder: "Merkle didn't run to second; the last run don't count; it's a tie game."

McGraw said that never in his life had he heard of a "no game" being called. "If we forfeited the game O'Day should have said so. As a matter of fact Merkle tells me he did reach and touch second. No Chicago player was on second base with the ball, anyway. It's simply a case of squeal. We won fair and square." —New York *World*

McGraw had some forcible comments after the game. "How can umpires decide it is no game?" asked Mac. "Umpires can't go out on the field and make rules. Either the game should be declared forfeited on account of the crowd overrunning the field and preventing further play, or it was won by us. The Chicago club can protest, of course, but they wouldn't have any grounds for a protest. The play in the ninth inning wasn't a question of interpretation of the rules, which is the only ground on which protest can be made. Emslie says he didn't see the play, and Merkle swears he touched the bag." —New York *Sun*

Minor league brains lost the Giants a game after they had it cleanly and fairly won.

The Cubs and Hank O'Day were primed for the situation, having been through it once before, in Pittsburgh. With one voice the Cubs set up a yelp like a cage of hungry hyenas, and O'Day, working behind the plate, ran to the pitching slab to see what came off at second base. Capt. Donlin realized the danger about to overtake the Giants, so he set off after the fat-headed Merkle while McGinnity, coaching at third base, butted into the fracas at the middle station.

The facts gleaned from active participants and survivors are these: Hofman fielded Bridwell's knock and threw to Evers for a force play on the absent Merkle. But McGinnity cut in and grabbed the ball before it reached the eager Trojan {Evers, who came from Troy, New York}. Three Cubs landed on the Iron Man from as many directions at the same time and jolted the ball from his cruel grasp. It rolled among the spectators who had swarmed upon the diamond like an army of starving potato bugs.

At this thrilling juncture "Kid" Kroh, the demon southpaw, swarmed upon the human potato bugs and knocked six of them galley-west. The triumphant Kroh passed the ball to Steinfeldt after cleaning up the gang that had it. Tinker wedged in, and the ball was conveyed to Evers for the force-out of Merkle, while Capt. Donlin was still some distance off towing that brilliant young gent by the neck.

Some say Merkle eventually touched second base, but not until he had been forced out by Hofman to McGinnity to six potato bugs to "Kid" Kroh to some more Cubs, and the shrieking, triumphant Mr. Evers, the well-known Troy shoe dealer. There have been some complicated plays in baseball, but we do not recall one like this in a career of years of monkeying with the national pastime.

—Charles Dryden, Chicago *Tribune*

It seems that a new magnate has "Jimmied" his way into the game and is trying to run baseball on entirely different lines than ideal ones. Charles Murphy, president of the Chicago club, has no sentiment for baseball, only for the money there may be in it for him. In fact, the "Chubby One" is considered a joke all over the National League, and nowhere more so than in Chicago. He is out for the "dough," and nothing else about the great sport appeals to him.

But, not being satisfied with trying to run his own club in his own city to the detriment of the baseball public, he comes to New York and endeavors to dictate how the game should be run here.

He will have a good, fat chance!

Directly after the argument on the field, which was brought about by Manager Chance and his fellow players developing that old yellow streak of claiming victories they can't win on the field, Murphy saw his opportunity to make a claim for yesterday's game on a cowardly technicality. Manager Chance and his players in fact incited a riot, and but for the fortunate presence of hundreds of New York's "finest" there would have been a serious riot.

Merkle did make a run for the clubhouse to escape the onrushing fans, as is the habit with the Giants, but he turned after going only a few feet and broke for second. Hofman did return the ball, but it went far over Evers' head, hit Tinker in the back and went on to Kling. Merkle was then on second with Mathewson, and as Evers, Tinker and Pfiester all rushed toward second, Matty, according to his own story, to which he will take an affidavit if such a ridiculous act is necessary, took Merkle by the arm and said: "Come on to the clubhouse; we don't want to mix up in this," and both Matty and Merkle left the base together.

Chance was frantic; he rushed up to both Umpires O'Day and Emslie in the endeavor to make them listen to his unsportsmanlike claim, but both those officials waved him away and said, according to bystanders and players, "We didn't see anything that warrants your claim or protest that Merkle didn't run to second. He was there the last we saw." And these were the words of both umpires, as hundreds will swear to.

Chance was insistent, however, and his doubled fists came dangerously close to O'Day's face. O'Day at last had to throw the irate Cub captain aside, and he was soon lost in the crowd, but was so angry he struck several citizens and was himself somewhat roughly used, as he by all right should have been. The police broke into the surging crowd and at last got O'Day and Emslie to their dressing room in the grandstand, Chance and his players gradually making their tumultuous ways to their dressing rooms.

And here is where the great Charley Murphy (in his own mind) bursts on to the scene.

I had hurried down from the press box to get an interview with the umpires. I found their door firmly braced against intrusion, but I managed to get my head through the open space of the door and I asked H.

O'Day, "Is it the Giants' game?" I understood him to say "Yes," but immediately after he said, "Wait until I am dressed," and the door was shut. I waited for O'Day to appear and was soon joined by several other newspaper men who also wanted to get the "latest."

While waiting anxiously, who should appear on the scene but his "augustness" (in his own mind) the "Chubby One," gorgeous in a Tim Woodruff vest and in his own vast conceit.

"How about this?" he said. "I want to know; the game wound up one to one, and we will have to play a doubleheader tomorrow." Looking for the money all the time. That never escapes his sordid mind. What did he care about the disappointed hopes of the army of New York fans who had seen their favorites win a victory fairly and squarely? Not a thing. If he could cause the Giants to lose on a technicality he would scheme that way if he could get the few extra dollars accruing to him by an extra game unfairly arranged.

—Sam Crane, New York *Evening Journal*

"If," Christy Mathewson said, "this game goes to Chicago by any trick of argument, you can take it from me that if we lose the pennant thereby, I will never play professional baseball again.

"I had started for the clubhouse when I heard Chance call to Hofman to throw the ball to second. I remembered the trick they had tried to play on Pittsburgh and caught Merkle by the arm and told him to go to second. Merkle touched the bag. I saw him do it."

—New York *Evening Mail*

———◇ FRIDAY, SEPTEMBER 25 ◇———

{On September 24, in New York, the Giants beat the Cubs 5 to 4. Winning pitcher, Wiltse; losing pitcher, Brown. Giants' standing: 88 wins, 50 losses, in first place.}

President Pulliam supported Umpires O'Day and Emslie and declared Wednesday's game a 1 to 1 tie. As neither club has an open date the tie contest will not be played off.

The end of the controversy, however, is not yet in sight, as President Brush has served notice that he will appeal from the ruling, while President Murphy claims the game by forfeit, 9 to 0, owing to the fact that the New York team was not at the Polo Grounds yesterday at 1:30 to play off the tie game. In announcing his verdict, Pulliam said he would stand by his umpires, regardless of the merits of the controversy. As the case stands the game will go on the records as a tie unless the Board of Directors of the National League takes action at its next meeting.

—New York *Times*

Amid the jangling of cowbells, the blowing of horns, unparalleled shouting of 25,000 "fans" in every tone of the scale, from a deep barytone to the highest soprano, almost continuous in its constancy throughout the game, on a darkened and gnat-swarmed field, the Giants came home a winner yesterday.

After the game had been apparently won in the first and fifth innings and the score stood at 5 to 0 the Cubs fell on Wiltse in the seventh session and collected three runs, with no one out. Then Mathewson, big, reliable "Matty," was rushed out to save the day, with Kling dancing on third like a performing bear after his triple. Kling scored but never again was home plate in danger from the Cub tread. "Matty" had saved the day and perhaps the pennant.

Baseball enthusiasm blew out another cylinder head yesterday. The "rooters" came armed with cowbells and horns, and from the bulging appearances of their pockets it was suspected that a few vegetables were concealed in convenient and accessible recesses. The general sentiment was that if a contingency should arise such as that of Wednesday those some distance from the umpire should not be handicapped by intervening space.

The other side, so to speak, was also reinforced, and about 100 bluecoats swung their sticks about the side lines. It was reported from the Bronx, Brooklyn and other outlying districts that many cowbells were missing and that so many cows had gone astray that the price of milk would probably go up two points in those regions in the near future.

Seldom has such partisan feeling been evidenced on a ball field as was displayed yesterday. When the Chicago team took the field they were jeered to the echo, and even the Putnam railroad engines in the distance hissed out steam at them. The names hurled at "Hank" O'Day when he took the field must have kept some "rooters" up all night thinking up the epithets, while the players constantly exchanged quips throughout the game.

"Three-Fingered" Brown was sent in to do the pitching for the Cubs. He worked so hard he almost lost another digit as he curled his fingers about the ball and sent up his best. He lasted only five innings, when Coakley {recently purchased by Chicago from Cincinnati} and Overall both tried to save the day but were powerless.

Donlin, next to "Matty," deserves credit for the victory. He made a double and triple which accounted for four of New York's runs.

In the seventh a mist settled over the field that all but obscured the outfielders from the grandstand. It was so dark "Matty" had to walk up to the plate to see Bresnahan's signals. In spite of this, Emslie, behind the bat, refused to call the game.

Every time Chance went to bat he was greeted with all sorts of names, and those greetings seemed to hang over the diamond in the humid atmosphere. As if attracted by the epithets hurled at Chance, ranging from "yellow dog" through all the various stages of head, from "in head" to "bone head," a swarm of gnats came over the diamond like one of the plagues of Egypt. One lodged in "Matty's" eye, delaying the game, while all the occupants of the right-field bleachers were fanning with handkerchiefs and newspapers, and here and there miniature campfires of newspapers were started to drive the pests away. Every time Chance was greeted with these pleasant titles his appearance reminded the "rooters" of Hank O'Day, and he would be pounced on again with renewed vigor.

—New York *Herald*

President Pulliam's now-famous decision that Wednesday's victory of the Giants over the Cubs goes as a tie game is not final, so local "bugs" and "bugesses" can keep their lingerie on.

President Charley Murphy, of the Cubs, claimed everything in sight, but, as usual with the "Chubby One," he overreached himself, and not only are the Cubs a good 13 points behind the Giants, but the disputed game he so confidently counted on is not his by a great big long shot.

And, moreover, the Giants have as good a chance to be credited with a victory as the Cubs have to have it called a tie, as poor Umpire Hank O'Day, after much weak-kneed wavering and careful consideration of National League politics, finally decided.

Formerly I thought Hank O'Day was like adament, and if he made up his mind one way he would stick to that through thick and thin, but I don't think so now—and that is letting Hank off easy.

President Brush is desirous of having the New York baseball public put right on the case. After yesterday's game he said: "There is no need of our patrons fearing that any such robbery as was attempted yesterday being carried through without our resentment and every possible measure in our power being used to prevent the Chicago club, or any other, taking our patrons' money and robbing us of fairly earned victories as well. The New York club will fight for its rights every inch of the way."

—Sam Crane, New York *Evening Journal*

Something happened at the Polo Grounds yesterday that never happened on a ball field before. The game was scheduled for 3:30. Before 2 o'clock there were 20,000 fans on the grounds. That's coming early to avoid a rush, isn't it? But it wasn't that.

Chicago had made a bluff that they would be lined up and ready to play the first game of a doubleheader at 1:30. This was in accordance with President Pulliam's ruling that Wednesday's game was a tie. A tie game has to be played out, and as yesterday was the last day the Cubs would be here, it was the only day on which the tie could be settled.

This looked even better than a bargain doubleheader. There might be trouble. Someone might take a punch at Chance. And it was in anticipation of a scrap that the crowd assembled so early.

A ball game and a free fight, all for the price of one admission, doesn't often fall to the lot of anyone.

But nothing like that. Not even an approach to it. Chance and his bunch lined up and went through the farce of making ready for a game, and that was all there was to it. All they got was the laugh.

—Gym Bagley, New York *Evening Mail*

The dispute that has arisen between two teams of the National League at the very climax of the baseball season may or may not be disheartening according to the point of view. It had not seemed possible that there could be any increase of interest in baseball, but just now it is the subject that seems to claim most of the attention the multitude of our fellow-citizens can spare from business and domestic affairs.

The decision of Umpire O'Day seems to an unprejudiced outsider fair and impartial. Merkle substituted his own judgment that the game was won after Bridwell's safe hit enabled McCormick to make a run, for obedience to the rules. He should have taken his second base. Undoubtedly if he had started for the base and fallen or even dropped dead, between the bases, McCormick's run would not have counted. Such an error of judgment could scarcely be overlooked in amateur sport. It would be foolish to expect professional players to overlook it.

The ensuing row in which a mob of spectators took part, overrunning the field, prevented the playing of another inning. We do not see how the umpire's decision can be set aside, unless the testimony of many unprejudiced eye witnesses is proved mistaken. But what a life the umpire leads!

—Editorial page, New York *Times*

Fred Tenney is playing solely on his nerve. His feet are in very bad shape, and his back is lame. Every time he stoops it is pain. But McGraw had enough of Merkle the day before and called on Tenney for his brains. A one-legged man with a noodle is better than a bonehead.

—Gym Bagley, New York *Evening Mail*

Oh, joy! oh, joy! John Ganzel and his Reds will be our guests in two games this afternoon, and Honest John will take his medicine like a sport. —New York *American*

————◇ **SATURDAY, SEPTEMBER 26** ◇————

{On September 25, in New York, the Giants lost two games to Cincinnati, 7 to 1 and 5 to 2. Winning pitchers, Spade and Dubuc; losing pitchers, Marquard and McGinnity. Giants' standing: 88 wins, 52 losses, in first place.}

Harry C. Pulliam, president of the National League, issued this statement yesterday:

"The umpires in charge of the contest {on September 23} filed their written reports at National League headquarters on September 24, stating that the game resulted in a tie score. The report was accepted in the usual manner without prejudice to the rights of either club.

"Under the constitution of the National League either club may appeal from the decision of the umpires within five days of the date of the game. The New York club has notified this office that it will appeal from the decision of the umpires.

"In compliance with the National League constitution, the protest of the New York club will be submitted to the Chicago club, and that club has five days in which to file its answer, if it so desires. The same procedure will prevail in the event that the Chicago club protests the decision.

"When the case is made up a decision will be rendered by the president of the league, which decision is subject to appeal within five days to the Board of Directors, whose decision is final."

—New York *Tribune*

The Gingery Giants lined up in a doubleheader against the Gingery Germans from Zinzinnati, and in both games we had to rap our poor, battered knuckles on the table and say "That's good," while Messrs. {Dick} Hoblitzel, Ganzel, Lobert, Schlei, {Bob} Beecher, et al., worthy Teutons all, were raking in the chips. Ach, du lieber!

The National League race is now a lulu—the luluest kind of a lulu what is. We are sailing grandly in the van with a juicy lead of one point, closely pursued by the Cursed Cubs and Peevish Pirates. They can't beat us until they catch us, and we are still peering downward, like Freedom from her mountain height, but we don't need to use spyglasses.

Mr. Marquard had stage fright, to be perfectly candid. {In the first game "Rube" Marquard made his major league debut.} He did not know what to do with his hands, and he wasn't quite sure what to do with the ball. First he tucked it under his right armpit, then he slammed it into his glove, then he spat on it, then he made a wild pitch with it, and then he aimed it over in the groove, only to see it soaring safe into the outfield.

Gentle Roger Bresnahan tried his derndest to hold up the young pitcher, and stopped more than one apparently wild pitch, but the kid was not quite ready for the ordeal, and after he had been clouted grievously, and had shown unmistakable signs of unsteadiness, he left the mound.

The Gingery Germans got away with a flying start. Marquard curved his first ball over the plate for a strike and was wildly cheered. But then he got too much ambish and put so much on the next shoot that it lit on the ribs of little Johnny Kane. {Dick} Egan popped to Herzog, and Kane stole second base. Lobert, the vest-pocket edition of Honus Wagner, tripled terribly, Kane scoring, and Lobert scored in a walk as Herr Beecher lammed out another three-bagger.

With two out in the fifth, the Gingery Germans got busy again. Spade singled to right, and little Johnny Kane also singled, the ball caroming off Bridwell's glove. Then Mr. Egan singled to center, scoring Spade and sending Kane to third. Mr. Marquard chipped in with a wild pitch, allowing Kane to tally, and when Lobert singled through the box, Mr. Egan scored. With Beecher at bat, Bresnahan got a fingernail nearly torn off in attempting to stop one of Marquard's wild heaves, and retired in favor of Needham. After this inning Marquard also retired and was replaced by {Louis "Bull"} Durham, another rookie from Indianapolis.

McGinnity was the pitcher that went to the well once too often in the second struggle, and before he had been relieved the damage was done. —William F. Kirk, New York *American*

Fred Tenney is quite lame, and he gave way to Merkle in the fourth inning of the second game yesterday. No plays came up in which Merkle had to think, so he got by.

—Jack Ryder, Cincinnati *Enquirer*

Fans who attended last Wednesday's game and saw or heard things which can help to establish New York's claim of a legitimate victory over the Cubs will confer a favor on the management of the New York club by giving their testimony as they enter the grounds today. The club's attorney, Mr. Sullivan, and a notary will be there to take this testimony, which will be put in the form of affidavits and used as evidence to support the New York club's protest. Many fans have stated that the umpires did not see the alleged play at second base and refused to call it. Their testimony will help greatly.   —New York *Globe*

CHICAGO, Sept. 25—During a fight over Pres. Pulliam's decision calling the disputed Giant-Cub game a tie the skull of Thomas Crocker was fractured. He is in the county hospital, probably fatally injured, and George Brooks is under arrest.

According to the police Brooks used a baseball bat to settle the argument. Brooks defended the claims of the New York team and Crocker upheld the contention of the Cubs. During the resulting fight Brooks is said to have struck Crocker with the bat, after declaring, "I'll show you how Mike Donlin makes a three-base hit."   —Boston *Globe*

◇ SUNDAY, SEPTEMBER 27 ◇

{On September 26, in New York, the Giants beat Cincinnati in a doubleheader, 6 to 2 and 3 to 1. Winning pitchers, Mathewson and Ames; losing pitchers, Ewing and Dubuc. Giants' standing: 90 wins, 52 losses, in first place.}

While the sun refused to shine on the Harlem meadow yesterday, it was anything but doleful for the 30,000 fans that saw the Giants redeem themselves and take a tighter grip on the narrow lead for the pennant. Cincinnati was just plain Sin-Sin-Natty this time. The Giants won two games almost as they pleased, with Christy Mathewson and Leon Ames doing the pitching.

Those who thought, after the double drubbing the Reds gave McGraw's men on Friday, that the Giants were cooped up in the elevator with all the doors locked and going down, have another guess. Nobody expected anything but a victory when Big Six appeared in the firing line for the opener. When Ames strolled to the rubber for the nightcap it was different.

Since Amesie returned to service he has been an in and outer, good one day and bad the next. Yesterday was one of Leon's good days. He was as steady as a rock and when it looked as though a pair of Redlegs might get to the plate he gave the boys behind him such easy grounders they couldn't do otherwise but accept them.

Fred Tenney was the hero with the willow. Fred was entitled to two home runs but could only land one because his legs are bad and interfere sadly with his locomotion.   —New York *World*

After Ed Reulbach, of the Chicago Cubs, had pitched the first game in Washington Park yesterday, in which Brooklyn failed to make a run, he volunteered to pitch the second, and Brooklyn did not make a run in that contest.

Reulbach's willingness to do overwork permitted Chance to give his other pitchers a much-needed rest. Instead of being compelled to use three men in Brooklyn, he got along with two, Overall and Reulbach. Brown, the three-fingered marvel, upon whom the final fight is likely to rest, will have four solid days of comfort in which to build up his strength.

No pitcher in the National League has ever been able to show such command over another team as Reulbach did yesterday. He has the record all to himself of two shut-out games in one afternoon. In the American League, Walter Johnson, of Washington, pitched three shut-out games to the Highlanders, but they were in successive afternoons. {No other major league pitcher has yet matched Reulbach's feat of pitching two shut-outs in one day. Johnson's three shut-outs, incidentally, although pitched in three consecutive games, were spread over four days, September 4, 5, and 7, 1908.}   —New York *Herald*

The New York National League club is engaged in one of its familiar fourflushes in an endeavor to convince the baseball public in Gotham that the Giants were robbed of a hard-earned victory on a mere technicality.

And because Broadway, from Times Square to the Battery, is the native heath of the fourflush; because New Yorkers have become so accustomed to it they take their hats off to a good one; because the average Gotham fan's knowledge of baseball is confined to the standing of the Giants in the pennant race and the number of games Mathewson has won; because in baseball, as in everything else, anything from across the Hudson, the Harlem, or the East River is regarded as barbarian and a rank outsider to be repulsed at any cost, the officials of the New York Nationals are likely to get away with this latest New York bluff.

Outside of Manhattan island, however, where baseball is considered a national pastime and not a form of paying tribute to New York, it is a recognized fact that the Giants lost that victory over the Cubs by a blunder more stupid than the rankest of fielding errors ever perpetrated.

If New York newspapers printed baseball news pertaining to anything outside Manhattan and Brooklyn, the Gotham fans might have understood from the Pittsburgh tangle what came off before their own eyes last Wednesday. Possibly, too, Merkle might have read about that play and have remembered it long enough to avoid duplicating Gill's bush league blunder. In that case the Giants would have another victory to their credit and would not be fourflushing about technicalities to cover the ignorance of the rules displayed by one of their players.

There was only one thing to do Wednesday after Merkle had been forced out. The decision should have been made known at once, the field should have been cleared, and the game finished in extra innings. There was plenty of light to go on with the battle, and there were less than 13,000 people at the game. Consequently with any kind of management the field could have been cleared.

But there are no screens or barriers to prevent Polo Grounds fans from pouring out on to the diamond as soon as they think a game is over, or nearly over, and there has been no real police protection there all season. The danger existing in this absence of regular policemen has been pointed out repeatedly and the league warned that it was courting not only serious trouble but actual scandal in permitting such conditions to go on unchanged. Now that the scandal has arrived there is no occasion for handing out sympathy.

If it had happened at any other grounds than New York there is no question but that the umpire would have forfeited the game to the visiting club on account of the crowd's interference. Anywhere else an umpire would have been assured sufficient police protection to enable him to do his duty as prescribed by the rules without endangering the wholeness of his scalp. One hates to think what would have happened to O'Day in New York if he had remained and tried to make the Giants resume the game. New York fans have been taught by years of tolerating McGraw-ism that New York is a law unto itself in baseball.

—I. E. Sanborn, Chicago *Tribune*

Here are several rules which bear on last Wednesday's game:

Rule 59. One run shall be scored every time a base runner, after having legally touched the first three bases, shall legally touch the home base before three men are put out; provided, however, that if he reach home on or during a play in which the third man be forced out or be put out before reaching first base, a run shall not count. A force-out can be made only when a base runner legally loses the right to the base he occupies and is thereby obliged to advance as the result of a fair-hit ball not caught on the fly.

Rule 77. Every club shall furnish sufficient police force to preserve order upon its own grounds, and in the event of a crowd entering the field during a game, and interfering with the play in any manner, the visiting club may refuse to play until the field be cleared. If the field be not cleared within fifteen minutes thereafter, the visiting club may claim, and shall be entitled to the game by a score of nine runs to none.

This, then, brings it up to the present situation. Umpire O'Day declared Merkle out for not going to second base on Bridwell's hit. It was a force play, pure and simple, as covered by Rule 59. Immediately after the umpire rendered his decision, the umpires were spirited away by the police, who assured the crowd there would be no further play. When the umpires finally broke out of captivity it was too dark to resume play. Frank Chance and his players did not remain on the field for fifteen minutes after the crowd broke restraint. In fact, they were swept aside by the angry tumult and were lucky to escape with sound skins when the fans found out what it was all about.

President Pulliam called the game a tie, and as a result it should have been played off as a postponement. But his decision was not reached until it was practically too late for the New York management to notify its players of a doubleheader the following day, if such had been desired. Frank Chance had notified the Giants he would lay claim to a game by forfeit if a doubleheader were not played, and he made good his threat. Pulliam by instructing his umpires not to report to the park till 3:30

practically eradicated the game from the schedule, despite a resolution adopted at the last National League meeting that each club must play 22 games with every other club during the season where such may be accomplished.

In declaring the game a tie, President Pulliam established a new precedent; in not ordering it played over and seeing that such was done after he made the strange decision he countenanced a fracture of the rules and gave Frank Chance good ground for a claim to forfeiture; and in leaving the matter to the Board of Directors of the National League, he has shifted an unwelcome burden from his own shoulders to those of others.

—New York *American*

Pending the final adjudication of the disputed game of Wednesday, Sept. 23, I want you to know why I assigned umpires for but one game at the Polo Grounds on Sept. 24, and why the provisions of the National League constitution governing the playing off of postponed and tie games were not enforced.

I was present at the game which ended in a scene of great confusion. With a desire to protect the interests of both clubs and to carry out the provisions of our laws, I sent for the umpires in charge of the game that night. They informed me that the game resulted in a tie.

While in conference with the umpires I received a formal protest from the Chicago club claiming the game by a score of 9 to 0. The moment this claim of Chicago was received I was estopped from taking any steps to have the tie game played off on the next day by the provisions of section 22 of the constitution, which provides that the claim, together with the accompanying proofs, must be furnished to the other club, which club has five days in which to reply.

A second communication from the Chicago club was received at or about 11 o'clock the next morning stating it did not desire to protest the decision of the umpires. It was then too late in my judgment to give the proper notice to both clubs that the game must be played over on that day, and therefore I did not assign umpires for two games.

—Harry C. Pulliam, in the Chicago *Tribune*

Christy Mathewson said this to the writer:

"Fred Merkle did touch second base, and I was there with him when he did it. He started directly for the clubhouse when Bridwell made his hit, but when he heard the shouting and took in the situation, he turned back and threaded his way through the crowd to the second bag. He touched it, and wanted to stay, but I was at his side and said, 'Come on, now, let's beat it to the clubhouse.' Then we went to the clubhouse together."

Umpire O'Day in a report to President Pulliam states that Merkle started for second base, ran part of the distance and then streaked for the clubhouse. As a matter of fact, Umpire O'Day didn't see anything in connection with Merkle's actions. Numerous affidavits filed with the management of the Giants will prove that O'Day saw nothing that happened on the diamond after he had seen Bridwell's hit! His back was to the field and the crowd from that instant until he crawled into his coop!
—William F. Kirk, New York *American*

——◇ **MONDAY, SEPTEMBER 28** ◇——

New York has eight more games to play with Philadelphia, and it is with the Phillies that the Giants expect to recover lost ground. The two teams have played 14 games, of which New York has won 11. For some reason the Quakers are the easiest team in the league for the Giants to beat, and it is due to this fact that followers of the Giants look to see their favorites increase their lead.

The one big advantage enjoyed by the Giants is that their hard games are apparently over. —New York *Times*

CINCINNATI, Sept. 28—President Murphy of the Chicago Cubs today made the following statement:

"I am making the claim that Chicago is now in the lead in the National League race, as the tie game of Wednesday went to us when the New Yorks failed to show up to play a doubleheader on Thursday.

"Under section 45 of the National League constitution, the New York club was obliged to play a doubleheader on Thursday, as it was the last opportunity we had of meeting the New Yorks this season. The section provides that 'a tie or a drawn game, or a game prevented by rain or other causes, shall be played off on the same ground on which scheduled during the same or any subsequent series, the date to be optional with the home club.'

"In the present instance Thursday was the only date left on which the game could be played, and when the Giants failed to come out to play the game they forfeited it.

"As a member of the Board of Directors of the league, I shall vote to have the game given to the Cubs, and I believe the other directors will do likewise." —New York *Globe*

Neither the Cubs nor the Pirates can play a game after next Sunday, October 4, not even if rain should prevent every game this week. Their season ends on that day. The Giants, however, have until Wednesday, October 7, in which to complete their quota of games. On Monday, Tuesday and Wednesday of next week the Giants are scheduled to play Boston. It is possible the result of the race will not be decided until October 7, and in such a case I can see the players of the Cubs and Pirates around the tickers, and a blamed sight more nervous than if they were on the diamond fighting to win.

The Cubs have only six more games to play, and it is therefore impossible for them to win more than 99 games, and if the Pirates should win the seven games they still have to play their total of winning games would be 99. But either the Cubs or Pirates will lose next Sunday, for they face each other then.

The Giants can, if they win all of their 11 games to come, have 101 victories. They can lose two out of the 11 and still win 99 games, the limit that either the Cubs or Pirates can get.

—Sam Crane, New York *Evening Journal*

Amid the wild, enthusiastic cheering of 20,000 delirious fanatics, Mike Donlin was presented the *Evening Journal*'s handsome loving cup for the most popular local player during the intermission between the first and second games between the Giants and Reds on Saturday. For fully ten minutes the applause lasted, and the outburst continued until Donlin took his position in right field at the beginning of the second encounter.

—New York *Evening Journal*

Larry Doyle is out for the season. He may be able to do a pinch-hitting stunt later in the week, but at present he is still on crutches.

—New York *Globe*

I have received many letters asking me about Charley Herzog's nationality and what Sunday school he plays. I answered one in which I replied that Herzog's forebears were his personal property and no one's business save his own.

But Herzog himself wishes it known that he is a Dutchman. So many fans wished him a happy new year Saturday it made him tired.

"They've got me wrong," said Herzy to me after the game. "I'm as Dutch as sauerkraut, but that's all."

What he meant by "that's all" is probably explained when he added:

"You see, when I was a kid, I fell off a cliff and broke my nose. It was never set properly, and that's what makes it stick out so now."

Herzy's nose does stick out a bit, that's a fact. When he slides to a base he must turn on his side. Otherwise he'd be so high off the ground he might as well try to make the bag standing.

—Gym Bagley, New York *Evening Mail*

I don't care whether the tadpole with the fish fell in love, at all;
Nor whether in slime they both did time, till they got the final call;
For that was so very long ago, that really no one knows.
Nor do I wot, for it matters not, that they dined at Delmonico's.
If a ship cuts the time of passage across the raging main,
Or she gets the gate, because too late to beat an aeroplane.
It wouldn't matter a cent's worth, you may believe me when I say,
If a ride on the cars from here to Mars would only take a day.
I wouldn't cough up a button to see an angel's face—

You can't get nourishment from these,
They're only gags for foolish gees;
And nothing like it, if you please—
When Merk touched second base.

The campaign doesn't bother me, I don't even read its news;
I wouldn't care if every hair in his whiskers votes for Hughes.
It's a pipe he'll be elected, he's nowhere now but there,
I'll put you wise, those other guys are not in it, but I don't care.
I wouldn't give a nickel to see Miss Liberty do a Salome dance,
Nor a suffragette—and it may be yet—spring Moe Levy pants.
I don't care whether Bingham only has his coppers for his toys,
Nor his bluff when he pulled that stuff about stopping the city's noise.
I haven't any tears to shed 'cause he beat it, our own Hal Chase.★
　　　But if you'll only tell me, Bo
　　　The thing that we already know,
　　　The thing that worries Murphy so—
　　　That Merk touched second base.

　　　　　　　　　　　　　—Gym Bagley, New York *Evening Mail*

———— NATIONAL LEAGUE STANDINGS ————

	W	L	PCT.	GB		W	L	PCT.	GB
New York ...	90	52	.634	½	Cincinnati ...	71	77	.480	22½
Chicago	93	54	.633	—	Boston	61	84	.421	31
Pittsburgh ...	92	55	.626	1	Brooklyn	48	96	.333	43½
Philadelphia .	77	65	.542	13½	St. Louis	49	98	.333	44

————◇ **TUESDAY, SEPTEMBER 29** ◇————

{On September 28, in New York, the Giants beat Philadelphia 7 to 6. Winning pitcher, McGinnity; losing pitcher, Corridon. Giants' standing: 91 wins, 52 losses, in first place.}

★The controversial New York Yankee first baseman who had recently jumped his team.

The gallant Knight of the Wallop, "Turkey Mike" Donlin, at about 5:35 P.M. yesterday saw a mud-covered baseball coming toward him through the gathering darkness. It came from the hand of Philadelphia Pitcher Frank Corridon, and it came just where Mike wanted it. Roger Bresnahan was on third base and the Giants needed a run to tie the score. So what did "Turkey" do? He just landed on that seal-brown sphere and hit it as hard as he ever hit a ball in his life. It traveled low and fast to the right-field fence. Roger walked home and Donlin half slid and half ran to third base, with 3,000 fans making about as much noise as 10,000 could under ordinary conditions. Then Cy Seymour walked up for a crack at the battered mud ball. Cy was as good as Mike. He slapped a liner to left. Only a single was needed to score Jack Barry, who had stepped in to run for Donlin, or Cy's crack would have been good for three bases. The Giants had pulled out of as tight a hole as they had been in for several days. —New York *World*

CINCINNATI, Sept. 28—While the Cubs rested in quiet seclusion, the Giants jammed the Chicago contenders back a couple of points in the frantic scramble for the pennant.

The Peerless Leader was disappointed because the champions had to remain idle though the sun shone. Fear of the deadly technicality microbe induced the Cubs to abandon playing off a postponed game this afternoon. The original intention was to remain idle today, and double up Tuesday. But while in New York Frank Bancroft of the Reds got Chance on the phone and arranged to play an extra game on Monday. Then occurred the rumpus at the Polo Grounds.

While the Reds were at the Polo Grounds on Saturday the wily John T. Brush tipped his mitt to Bancroft by asking a number of questions about switching the game here. That set Bancroft to thinking. This morning he and Garry Herrmann looked up the rules and found that tie games "shall be played off in subsequent series."

Notice the delicate point John T. Brush is flirting with. Our present series here does not become subsequent until tomorrow. Hence if a postponed game was played today Brush might subpoena a bunch of ham-fat actors and such and have the combat thrown out as illegal on the ground it was not subsequent according to Hoyle. After talking the matter over with the Peerless Leader and others, Mr. Murphy decided not to take a chance. Today's game will be played on Friday.

—Charles Dryden, Chicago *Tribune*

When Barry, running for Donlin, danced over the rubber on Seymour's hit yesterday, the game was won. As he ambled home, Barry stopped just short of the plate and then jumped on it. But even that didn't satisfy Donlin. He ran out and took Barry back and made him stand on the pan, at the same time pointing to the act and calling Klem's attention to it.

"He is touching the base, isn't he?" asked Mike of Klem.

Klem smiled and said, "Yes."

"Just so nobody can protest it," quothe Mike.

—Gym Bagley, New York *Evening Mail*

———◇ **WEDNESDAY, SEPTEMBER 30** ◇———

{On September 29, in New York, the Giants split a doubleheader with Philadelphia, 6 to 2 and 0 to 7. Winning pitchers: Mathewson and Coveleski; losing pitchers, McQuillan and Crandall. Giants' standing: 92 wins, 53 losses, in second place.}

More in anger than in sorrow, it has to be reported that Philadelphia sprung something yesterday. It was named something unpronounceable, and spelled C-o-v-a-l-e-s-k-i {a misspelling of Coveleski's name}. It pitched, and that's why we're in second place.

Two games were scheduled at the Polo Grounds yesterday between the Giants and Quakers, and one of them was played and won, 6 to 2. In this game, Mathewson pitched, and without having to extend himself, he made the sluggards from the Schuyl-kill look their class. And none of the 15,000 crowd so much as gaped at the result. It was to be expected.

That was the way it went in the first game, with Matty pitching about as he liked, easy and graceful and not too exertful, and everybody in good humor, and the fans wondering whether Matty wasn't going to pitch another nine innings, and the grill at the back of the stand coming in for a strong play, and a lot of new celebrities in the new grandstand, and only the laziest sort of interest in the Pittsburgh and Chicago scores, for we're going right along now, fellows, and we don't have to be geographical to be happy, and something of this confident feeling gets into the cosmos of old boy McGraw, and he grows indulgent and says to that minor child Crandall—which is only 19 years old, so they say, and pitches like it exactly {Crandall would in fact celebrate his twenty-first birthday on October 8}—says McGraw, then, "Go on in, Otey, for this second game, and you can win it all right, son, for you're the strong, hefty infant, and they'll never get to that stuff of yours, and even if they did, we can hit anything they bring out, and we can always fall back on Matty to help you out, so you go on and show these Philadelphians that New York can celebrate a bit on its own account on Founders' Day."

And Otis Crandall, big and kiddish and important, and without a pitching thing in this big world to recommend him, gets into the game, and they kill him fatally.

Philadelphia put one over on us. His name was Covaleski. Crandall starts and retires the first three men and that's all right. Umpire Klem gets out in front of the grandstand and sneezes three times, and then somebody says: "Tell us the name of Philadelphia's pitcher," and then Klem says, sort of shortlike and resentful: "I done told you his name; it's —" and he sneezes some more, and a gentleman in the grandstand who is a linguist by day, says: "Why that must be Mr. Covaleski," and there isn't anybody can argue the point.

Mr. Colvaleski comes from the Warsaw team of the Plander Leaguesky, and they say that all along the Nevsky Prospekt his name has got it on the Goldbrick Twins for being a household word. Last time out in his own country he shut the Kischeneffs out, and made the flower and glory of the Moscow sluggers look anemic. Bar a couple of strikeoutskys in the course of the afternoon, this gentleman was all to the pitchovitch.

Everybody has a funny little something to say about the pitcher for Philadelphia, and the pitcher for Philadelphia has a funny little something to hand out to most of the crowd, including Giant batsmen. When the fifth inning has come around, and we have failed to score, we're beginning to believe this fellow has something. In the fifth we set out to win the game and stop our fooling and send Covaleski back to the coal mines. Devlin leads off with a two-bagger to the left-field fence, and right on top of this Merkle drives out a double to right. Now, you who did not see the game are saying: "Ah, that is where Devlin scored." You are wrong. Devlin did not score. Devlin has not scored yet. Devlin made a play that for pure asininity overlaps any of the inexcusably bad throws he has made in the last three days, and everybody knows these errors have been hard to beat. When Devlin doubled and Merkle doubled Devlin stood still as long as he could without taking root, and only got off second base when Merkle came crashing around and gave the signal to clear the track. Even at that it looked as if we couldn't possibly help scoring. Two on base, nobody out, Bridwell up. And Bridwell lines to {second baseman} Knabe, doubling Merkle off second, Crandall is thrown out by Cov. & Co., and there are no runs, and maybe Devlin is popular, eh?

And right on top of this, the sixth inning, Philadelphia gets nine men up, with the first man, Cov., & Co., making three bases as Merkle chases futilely around right field for the ball, and they score five runs. Doggone these foreigners anyway. Why don't they confine themselves to skat or ski-balling or whatever their national game is, and leave America for the Americans?

—W. W. Aulick, New York *Times*

The National League race is more of an enigma this fair September morning than it has ever been. The three leading teams are grouped in a cute little bunch, like a tangled ball of yarn. What the outcome will be, no sage can say. But the Giants are still there, and don't forget it.

The team that crawled up by inches from the second division to its present advantageous position is anything but a perfect team as it stands today. Three or four seasoned regulars are playing on their nerve, when they ought to be taking a vacation. Tenney is sticking to his position because the season is drawing to a close with the heartbreaking race still unsolved. Roger Bresnahan, who was hurt again yesterday, is in the cast of characters simply because his presence is needed. Mike Donlin, who got a little wrench of his bad ankle in Monday's struggle, wanted to play until Dr. Creamer said it was out of the question. That's the kind of boys, New York fans, who are keeping us on the baseball map.

—William F. Kirk, New York *American*

NEW YORK, Sept. 29—In yesterday's game McGraw acted like a wild man and passed several remarks to many Phillies, which has aroused their fighting spirit. It is now anything to down New York.

Also, just know, Bresnahan's injury was due to his attempt to cripple {Red} Dooin. While {shortstop Dave} Shean was tossing Seymour out in the fifth inning of the first game, Bresnahan, on third, made a dash for the plate. Bransfield relayed the ball home to head him off, and as Bresnahan slid he came feet forward right at Dooin's legs. The shock of the collision sent Bresnahan rolling away from the plate, and Dooin was spiked. But, as it afterward proved, Bresnahan got the worst of his attempt to cripple Dooin.

—Philadelphia *Inquirer*

Now here's a problem: If Bresnahan had caught the second game, would the Giants have lost, Covaleskie to the contrary, notwithstanding? Would the Bresnahan nut, if he could have stood up behind the bat on that bum gamp for nine innings, have pulled his team through?

There was one way for him to stay in, not to hit the ball and in consequence be compelled to run the bases. He could have intentionally struck out each time up. Even if he was of no use at the bat, he would still have been the directing hand and mind.

But the first time up he singled. That was his undoing. He had to hopscotch it to first. He could only put down one leg. Now it stands to reason that a guy getting to first on one leg would have to hit far away. But Bresnahan didn't. It was an infield which he beat out—on one foot.

Both Shean and {second baseman} Knabe went after the ball. They committed no error on the hit. And Roger was on the bag long before the ball was returned.

I'm no mind reader, but if the truth were told, I'd gamble a bag of Harry Stevens' gubers that when Shean and Knabe saw Bresnahan hobbling so painfully down the line they came to the conclusion that it would be a shame to throw out so game a player.

Roger had to give in for a pinch-runner, and of course that put him out of the game.

—Gym Bagley, New York *Evening Mail*

The electric light plant for playing midnight baseball will be ready for use in the Reds' park in two weeks. Mr. Herrmann is investing $4,000 in the scheme. Should the idea prove a failure the lights will enable the park to be used for political meetings. Three huge light towers have been erected in the yard. {Night baseball in the major leagues indeed began in Cincinnati, but not until May 24, 1935.}   —Chicago *Tribune*

─────◇ **THURSDAY, OCTOBER 1** ◇─────

{On September 30, in New York, the Giants beat Philadelphia 2 to 1. Winning pitcher, Ames; losing pitcher, Moore. Giants' standing: 93 wins, 53 losses, in first place.}

The stirring, nerve-racking fight for the National League pennant took a sudden turn yesterday that makes New York's chances look bright again. The Giants won from Philadelphia, but the change in the situation came in the ninth inning of a game in Cincinnati, when the Reds batted out a startling victory over Chicago, forcing the Cubs, who started the day in the lead, into third place, Pittsburgh having won an uphill game from St. Louis. The strain on the Giants is nonetheless acute, although they can lose two more games of the seven they have to play and still tie with Chicago if the Cubs win their remaining games. If, however, Pittsburgh cleans up, the Giants must win six of their seven.

—New York *Tribune*

Yesterday's Polo Grounds triumph was a game in keeping with the day. A fair game on a fair afternoon, with cool air sending a tingle through your veins, and just enough folks in the stand to make things clubby, and old boy Donlin in right field with his whip in his hand, making throws to home plate and third base that up to this time have been peculiar only to Right-Fielder Catapult of the Julius Caesar League.

Also, it's only justice to say, in a few brief but well-intended words, that Leon Ames pitched baseball yesterday, and pitched it the last time out, and looks for all the world as if he were gaited up for championship class.

As for runs, we got ours in the first, Herzog walking and going to second on Pitcher {Earl} Moore's throw and scoring when Shean threw McCormick's hit into the stand. McCormick scored on Devlin's hit to right.   —W. W. Aulick, New York *Times*

CINCINNATI, Sept. 30—Mr. H. Lobert, the finely trained athlete, turned a cruel trick on the Cubs this pleasant afternoon. In the ninth round with the bases full he smote a single that tallied two runs and beat the champions, 6 to 5. Tonight they repose in third place, 2 points behind the Pirates, and 6 in the rear of the hated Giants.

The champions still have a chance, but it is thinner than the ham in the sandwiches at the Philadelphia ball park. Only those who have inhaled said sandwiches know how thin that is. But the game is lost, so what's the use of beefing? Moreover, the gents who did not score behind or in front of Lobert's swat went on and touched the next base.

                                        —Charles Dryden, Chicago *Tribune*

CHICAGO, Sept. 27—It certainly is staggering to some of us old-timers to look back 15 or 20 years and, by comparison, force one's self to realize the vast growth of the national game. How many of us, for instance, ever saw or heard of a political campaign for the election of a President of the United States held up by greater interest in a baseball campaign?

Yet that is the situation in which the country finds itself now. There is more interest today in what clubs are going to play for the world's championship than in the outcome of the November election. It is absurd in a way when one thinks of it that the decision of a baseball pennant, which means almost nothing to the welfare of the country or its citizens, should obscure even for a minute that which affects every man, woman and child in the land.

Politicians are complaining about it, sages are writing about it in their political reviews and editorials are being penned about it, so there can be no mistake in thinking such a situation exists. One local politician told me that four out of every five times he asked someone what he thought would be the outcome of the next Presidential election the reply would be: "Oh, to —— with that. Who's going to win the pennant?"

                                        —I. E. Sanborn, *The Sporting News*

———◇ FRIDAY, OCTOBER 2 ◇———

{On October 1, in Philadelphia, the Giants split a doubleheader, winning 4 to 2 and losing 6 to 3. Winning pitchers, Mathewson and Coveleski; losing pitchers, Corridon and Wiltse. Giants' standing: 94 wins, 54 losses, in first place.}

Another crimp was put in the pennant aspirations of the tribe of McGraw by the Phillies yesterday.

After the first session of a doubleheader had been chucked into the maw of the hungry New Yorkers by {left-fielder} Sherwood Magee {by muffing a line drive that let in the winning run}, the Murrays copped the second chapter by whaling the horsehide while Covaleski, fresh from having dosed the Giants with whitewash over on Papa Knickerbocker's isle, again mowed them down.

It's in the dope that Covaleski, the Phillies' "Iron Man," will prove the undoing of the Giants. They are afraid of him, and as he is likely to twirl again tomorrow, the McGrawites are expected to take a tumble. All the faithful say that defeat for New York will be spelled C-o-v-a-l-e-s-k-i.

Probably not since the Athletics and Giants clinched for the world's championship has there been such an influx of dippy ones from where the white lights dangle. Everybody who could get away or had the price seemed to have beat it over from Manhattan to work their lungs for McGraw's bunch, and many a gloom-nipped Gothamite hiked it back Madison Squareway, green hats and all, with dope tucked away in their thinktanks that New York's chances of swiping the bunting are getting more emaciated every day.   —Philadelphia *Inquirer*

PHILADELPHIA, Oct. 1—While the Giants still figure prominently as pennant winners, there is no question that the team is now a sadly battle-scarred lot of ball tossers. If the pets from the Polo Grounds can win tomorrow and Saturday, it will be on nerve and nothing else. Bresnahan's lameness may keep him out for the remainder of the season, though the fiery backstop wants to work if there is a chance for him to appear behind the plate.

Donlin's leg is so bad he ought to be on crutches. Seymour got a slight twist in his right leg today, which slowed him up and caused him a good deal of pain the rest of the afternoon.

About 8,000 people saw the game, not as large a crowd as the Philadelphia management had hoped to see. It seems, however, that our beauties and their rivals were playing against several competing attractions. There was a football game somewhere, a special matinee somewhere else, and besides the residents of this quaint old city are all wrought up over a coming festival to be known as "Founders Day."

Hundreds of business houses and dwellings are profusely decorated with bunting, strangers are pouring into town, and there isn't much time to talk baseball. Nobody seems to know just who the "Founders" are or why any body of men should get a "day" for founding Philadelphia.

As a result of the second struggle's sad ending the three contenders are squeezed into the funniest little corner you ever dreamed of. Never was there such a race before. The baseball public is on the verge of dementia doperina, and the players of the three leading clubs are worn to a frazzle. Chances are that this week will tell the tale.

—William F. Kirk, New York *American*

It's a funny thing when you have to spring the dope that Mike Donlin lost a game. But that's just what happened in the second session of the doubleheader here in Philadelphia yesterday. But it wasn't Donlin's fault. It was the fault of his bum ankle. At least four runs came across in that sad, sad story of the second spasm because Mike couldn't shag flies.

It was pitiful, that is pitiful for the bunch of New York bugs who journeyed to this burg to see the Giants clean up the Phillies and cinch the old rag. Rockets that ordinarily Donlin would make a pie of fell safe many feet from the crippled right-fielder. He just couldn't get to them.

But McGraw had to keep him in on the chance that his batting eye would pull over a run or two at a critical moment.

And this same thing did happen in the sixth inning. Mike packed a double which brought across a couple of runs.

—Gym Bagley, New York *Evening Mail*

The only way in which McGraw can beat that gentleman with the Russian suffix to his name, which is pronounced like an automobile with its muffler off, running on three cylinders, is to dress his team in kimonos and disguise them as Japs. Then, if the same disguised ball players make a noise like the Mikado's army, Covaleskie might dig for the tall timber.

—New York *Herald*

———◇ **SATURDAY, OCTOBER 3** ◇———

{On October 2, in Philadelphia, the Giants won 7 to 2. Winning pitcher, Ames; losing pitcher, McQuillan. Giants' standing: 95 wins, 54 losses, in second place.}

After a week of deliberation President Harry C. Pulliam last night rendered a decision on the protested New York–Chicago game of September 23. President Pulliam rules the game a tie and says the Chicago club has no claim for a forfeited game on September 24. The text of the announcement is:

"The game was played at the Polo Grounds and was declared a drawn contest by the umpires in charge.

"Against this decision the Chicago and New York clubs filed protests, as follows:

"Sept. 23, 10:00 P.M. Chicago appeals from decision declaring a draw and claims forfeiture.

"Sept. 24, 11:00 A.M. Chicago serves notice it does not protest decision.

"Sept. 25. Chicago claims a forfeiture by 9 to 0 for failure of New York club to play off on Sept. 24 the tie of previous day.

"Sept. 25. New York club gives notice of appeal from decision of umpires and at expiration of time limit files briefs, together with documentary evidence.

"Sept. 30. Chicago formally waives its right to five days in which to reply to New York, resting its case on the report of the umpires, and claiming thereby a forfeited game on Sept. 24.

"The contentions of Chicago for a forfeiture on Sept. 24 will be disposed of first. When Chicago filed its original claim it tied the hands of the president of the league in his endeavor to reach a speedy adjudication. Under the constitution the filing of the claim precluded the president from taking any step looking toward the immediate playing off of the game.

"There was nothing to do but serve notice of claim on New York and wait five days for reply. When Chicago filed its second communication, it was too late to insist on playing off of the game on a few hours' notice.

"Since the last and final claim for a forfeiture, filed by Chicago Sept. 25, cannot be entertained, the same is hereby dismissed.

"Before going into the merits of the protest filed by New York against the decision of the umpires, I shall quote the rule governing the scoring of runs:

" 'Rule 59. One run shall be scored every time a base runner, after having legally touched the first three bases, shall legally touch home base before three men are put out; provided, however, that if he reach home on or during a play in which the third man be forced out or be put out before reaching first base a run shall not count. A force out can be made only when a base runner legally loses the right to the base he occupies and is thereby obliged to advance as the result of a fair hit not caught on the fly.'

"The play: Bridwell at bat, McCormick on third, Merkle on first, and two out. Bridwell hits the ball, which results in a fair hit not caught on the fly.

"What is necessary to score this run? Bridwell must reach first safely, so must Merkle reach second, he being forced in advance on Bridwell's hit.

"Under the rules the umpire is sole judge of the play, and on this play both ruled that Merkle was forced out for failure to touch second— O'Day on his personal observation of Merkle and Emslie by information received from O'Day.

"This left the game a tie, and O'Day in his report gives the reason why the game was not continued. He says: 'The people had run out on the field. I did not ask to have the field cleared, as it was too dark to continue play.'

"New York, in support of its claim for the game, contends: First, that neither O'Day nor Emslie saw the play; second, that as proof of this claim the fact is cited of the umpires' failure to order the field cleared for the purpose of continuing the game; third, that no decision was rendered on the field to the effect that the run did not score.

"No claim is made that Merkle touched second base, it being held by inference that this requirement was a technicality. Numerous affidavits by players and spectators are submitted in support of the contentions of the New York club. Among the affidavits of players are those of Bridwell and McCormick, but none from Merkle.

"The question to be decided is: Shall the decision of the umpires be upheld, or shall it be set aside on the evidence submitted by players and spectators?

"In a similar case, covering the identical play under the same conditions, in a game played at Pittsburgh Sept. 4, with Chicago, the latter club protested the decision of the umpire, and submitted affidavits by players and newspaper correspondents. My ruling in this case was as follows:

" 'This is a case simply of fact and judgment, and the ruling of the umpire is final. The question of whether there was a force play or not cannot be substantiated by evidence of spectators. It rests solely with the umpire. The umpire, by allowing the winning run, ruled that there was no force at second, because if there had been the run could not have scored.'

"At Pittsburgh there was but one umpire. At New York there were two, and the purpose of the double-umpire system is to cover all plays. This play in question, missed by Emslie, was seen by O'Day, who, being the umpire-in-chief, ruled that the run did not count.

"Much as I deplore the unfortunate ending of a brilliantly played game as well as the subsequent controversy, I have no alternative than to be guided by the law. I believe in sportsmanship, but would it be good sportsmanship to repudiate my umpires simply to condone the undisputed blunder of a player?

"The playing rules say that the decision of an umpire on a question of fact is final. This whole controversy hinges on a simple question—Was Merkle forced out at second base? Umpire-in-chief O'Day says he was. O'Day is no novice, and there is no reason to doubt his accuracy in his decision. As an umpire he ranks second to none; his integrity has never been questioned.

"My decision in this matter is just as it was in the Pittsburgh decision and as in every other protest that has come before me—to uphold the umpire on questions of fact.

"I rule that this game ended in a tie score and that Chicago has no claim for a forfeited game on Sept. 24.

"This ruling is subject to appeal to the Board of Directors, and in that event a meeting of the board will be called for Monday, October 5."

—New York *American*

PHILADELPHIA, Oct. 2—Flying at the throats of the Phillies like nine wildcats, the Gingery Giants made enough runs in the first inning to make victory a certainty.

It was a cold, windy day, more fitted for football than baseball. McQuillan and Foxen, the first two men sent to the slab by Manager Murray, couldn't get warm enough to pitch and couldn't pitch enough to get warm, and, thanks to their lack of control and general ineffectiveness, we piled up our commanding lead.

Ames pitched for the Giants, and Leon was at his best. The powerful young redhead didn't let himself out any more than he had to, realizing that the sudden change in the weather wasn't the best thing in the world for a pitcher's salary limb, but when he had to use the old steam he certainly had it to use.

The fireworks began promptly at 3:30. Mr. McQuillan, who has sent many a Giant back hitless to the water bucket in days gone by, strolled to the mound and squared off at his foemen like a real, honest-to-goodness winner. He patted the new white ball, talked to it a moment and then tried to get it over the plate. Mr. Tenney waited, and waited, and waited, and then walked. Young Herzog, who was the candy child today, clouted an inshoot one good, sincere clout. The ball started like a flash of light for centerfield. Tenney walked home, and the estimable Mr. Herzog never stopped till he pulled up, panting, on third base. Harry McCormick singled to center without seeming to exert himself, and Herzog waddled homeward with a shining countenance. Captain Mike came mighty near ripping off a long, safe one when he pulled a hard grounder over first base, but Bransfield made a fine stop, touched first and threw out McCormick at second.

If you had been there, gentle reader, you would have leaned back at this stage of the game with the remark that two runs look pretty good for a starter. The Giants, however, were out for more plums. Cy Seymour drew a base on balls, and Knabe fumbled Devlin's hard grounder. Mr. McQuillan began to get white around the gills, and presented Roger Bresnahan with a complimentary, filling the bases. Bridwell went up with the firm intention of cleaning up, but he, too, ambled to first on four balls, forcing in Seymour. McQuillan didn't do any more flinging, Mr. Foxen taking up the burden. Foxen was no great improvement. He began by walking Ames, thus crowding Devlin into the harbor. He kept up the good work by giving Tenney his second base on balls, Bresnahan paddling homeward.

The ingenious manager of the scrapplers decided it was not Foxen's day and sent in Moren. Herzog didn't falter in the presence of the newcomer, clouting another single, scoring Ames and Bridwell. Two hits for one young fellow in one inning is a notable achievement, and Herzog was in bad with local fans for the rest of the afternoon. McCormick ended the inning by making the third out. This is how the Gingery Giants made their seven tallies, and that is how they won the game.

—William F. Kirk, New York *American*

"I am sure Mathewson will send us up the ladder a little further today," said McGraw this morning. "They can talk about him being tired or overworked, but he isn't. Once Matty gets loosened up in the pitcher's box it will be only a question of making runs behind him. The Phillies hit him the other day because he started slowly, but I will see that he is well warmed up today. The weather is a little cool, and a pitcher's arm is apt to stiffen up with a cold wind blowing. Let Matty get up a sweat and he will go through the Phillies like a rifle bullet through a cigar box."

—Sid Mercer, New York *Globe*

PHILADELPHIA, Oct. 3—So worked up was the populace that one New York fan who rooted for the Giants too exuberantly got a severe thrashing, although he put up a game battle and delivered many telling punches before he was finally knocked into dreamland. There was one Philadelphia policeman who didn't interfere until he saw the New Yorker getting the best of it, and then he held the latter's arms while the frantic Quaker fans made a punching bag out of the stranger.

Oh, I tell you, this race is a peach. But what a great big laugh we will give 'em when the Giants cop the rag.

—Sam Crane, New York *Evening Journal*

PHILADELPHIA, Oct. 3—Manager McGraw is ill in his room at the Continental Hotel and may not lead his team to battle in the final game with Philadelphia this afternoon.

"He has worried himself sick," said Secretary Knowles. "No man ever worked harder against difficulties and bad luck than McGraw has in the past month, and as game as he is the strain is breaking him down. I will be glad when it is all over."

But unless positively forbidden by the doctor, McGraw will be in uniform today. He feels that as long as cripples like Donlin and Bresnahan are hobbling around in their appointed places nothing but sheer physical incapacity should make him give up the active leadership.

—J. W. McConaughy, New York *Evening Journal*

ST. LOUIS, Oct. 2—Manager Clarke of Pittsburgh tonight declared that should Pittsburgh lose a game tomorrow or the game on Sunday in Chicago through his players being in bad shape, and if losing these games loses the pennant, he will sue the Pullman Company for heavy damages.

The Pittsburgh team reached here this morning after having been up almost all night trying to keep warm or from being burned to death by a fire a porter insisted on building in a blind stove. The team had to get out twice and help extinguish fires which were burning the car. There was no steam in the car all night and the players were badly frozen.

—Chicago *Tribune*

Fifty thousand dollars for Christy Mathewson!

That is the stupendous sum offered by Charles W. Murphy and Frank

L. Chance, of the Chicago Cubs, to the New York club for Mathewson. The New York management promptly spurned the offer and remarked that they would not sell Matty at any price.

—New York *Evening Journal*

A correspondent writes, "Mr. Marquard carries documentary assurance from the New York club that guarantees him a full share in the world's series money if the Giants win." He was smart enough to make that provision before leaving Indianapolis, and yet they call Mr. Marquard a Rube. He is foolish like a pawnbroker.   —*Sporting Life*

———◇ SUNDAY, OCTOBER 4 ◇———

{On October 3, in Philadelphia, the Giants lost 3 to 2. Winning pitcher, Coveleski; losing pitcher, Mathewson. Giants' standing: 95 wins, 55 losses, in third place.}

Great is Covelaski.

Covelaski, the gunner from the Tri-State field, who shot three holes through the Giants' armor in one week's time and has shoved McGraw and his tribe down to third place.

If New York loses the championship nobody can the Giants blame more than the same Covelaski. Three victories from New York in one week is going some, especially when the Giants were going at a pace which would have beaten the majority of pitchers in either big league.

And to make Covelaski's achievement all the greater, he easily outpitched the great Mathewson from beginning to end. The Giants would have been lucky to have scored yesterday had the outfield of the Murrays been on their toes. A fumble by Magee on Tenney's single in the opening inning greatly aided the Giants to their first run, while in the ninth a juggling act by Osborne, followed by Titus letting McCormick's single go through him, gave the New Yorks their last tally.

And to show he possesses the stuff which great pitchers are made of, he kept his nerve about him in the ninth when, with McCormick on third base and none out, he prevented the Giants getting the tying run across. Donlin hit a weak little fly to Osborne. Seymour tapped one to Knabe and McCormick was run down between third and home. Then to wind up his brilliant performance Covelaski fanned Devlin, and the Giants fell to third place.

When Devlin whiffed on the third strike the crowd of 6,622 fans went wild with joy and swarming on the field, surrounded Covelaski and followed him to the clubhouse, patting him on the back and going through other wild demonstrations. The exhibition of joy by the fans would lead one to think the result of the game had won the championship for Philadelphia. But as long as it had put the Giants out of the running for the time being the crowd was satisfied. McGraw never was a favorite here, and whenever he is licked the victory is doubly relished by local fandom.

The "Joints" {Out-of-town writers often referred to the Giants as "Joints," mocking the way some New Yorkers pronounced the word: "Joy-ints."} were a sore lot when they left the field, and Devlin was perhaps one of the worst ones with a grouch. As he was about to go in the clubhouse a small boy hurled a remark at him and this aroused his ire and he kicked the youngster. The crowd quickly swarmed around the entrance of New York's dressing room after this and waited for the Giants to appear on the "Hump" from the Broad street door. But outside of jeering every member of the New Yorks and unmercifully "kidding" McGraw as he worked his way to the North Philadelphia Station the crowd went to their suppers peacefully.

—Philadelphia *Inquirer*

PHILADELPHIA, Oct. 3—There is an end to human endurance. Mathewson, the grandest Roman of them all, had been called on once too often. No arm can stand the strain of constant use, and Matty had worked more than his share. For half the game Mathewson was the same cool, deliberate, unsolvable mystery as of yore. Then the great strain told. Covelaski had settled down to his arduous task after the first inning with all the novel cunning for which he is now noted.

—New York *American*

If the Pirates win today, they will win the pennant even if New York wins all three from Boston. If the Cubs win, the best the Giants can do is to tie them for first place. This is not counting on what action the Board of Directors may take in deciding the disputed New York–Chicago game. Both clubs have appealed from President Pulliam's decision, and the board will meet in Cincinnati tomorrow to make a final decision. A decision in New York's favor and three games from Boston would mean that New York could win the pennant provided the Pirates lose today. Should the Pirates win today and the decision of the board be in New York's favor, the latter could tie Pittsburgh by winning three from Boston.

—New York *Sun*

If the Giants lose the pennant, Coveleski deserves the credit for defeating them. He seems to have the Indian sign on the stickers, big and little, from Coogan's Bluff. He hails from Shamokin, Pa., in the coal field, and is a Polak. Last summer he was twirling for an amateur team in Wildwood, N.J., having graduated from a coal miners' aggregation. In the Jersey marshes Murray picked him up last Autumn, and this Spring he was very green. In the early part of the season the Giants drubbed him 14 to 2.

He spent the Summer in the Tri-State League and as an alumnus of that organization he has developed into the man who has put such a crimp in the New York pennant aspirations. {Beyond these three victories against the Giants, Harry Coveleski won only one game for Philadelphia in 1908. When he completed his nine-year major league career in 1918, he had gained 81 victories. He was an older brother of Stanley Coveleski, the American League spitball pitcher elected to the Hall of Fame in 1969.}

—New York *Herald*

——◇ MONDAY, OCTOBER 5 ◇——

{On October 4, the Giants were not scheduled to play, but in Chicago the Cubs beat the Pirates 5 to 2, providing the Giants with the chance to tie for first place.}

CHICAGO, Oct. 4—Chicago's Cubs, world's champions, closed their dramatic struggle to retain their title with a victory over Pittsburgh. Before the greatest crowd that ever saw a baseball game, the two teams engaged in one of the most desperate and determined games in the history of baseball.

The game, climaxing the heartbreaking race of the last two months, saw two of the gamest clubs in the league locked in the death combat. Loss of the game meant hopeless defeat to either, victory meant the pennant for one and in all probability for the other. All the strain and effort, all the brains and energy and hard work, the suffering and sacrifices that the two clubs have endured, were wasted for the defeated one, and well endured by the winner. And before 30,247 maddened fans they fought it out to the finish, and Chicago won.

The finish of the battle for the championship of 1908 was perhaps the most thrilling event of all the long, strenuous season. Piled in the immense stands were nearly 20,000 persons, and banked in immense solid masses around the great field, twenty deep, stood an army. They realized the situation, and that the 18 men in uniform on the narrowed space of green were doing battle for the honor of their cities, for the championship of their league, and perhaps of the world, and that to each man the game meant $2,000 in cash.

Chance had chosen Brown to lead, and Clarke had gambled the whole season on Willis. They had met before again and again and Brown usually was victor, but this time in a strain that shook the nerves and tried the souls of men both managers were confident, and Brown won. Pitching with wonderful nerve and coolness, backed in superb style by Evers and Tinker and Chance especially, with Kling catching in grand form, Brown proved too much for the Pirates.

The game was grandly played. Chicago outplayed, outhit and outran the Pirates. They won the game on class and nerve, and demonstrated that they have the best ball team in the league.

Twice, when hits were desperately needed, Schulte, who almost got interested in baseball at last, pounded out singles that drove in runs. The Cubs were away in front and Schulte's two drives gave them two tallies before the Pirates could score. And then, in the sixth, came danger. For a few moments it looked as if the Pirates in one rally might ruin all the grand work the Cubs have done in the last month, and the crowd became scared and apprehensive. Twice men smashed out hits after two were out, and each after two strikes had been called, and the score was tied.

There the fighting spirit of the Cubs asserted itself and Brown himself won the game. It was in that inning that the season's race was decided, and Willis and Clarke made a move that brought disaster on them.

Two men were out when Tinker drove a double into the crowd to left—a hit that might have been a triple but for the crowd. Kling was next, and Willis chose to pass him and face Brown. It looked like good generalship, but it proved bad, for Brown is one of those men who get mad when others affect to despise them, and, gripping his bat tighter he drove a screaming hit to right that scored Tinker, and gave the Cubs the lead, never to be lost.

The defensive work of Chicago was grand, the stops of Evers and Tinker setting the crowd mad with applause. But for Chance was reserved the major honors, for in the eighth, by one of the most astounding plays ever made, he stopped the Pirates.

Leach hit a fierce line drive straight over first, and it looked a sure double until Chance, with a running jump, shoved out one hand, turned backwards and clung to the ball. Against that kind of defensive work Pittsburgh had no chance.

The Pirates quit while fighting, but when Wilson hit a hard bounder straight at Tinker and the ball flashed to Evers on top of second, forcing {Alan} Storke, the crowd broke. With a roar like an ocean breaking a dike the thousands poured down in the battleground in the wildest, craziest demonstration of the year. Brown, carried aloft on the shoulders of admirers, was borne around and around. For 15 minutes the players, unable to escape to the clubhouse, were carried over the field, while the air was black with cushions, hundreds of men—women, too—hurling the cushions high in the air, throwing coats, screaming and flinging hats.

But even then the demonstration was not over, and an hour after the game was done a thousand fans still waited outside the park. As Chance backed his automobile out hundreds swarmed around him, cheering wildly. Evers escaped to a cab, with a hundred men trying to unhitch the horse and pull the cab themselves, and as for Brown, who tried to slip across to Joe's and wash the dust of battle from his throat, he found about 500 there waiting, each wanting to buy him a keg.

—Hugh S. Fullerton, New York *American*

There was a decided novelty yesterday at the Polo Grounds. It was the sight of a crowd of 3,500 New York baseball fans rooting hard for the Chicago Cubs to win a game. The game was reproduced on two electric scoreboards, placed near home plate. By following the twinkling of small bulbs the fan could figure out play by play.

When Gibson, the last Pirate up, forced Storke at second the fans shook hands all around and yelled: "The Giants will get them yet."

—New York *World*

For the first time in Pittsburgh evening papers printed extras Sunday, giving an account of the final game. —New York *Times*

Fred Knowles, secretary of the Giants, is thinking of having a sign placed on the Polo Grounds reading: "Miners not allowed here." The placard will have special application to Mordecai Brown and Harry Covaleski, who wielded the pick and shovel before they entered the national game. —New York *Press*

What with accidents and the sudden lapse from his superb midseason form of George Wiltse, it is safe to say that McGraw and his Giants would have been in a sorry case in the last ten days of the desperate fighting had it not been for the splendid work of Leon Ames. He came suddenly into his best form a week ago, and has since beaten Cincinnati once and Philadelphia twice. He and Mathewson have been the only victorious New York pitchers since Wiltse, despite an awful beating, was saved from defeat in a Pittsburgh game by the terrific hitting of the Giants. —New York *Tribune*

──────── NATIONAL LEAGUE STANDINGS ────────

	W	L	PCT.	GB		W	L	PCT.	GB
Chicago	98	55	.641	—	Cincinnati	73	81	.474	25½
Pittsburgh	98	56	.638	½	Boston	63	88	.417	34
New York	95	55	.633	1½	Brooklyn	52	98	.347	44½
Philadelphia	80	70	.533	16½	St. Louis	49	105	.318	47½

──────◇ **TUESDAY, OCTOBER 6** ◇──────

{On October 5, in New York, the Giants beat Boston 8 to 1. Winning pitcher, Ames; losing pitcher, Tuckey. Giants' standing: 95 wins, 55 losses, in third place.}

The Board of Directors of the National League is skating on very thin ice. Whether the decision of the league umpires shall be upheld and the president of the league sustained in his rulings, or playing rules cast aside in favor of baseball by affidavit, is the grave question before this body, and the directors are hemming, hawing, delaying and pondering on the affidavits of partisans. As a result of this shaky condition of mind on the part of the directors, the decision in the disputed game of September 23 is still in abeyance. The directors are taking a night to think it over and determine whether they shall enforce the league rules and sustain their umpires and their president or yield to extreme pressure brought on them by argument by affidavit and by shrewd legal cross-questioning, and hand a decisive game to a club which threw it away through a stupid performance on the part of one of its players. The extent of the pressure is shown by the fact that the directors refused to announce a verdict last night after a session lasting for eight hours with no intermission for dinner. They will meet again this morning and endeavor to make up their minds. Meanwhile the entire baseball world waits eagerly.

The board consists of Messrs. Herrmann, of Cincinnati; Murphy, of Chicago; Dreyfuss, of Pittsburgh; Ebbets, of Brooklyn; and Dovey, of Boston, with President Pulliam as chairman ex-officio. All were present when the meeting was called to order by President Pulliam at the Sinton Hotel at 10 o'clock yesterday morning. Mr. Pulliam's first act was to rule that Messrs. Murphy and Dreyfuss were ineligible to vote on account of being directly interested in the case. Mr. Murphy retired at once, but Mr. Dreyfuss claimed a right to vote on the ground that the case did not concern his club. Mr. Pulliam pointed out that a vote for New York might enable Pittsburgh to finish the season tied for first place and that, therefore, Mr. Dreyfuss was directly interested. The other three directors sustained the president's position, and Mr. Dreyfuss was barred. He left for home, declaring he would have voted in favor of a forfeit to Chicago if he had been allowed to do so.

President Pulliam retired from his position in the chair, stating he felt it improper to preside in a case in which protests of his own decision were being considered. Mr. Ebbets was appointed chairman of the meeting, and the board got down to hearing testimony. President Brush made his argument in favor of having the game declared a victory for his club, assisted by Attorney Thomas Cogan of this city, his legal adviser. Mr. Brush presented a large number of affidavits from persons who saw the game, some of which declared that Merkle ran down and touched second base, others claimed that O'Day never walked into the diamond, but went straight to the dressing room and never called the game a tie. These affidavits were accepted and carefully considered. Among them were several from New York players, including Fred Merkle, who swore that he started for the clubhouse, but did not go far without returning and touching second base. This last affidavit was not presented in President Brush's original protest to the league president, but was obtained in time to offer to the Board of Directors.

President Murphy advanced his claim in favor of a forfeit to his club because the New York club refused to play off the tie of September 23 on the following day.

The umpires who officiated were then called and subjected to a very rigid cross-examination, including searching questions as to what they did before and after the game and on the following day, as well as their actions at the crucial period of the disputed play. Both O'Day and Emslie testified separately to the main facts, namely, that Merkle did not touch second base until a play had been made on him there and he had been declared out by Umpire Emslie, and that O'Day called the game a tie before leaving the diamond. They could not be shaken on these important points, though every effort was made to muddle them by severe cross-questioning on unimportant details. When Umpire Emslie, the first to be examined, came out of the directors' room, he said:

"I would never have believed that men could swear to such statements as are made in some of the affidavits presented by the New York club. Several of these affidavits are absolutely false. It is a revelation to me that such documents could be obtained."

Umpire O'Day, after his ordeal of cross-questioning, simply shrugged his shoulders. He was evidently highly disgusted with some of the statements to which he had listened.

The umpires agreed on the details of the decision, declaring Merkle out at second and the score a tie. They declared that O'Day's decision of a tie score was made while he was in the center of the diamond and that his declaration on this point caused him to be hustled and jostled by the crowd as he retired to his dressing room. After the umpires had been examined the directors took a recess for dinner.

The board met again at 9 o'clock and remained in session for an hour and a half and then adjourned until this morning at 10 o'clock.

Mr. Ebbets said: "This is a very important matter, one which will establish a precedent for many years to come. We cannot be too hasty in our decision." Mr. Herrmann declared that the directors had not had sufficient time to consider all the affidavits presented by the New York club. None of the directors attempted to explain why affidavits of players and partisan spectators were entitled to be considered as evidence.

—Jack Ryder, Cincinnati *Enquirer*

The Gingery Giants, playing before one of the largest Monday crowds ever seen at the Polo Grounds, began their series with Boston in rosy fashion. The young pitching prodigy named Tuckey, who has been touted as another Covaleski, tried to outpitch Leon Ames—and a mighty swell chance he had! In the words of the immortal Milton:

> *On a perfectly fine Autumn day*
> *Pitcher Tuckey attempted to play;*
> *Perhaps we were lucky*
> *With said Pitcher Tuckey,*
> *But we certainly tucked him away!*

Everybody East and West is pulling for the Giants to win, except people that dwell in cities where they have major league baseball clubs, and people that live in cities where they have minor league baseball clubs, and people that reside in cities where they have amateur baseball clubs. Otherwise, the Giants are all right.

The gathering yesterday was surprisingly large. Monday, as we have frequently observed, is a bad day to take your girl to the ball game. If she goes to bed early Sunday night she has to run the washing machine, and if she doesn't have to run the washing machine she doesn't go to bed early

Sunday night, and in either event there isn't much doing at the old ball game. Furthermore, as campaign orators say, no true gent would feel like going to a ball game on Monday if Sunday is his day off. But the crowd was there.

Leon Ames was in rare form. Leon is a great help to the folks these days. When Ames has control—and he has it these days—there is no beating him.   —William F. Kirk, New York *American*

CINCINNATI, Oct. 6—After the three voting directors of the National League reconvened today to consider the appeal from the decision of President Pulliam declaring the Giants-Cubs disputed game a tie, it became known that two of them had voted to award the game to New York.

The third of the directors, however, steadfastly refused to vote with the other two. He advanced many reasons for his attitude and up to latest accounts had not been won over.

A unanimous vote is necessary for a decision.

Garry Herrmann, who has the reputation of being the fairest man in baseball, was put down as favoring New York.

"I don't think a team should lose a game because a man did not run to second base on a clean hit when there was no chance to get him out if he did," he is reported to have said to friends last night.

President Ebbets, of Brooklyn, to the great surprise of dopesters, is put down as strongly in favor of supporting Pulliam. His opinion is not based on a study of the case so much as a feeling that the head of the league should be sustained on a question of rules.

The third member of the board, George Dovey, of Boston, is openly in favor of declaring the game a tie and wants it played over.

"In a broad sense New York has the best of it," he says. "The fair way out of it, it seems to me, is to have them play it over."
                              —New York *Evening Journal*

A hush fell upon 80,000,000 people. The wheels of industry had ceased their whirr, the marts of trade had stopped marting, money had forgot to change, husbands halted on their homeward way, wives let the dinner grow cold, children choked off their prattle and the dogs no longer wagged their tails.

What had happened?

Was all the campaign dope upset and Bryan elected?

Had war been declared between the United States and Japan?

Had Wall street once again played its little joke and plunged the country in a panic?

Had all of man's precious prerogatives, since Eve crabbed his laziness by making him eat an apple (it was a crab apple), been tossed into the discard and woman at last allowed to vote?

Was it come to pass that New York City had become a state and was free?

No, little one. None of these. Something of far greater importance.

All things had stopped, even the clock, in a stilled and silent wait for the decision on that tie game.

What was war or panic or the oft-recurring election of a President to this?

Peanuts.

The board is stalling for a result that will relieve it of the responsibility. The Giants might drop a game to Boston. That would end the controversy on the field and allow the board to escape from the rebuke of deciding play in a lawyer's office.

But after yesterday's game it doesn't look as if the board has a chance to escape.　　　　　　　　　　—Gym Bagley, New York *Evening Mail*

If the Giants are legislated out of the championship of the National League, it will make more American League fans in this city than the Yankees have ever converted. Hundreds of New York fans have sworn they will never set foot on the Polo Grounds again if this travesty is allowed. The sporting editor of the *Globe* has received scores of letters on this subject. The following is a fair sample of how the fans feel:

Dear Sir—Put me on record!

If the Giants lose the pennant through the yellow claims of Charles Murphy, Evers, Chance, et al., I will never attend another game played by National League clubs.

I am not an American League or a National League "fan," but a baseball enthusiast who insists on fair play, common sense and the elimination of politics.

There is a new major league forming!

If the National League is so enmeshed in politics that a "technicality" wins a pennant, fair play, common sense, and justice no longer prevail.

By all means endorse the withdrawal of McGraw and his game players from the National League to the new major league that is just forming so that the many fans who would never patronize a league so dishonest as the National League would be given an opportunity to still encourage and applaud McGraw and the Giants. {The "new major league," the Federal League, began operating in 1914 and lasted for two seasons.}

—New York *Globe*

In the personal column of the want ad section of the *Tribune* this morning appears the following paid advertisement:

"Personal. Wanted. Heavy rain at the Polo Grounds, New York, on the afternoon of Wednesday, Oct. 7." {Rain would eliminate the Giants' final game and prevent them from finishing in a tie with the Cubs.}

—Chicago *Tribune*

———◇ **WEDNESDAY, OCTOBER 7** ◇———

{On October 6, in New York, the Giants beat Boston 4 to 1. Winning pitcher, Wiltse; losing pitcher, Ferguson. Giants' standing: 97 wins, 55 losses, in second place.}

After two days of deliberation the National League Board of Directors reached a conclusion yesterday afternoon in the matter of the disputed game of September 23. The directors upheld the decision of the umpires and of President Harry C. Pulliam and declared the game a tie. They ordered it to be played off at the Polo Grounds tomorrow afternoon, or as soon thereafter as the weather will permit. Though the decision stretches the league constitution slightly, by extending the season beyond the date set by the regular schedule, the directors felt it was no more than fair to both clubs that this important contest be played off, and in this decision they have the baseball public with them.

A remarkable state of affairs may result from this decision, and that is the possibility that three clubs may be tied for first place by tomorrow night. This condition will arise if New York loses to Boston today and beats the Cubs tomorrow. In that case the Cubs, Giants, and Pirates will be tied for first place, and a three-cornered series will be necessary to determine the winner of the flag. There would have to be some tall hustling to get the Pirates together again to play off a triple series, which would take at least nine days, and would delay the start of the world's series until late in October.

The claim of Chicago that it was entitled to a forfeit was not allowed for reasons made perfectly clear. President Charles W. Murphy was very much disappointed over this, but after a conference with Manager Chance he issued this statement:

"We will play them Thursday and we'll lick 'em too. We'll make it so decisive that no bone-headed baserunning can cast a shadow of doubt on the contest. We want to win the championship on the playing field. Manager Chance and his players are in good condition and will have no excuse if we fail to bring the third successive National League pennant to Chicago."

The decision of the directors {in part} is as follows:

"There can be no question but that the game should have been won by New York had it not been for the reckless, careless, inexcusable blunder of one player, Merkle. In order that a run could have been scored the following rule applied {Rule 59, presented earlier, is now quoted}.

"This rule is plain, explicit and cannot be misconstrued. While it may not have been complied with in many other games, it did not deprive the Chicago club of the right to do so if it so be desired, notwithstanding that it might be termed winning or tying a game on a technicality.

"Merkle should have had only one thing on his mind, to reach second base in safety. The evidence clearly shows the following: After Bridwell hit the ball he ran to and over first base; McCormick started for home and crossed the plate; Merkle started for second and when about halfway to the base turned and ran in the direction of the clubhouse without having reached second base. Emslie was officiating back of the pitcher, O'Day back of the catcher. When the hit was made Emslie fell to the ground to escape being hit by the ball; he got up and watched the play at first base and saw the batter had run out his hit. In the meantime the ball was fielded in by Hofman and eventually fielded to second base to Evers for a put-out on Merkle. Tinker notified Emslie that Merkle did not run to second base. Emslie stated he did not see the play; and then went to his colleague, O'Day, and asked him whether he had seen the play. O'Day answered in the affirmative, and then Emslie asked whether Merkle had run to second, and being informed that he had not, Emslie declared Merkle out. It may appear as rather peculiar that Umpire O'Day should have been watching the play at second. For this reason, we quote from O'Day's testimony:

" 'Mr. Murphy: I would like to ask you, Mr. O'Day, if the matter at Pittsburgh had caused you to anticipate a play of this sort?'

" 'Mr. O'Day: Yes, sir; and I came within an ace to tell Bob {Emslie}, but I thought I had no right by actions to tell the players what to do or to give them an inkling of what I thought.'

"To set aside an umpire's decision by evidence from persons in attendance, would, in our mind, be establishing a bad and dangerous precedent. In this case, however, there is not a single line or word of testimony offered by the New York club that could even by inference be construed to mean that Merkle reached second base at any time, excepting the affidavit of the player himself, which was not made until after Mr. Pulliam had passed on the case. We can, therefore, come to no other conclusion than that the New York club lost a well-earned victory as the result of a stupid play of one of its members.

"Query was submitted as to why the umpires did not proceed with the game after they had decided that Merkle was out and the game was a tie. In answer to this query both umpires contend it was growing dark very rapidly, and that there was the utmost confusion and uproar on the grounds; that it would have been an impossibility to clear the grounds in time to proceed with the game. We believe the umpires acted wisely under the extraordinary circumstances and conditions in calling the game when they did.

"Coming to the appeal made by the Chicago club. This, to our mind, should not be given any consideration. If there was a violation of the constitution by the New York club in having failed to play off a tie game on the only available date, the Chicago club is to be blamed. On the night of the game in question the Chicago club filed a claim with Mr. Pulliam for a forfeiture. This claim on their part tied the hands of the president and prevented the playing off of the game on the following day. Also on the day after the game in question the New York club conferred with Mr. Pulliam and asked him whether they would be required to play off the tied game and were told that they would not be required to do so. By this action the New York club clearly indicated they were ready to play off the game if required to do so.

"We hold that the New York club should in all justice and fairness be given a chance to play off the game in question. For that reason we order that the game be played on the Polo Grounds on Thursday, October 8, or as soon thereafter as weather conditions will permit."

—Jack Ryder, Cincinnati *Enquirer*

Beating Boston again the Giants won the second of three games necessary to enable them to tie Chicago.

Ferguson pitched great ball against his old team for five innings, but a good mixture of luck and timely hitting gave the Giants the lead in the sixth inning, and in the seventh they made sure of the game by scoring three runs. Wiltse would have shut Boston out had it not been for Seymour's muff of a short fly in the eighth.

—New York *Tribune*

Manager Frank Chance and the nearly-champion Cubs, accompanied by President Murphy, will leave for New York this afternoon on the Twentieth Century Limited.

Chance and his teammates, who had expected nothing worse than a series of three games against the Giants in the event the latter won all three games from Boston, as now seems probable, were incensed at the action of the triumvirate compelling them to play one game on the home field of their rivals.

In the heat of his anger Chance told of alleged actions and words of President Ebbets of Brooklyn, one of the men who gave the Cincinnati decision.

"Ebbets was not qualified to pass on our case," said Chance. "He is prejudiced and would surely give us the worst of it. Before the last Chicago series against Brooklyn Ebbets called his whole team together and told them he wanted the men to play their hardest against us and that he would see that any player playing 'soft ball' was barred from baseball for the rest of his career. That was all right, but when he added he hoped the Giants would win the pennant he gave his players a hunch the point of which cannot be overlooked.

"On another occasion Mr. Ebbets went so far as to say to a friend that he was sorry he did not let the crowd kill me at the time of my trouble in Brooklyn last year when fans threw pop bottles at me and I was saved from serious injury or even death only by a police guard."

—Harvey T. Woodruff, Chicago *Tribune*

CINCINNATI, Oct. 6—President C. W. Murphy, of the Chicago club, is not satisfied with the decision of the National League directors.

"The decision makes the tangle worse than before," said he, "and throws open the pennant race to a possible victory for all three of the leading teams, when the Giants were legally out of the race last Sunday. The Giants were given as much as possible the best of it without giving them the game direct."

{If required to play the Giants, Murphy and Chance wanted a three-game series, as provided in the National League constitution for pennant playoffs. The Giant-Cub game would not, however, be a playoff game, which occurs after two or more teams have tied at the end of the season, but the replaying of a regularly scheduled contest which had ended in a tie. On two other occasions in 1908, July 28 and August 5, Giant games ended in a tie and were replayed.} —New York *American*

There is a deep well-founded opinion among the majority of Manhattan lovers of baseball that the New York club should refuse to play off a game that has once been rightfully won by all the ethics and precedents of honest baseball.

The New York club, or rather those officials now in the city, Manager McGraw and Secretary Knowles, are personally "dead set" against giving Charley Murphy or the Cubs a chance to gather in any more New York money or giving the Cubs the unfair opportunity of having another try at the pennant they have rightfully been beaten out of, according to President Pulliam's previous decision on a like play when he decided that games should be won on the diamond.

But Manager McGraw and Secretary Knowles, putting aside personal feelings, rightfully consider that the players of the team, who have been deprived of what rightfully belongs to them, should decide what they will do in the unfortunate dilemma that has been thrown up to them.

President Brush is on the road from Cincinnati, and the whole situation is of necessity left to him to decide.

In earlier days of baseball there was a sentiment attached to the national game that made games take on the appearance of a real battle between cities and sections, but sentiment no longer figures in the sport. It is now only a battle of dollars. The business end of baseball has so superseded the real sport that used to cause legitimate and honest rivalry for sport's sake alone I personally wouldn't care if the whole foundation of the national game went to the dogs. And this bluff of Charley Murphy of beating out the Giants on a game fairly won—and getting away with it— shows conclusively that baseball is not as it used to be, when "Old Uncle Nick" Young, a man who really loved the game, was president of the grand "old" league. You see that I say "old." The "new" dispensers of rules and regulations by which the great national game is conducted I have no use for.

Charley Murphy and Barney Dreyfuss—bah and bah again. And Charley Ebbets, booh! and bah!! Mr. Ebbets is from Brooklyn, the city that has coined more money out of Manhattan fans in the last few years with a tail-end team than any Brooklyn magnate would have even dared to do. Those much-vaunted $20,000 improvements made on Washington Park last Spring have been paid for by money Manhattan fans paid by reason of the most favorable schedule that the schedule-making Mr. Ebbets could make to give the Brooklyn club the advantage of holiday dates with this same New York club he voted against.

Mr. Charley Ebbets, in my opinion, has not feathered his nest in Brooklyn a little bit by the Giants losing the game that rightfully belongs to them.

I am sore, and I acknowledge it, over that decision.

It may be that the ones who robbed the Giants out of the game may say their president must be upheld for the good of the game, and President Pulliam will, of course, uphold his umpires for the same reason, but that does not excuse the fact that Umpire O'Day made an overnight decision and sent in a report the next morning directly contrary to what he told me after the disputed game was played.

No matter what technical construction has been put on rules, the Giants fairly and honestly won the disputed game, and the mushy weak-kneed straddle the Board of Directors made on their decision showed to me conclusively that they really thought the game belonged to the Giants rightfully and were ashamed of the final conclusion they arrived at. They should be, anyhow.　　　　　—Sam Crane, New York *Evening Journal*

———◇ WEDNESDAY, OCTOBER 8 ◇———

{On October 7, in New York, the Giants beat Boston 7 to 2. Winning pitcher, Ames; losing pitcher, Flaherty. Giants' standing: 98 wins, 55 losses, tied for first place with Chicago.}

The Giants brought their wonderful fight for the pennant to an end, so far as the regular season goes, by winning the third straight game from Boston.

Just at the start it looked as if Boston, in a dying gasp, was to make a triple tie possible by beating the Giants, but after the first inning Ames pitched as no one imagined he would ever learn to do, and, backed by some fielding that was startling in its brilliancy, kept the visitors from getting near the plate. He helped to win the game with his batting, too, delighting the crowd by smashing out two pretty singles.

　　　　　　　　　　　　　　　　　　—New York *Tribune*

The most bitterly contested championship race in the National League's history will reach a climax this afternoon. When John T. Brush arrived home yesterday morning from the directors' meeting in Cincinnati it did not take him long to announce that the New York club had consented to play the game, and the momentous battle will begin at 3 o'clock.　　　　　　　　　　　　—New York *Sun*

Mathewson was anxious yesterday to pitch against Boston as well as against the Cubs today, but McGraw had faith in Ames and saved his star. Mathewson warmed up a little yesterday and looked strong and rested. He has not pitched since Saturday, and the rest, the longest he has had for weeks, seems to have done him lots of good. At his best, Mathewson should be able to win. If he should be hit hard, however, McGraw might call on Ames to relieve him, as the latter saved himself yesterday and got through the game without undue effort. Wiltse, too, will be on the bench, and McGinnity, Taylor, Crandall, Marquard, and Durham are other New York pitchers in reserve. —New York *Tribune*

Never before have two teams been tied at the end of a season. Never before has the race been so close. Never has it been necessary to play off the tie of six months' baseball in a single gigantic battle.

That the game will be a struggle to the death is certain. The town is in the grip of the greatest excitement, fringed with nervous prostration. It is rumored that several sanitariums are constructing additions to take care of baseball "bugs" resulting from the last few weeks of the campaign.

Tonight there may be rejoicing and the blare of trumpets in the streets, the burning of colored fire and the shooting of skyrockets. There may be a display of crepe, the wearing of mourning, and the strains of a funeral dirge. There may be nine heroes or nine corpses up at the Polo Grounds. Whether the city will be gay with a rejoicing crowd or plunged in sadness depends entirely on the outcome of the game.

—New York *Herald*

While the players will not participate in the financial returns of to-day's game, members of the winning team will receive about $2,000 each as the result of the games for the world's championship which follow. The contest will therefore be for a $40,000 stake for the players, and an almost equal amount for the owner of the winning club.

The management, knowing the ardor of the enthusiasts, threw out a strong cordon of watchmen last night to prevent the bleachers from filling up overnight. About a dozen extra men were strung out about the fence on the inside of the grounds, and they spent most of the night digging small boys from under seats and the grandstand, and repelling those attempting to climb the fence under cover of darkness.

The final round-up will come with daylight. It is expected that every nook and corner will give up youngsters and perhaps older but just as enthusiastic fans.   —New York *Times*

Despite the mandates of Governor Hughes and civic authorities, more money will be bet on the game than has been wagered in the old town since the lid was put on horse racing. The West is well represented, and in true Western fashion is backing the Cubs to the limit. Several large personal wagers were laid last night at even money. In all probability the Giants will be a 10 to 9 favorite, for the unlimited financial strength of an overwhelming home following is bound in time to stop the outsiders. Gotham is loyal to its team, and, though holding out for even money, is doing so in nowise through fear of the ultimate outcome. Everyone in this city has unlimited faith in McGraw, in Mathewson and in each and every individual on the Giant roster.

—W. J. McBeth, New York *American*

Manager Frank Chance and the Cubs, overflowing with confidence, are speeding toward New York on the fastest train ever taken by a baseball club. They will arrive on Manhattan island this morning shortly after their Chicago admirers have finished breakfast.

As the hopes of local fandom climbed aboard the Twentieth Century Limited at the Lake Shore Station yesterday afternoon they were given a rousing reception by several hundred fanatics who had assembled to pay homage.

Sixteen players composed the party, in addition to President Murphy, Treasurer Williams and newspaper correspondents. The distinguished guests were assigned to a special car, which significantly was placed by railroad officials just before the diner.

The expense of the trip, one way, will be about $600, an extra item of about $200 on account of taking the limited. Baseball teams making the trips on regular trains with a 28-hour schedule are given the usual ten-party rate of $18.75. Passage on the limited requires a straight rate of $20, with an extra fare of $10 per person, so the excess cost figures $11.75 each for the party of 18. Berths and meals are about the same, though Johnny Evers figured that a person ought to eat faster on such a fast train.

But the item of expense, which cuts 10 hours off the running schedule, and appears picayune in comparison with the New York money Mr. Murphy will bring home as the Cubs' share of the receipts, was the last thing Chance or any of the players were thinking of. In small groups they stood around, talking with friends or one another, and baseball was the only topic.

Jack Pfiester is chosen in advance by Manager Chance to occupy the slab in the crucial game as the New Yorkers have been found less effective against the sidewheel delivery. Left-handed Jack has been successful in his last efforts against the chesty Giants.

If the star southpaw shows signs of weakening, or if a tense situation arises where heart and nerves of iron are required, Brown, three-fingered Mordecai, who destroyed the Pirates' hopes last Sunday, stands ready and anxious to jump into the breach.

—Harvey T. Woodruff, Chicago *Tribune*

The *Tribune* will show Cubs vs. Giants game on Electrical Baseball Board at Orchestra Hall today. For the benefit Tribune Hospital Fund. Seats now on sale at box office, Orchestra Hall, and 326 Tribune Building. Admission 25 cents and 50 cents, box seats $1.

—Advertisement, Chicago *Tribune*

When the largest crowd ever gathered in the world for a sporting event—fully a quarter of a million—were surging in and around the Polo Grounds, the occasion was marred by a fatality.

Losing his balance as he hung on to a pillar of the elevated structure at Eighth avenue and 159th street, a man supposed to be Henry T. McBride, a fireman, fell and was instantly killed. The man was on the structure in order to look over the fence at the game.

Hardly had the man breathed his last when there surged forward a score or more frantic in their daring just to get a glimpse inside the grounds, who vainly endeavored to climb up on the pillar, in falling from which McBride had just died.

Only the vigorous use of clubs by the police cleared a small circle around the dead man and kept others from climbing the pillar.

In the terrible jam in the bleachers, Edward Wheeler, 34 years old, a restaurant keeper from Brooklyn, either fell or was pushed from the top seat on the grandstand and fell to the ground, about 15 feet. His right leg was broken and he was badly cut and bruised.

The estimate of 250,000 in and around the field is, if anything, below the actual figures. There were fully twice as many persons immediately outside the fence around the grounds as there were inside, and every foothold and balancing handhold on structures of every kind with even a glimpse of the grounds was fiercely held against any newcomer.

From the press box the skyline everywhere was human heads. They were located on grandstand, roofs, fences, "L" structures, electric light poles and in the distance on smokestacks, chimneys, advertising signs and copings of apartment houses.

On the viaduct, the Speedway and cliffs back of the grandstand there was practically a solid mass of people. The partially completed addition to the grandstand, converted from a section of the bleachers to the north, seated 2,500.

A four-car "L" train which stood on a siding by the grounds, affording a fine view of the whole amphitheater, and which was covered inside and on the roofs, was suddenly moved out by the railroad company, and the fans were carried rapidly downtown.

Commissioner Bingham had placed all the police arrangements in the hands of Inspector James F. Thompson. He had 300 policemen and five mounted men under him. Fifty special policemen were also hired by the baseball management.

There was something fascinating in watching the filling of the picture by the constantly growing inpour of people. Every possible vantage point, however precarious, came to have its human cluster. The unusual number of women gave relieving touches of color here and there. And in the center of it all, in the middle foreground, the empty diamond.

Half a dozen ambulances came along and were sent inside the grounds, each loaded with doctors. People besieged the ambulances, some offering as much as five dollars to be taken aboard.

At 12:45, two and a quarter hours before the game would begin, orders came out to the police in front of the Polo Grounds to close the gate as the grounds were jammed to their utmost capacity.

Meanwhile hordes kept coming in every conceivable kind of conveyance. Every surface car that crept up to 155th street had dozens hanging on whatever a hand could find an inch to grip, not to speak of many lying flat on the roofs of cars with only a few inches between their heads and the elevated structure.

As for the elevated railroad, it is safe to say that today's traffic broke all records in its enormity.

Inside the grounds trouble started early and every few minutes one of the gates would be slightly parted and another battered citizen would emerge to be conveyed to the West 153d street police station by a husky bluecoat. Many of those inside tried to get out to meet friends for whom they had bought tickets, but as the only chance of getting out was to be arrested they stayed in.

The Cubs made no demonstration in coming to the Polo Grounds. One by one they dropped off the "L" train, quietly made their way to the clubhouse of visiting players and put on their uniforms. Most of them were unnoticed by the crowd, who failed to recognize the players in street garb.

When two o'clock came and there was no sign that the gates would again open to the tens of thousands packed in Eighth avenue many small-sized riots, started by various fights, followed. Most were brought about when a gullible person would buy a ticket from a speculator down at 155th street, only to find when he had struggled half a block further north that there his journey ended.

He would then wriggle back toward the speculator and if he could get near enough to him would invariably take a swing at him. But the speculators kept right on selling—and fighting. They were getting such prices that they could afford to throw in a little fight with each ticket.

The inevitable comic side of such gatherings was not long in eventuating. Some ingenious person conceived the idea of bridging the space between the elevated structure and the Polo Grounds fence with a plank up at about 158th street, and it was not long before there was a crowd rushing to buy downtown "L" tickets only to walk up the track and "walk the plank," dropping over the fence into the grounds. Naturally, the guards inside soon lined up at the dropping place and escorted intruders rather forcibly to the nearest "chute," through which they were unceremoniously jammed back into the crowd outside. Finally an officer of the elevated railroad appeared with a club and put a stop to that traffic on the first plank, but immediately another appeared 50 feet away, which a strapping big negro had spanned from the drop pan under the "L" to the fence.   —New York *Evening Telegram*

Police Commissioner Bingham has given orders that the crowd must be kept off the field for at least three minutes after the game, giving the players time to escape to the clubhouse. This precaution has been taken on account of the riot that followed the famous game of Sept. 23.
                                                            —Chicago *News*

Merkle's best chance to go down in baseball history is for the Giants to lose today. At least a dozen persons will then remember him for life.
                                        —John E. Wray, St. Louis *Post-Dispatch*

If the Cubs don't win the pennant—tragedy! Despair, insanity, suicide, coroner's inquest, and a new chapter in baseball history.

That is the prophecy of Coroner Peter M. Hoffman in speaking of some fans who go the extremity of being irrational.

"To tell the truth I shouldn't be surprised if we had a suicide or two right here in this office," the coroner added. "One of my deputies, I am sure, will commit suicide if the Cubs don't win."
                                                            —Chicago *Tribune*

You never saw such a sore lot of losers to grace the big town these lovely autumn days. There is all sorts of silly trash to be read in the yellow newspapers about the Cubs, the Pirates, and Harry Pulliam's decision, and the long-nosed rooters who have made the Polo Grounds this summer look like the market place in Jerusalem are simply devouring the stuff like so many hungry wolves. We are told that the Cubs and Chubby Murphy are cheap sports and skinflints who are winning games on suspicion. We are also informed that Barney Dreyfuss controls the entire situation and can make Pulliam dance a jig. Furthermore we are solemnly tipped off that if the league's directors do not hand the pennant to McGraw's men, John Tooth Brush will take his club to the American League, bag and baggage.

Nobody seems to be fair enough to realize that the Giants have been lucky to stay with the leaders so long. Had it not been for Mathewson and Wiltse, the Giants would have been where Philadelphia is. As far as team play goes, the Giants never classed with the Cubs, who, despite many accidents, have risen to the top by dint of superb ball playing.

—Joe Vila, The Sporting News

———◇ THURSDAY, OCTOBER 9 ◇———

{On October 8, in New York, the Chicago Cubs won the National League championship of 1908 by beating the Giants 4 to 2. Winning pitcher, Brown; losing pitcher, Mathewson.}

One terrible inning brought the Giants the sting of final defeat after a season of glorious struggling in the face of every possible discouragement and handicap. Fighting for a pennant already won, as far as baseball on the field is concerned, it was the fate of McGraw's gallant band to lose the crucial struggle through the wavering for a moment of the great pitcher whose splendid skill and still more splendid courage have done so much to make this the most wonderful fight the game of baseball has ever known.

It lacked 15 minutes of 3 o'clock when Klem called play in the struggle on which the attention of the whole nation was centered. As warm as on a perfect August day, with a blue sky above, conditions could not have been more perfect. Fifty thousand pairs of eyes were focused on the field where the tense gray players of Chicago, fighting to lead the league for the third time, awaited the issue, and fifty times that many gazed at bulletin boards, at tickers, at electric boards that showed every play, and at other countless devices waiting all over the country to carry the instant word of the fight from the living, throbbing wires that began at the ends of nervous fingers in the press box.

Sheckard faced "Matty" for the first ball of the game, and a great sigh—the tension was too great for a cheer—went up as Klem's raised hand flashed a strike. A moment later tense tongues loosed in a mighty roar as Sheckard swung wildly at a slow, floating ball and went back to the bench. Two strikes were quickly called on Evers, and then he shot a bounding hit to Herzog, which was thrown to Tenney for the second out. Schulte was the next man, and Mathewson, exulting in his strength, struck him out.

It was a superb start, and when the first ball that Pfiester pitched hit Tenney on the arm a great roar of joy filled the air. Herzog walked on four balls, and the crowd fairly shrieked at Bresnahan for a hit. But the third strike fooled the great catcher completely, and Herzog, foolishly dancing off first base, was thrown out by the deadly arm of Kling, completing a play that may have cost the game. Donlin was next up, and when he smashed the ball down the right field foul line for two bases the crowd was lost in such transports of joy as Tenney scored that it could hardly take the time to hoot Chance for shrieking that the ball was a foul.

Then came a base on balls to Seymour, and after a long conference Chance sent for Brown, and Pfiester walked sadly to the bench. The crowd went wild with joy, but its rapture was short lived, as the three-fingered pitcher ended the inning and a great chance to break up the game by striking Devlin out.

Chance whipped a single to left to start the next inning, but a lightning throw by Matty caught the Chicago manager off first base, and the roar from Chance on the decision seemed likely for a moment to break up the game. He argued with Johnstone for five minutes, and the umpire threatened twice to put him off the field—which he would have been justified in doing. Chance came back wringing his hands, and Hofman, waiting his turn at bat, threw his bat on the ground. He had said nothing, but his act was evidently thought more serious than his manager's unless it is that Klem is made of sterner stuff than Johnstone, for the doughty umpire behind the bat ordered Chicago's centerfielder off the grounds. Then Steinfeldt and Howard, who had replaced Hofman, struck out.

Schulte helped Brown in the second inning by two fine catches in right field, the second, of a hard drive by Bridwell, being a really great play. Tinker gave more help by a fine stop of Matty's hard grounder, and all was ready for the tragedy that was to turn wild joy and rosy hopes into gloom.

Here was Tinker, swinging the mighty bat that had so often made trouble for Mathewson, and once more he swung it with fatal effect. Matty had looked around as he prepared to pitch, and waved his fielders back, but Seymour had paid no heed, and as Tinker smashed the ball far away to left center, Seymour saw his fatal error even as he raced back. He made a great leap for the ball, but just missed a catch that would have been easy had he been ten feet further back.

Tinker was safe on third when the ball came back and almost walked home when Kling singled viciously to left. Brown sacrificed, and Sheckard raised a fly that Seymour caught, being where he belonged this time. On such small things do great issues hang. Had Seymour been ten feet further back and taken Tinker's fly, the inning, and the game, would have ended with Sheckard's fly, without a score. But, as it was, there was still a man to be put out, and before he had been retired, Evers had walked and Schulte and Chance had doubled, sending in three more runs and winning the game, as it turned out.

Gloom was in the crowd everywhere, but not on the New York bench. Matty had been hit hard, but McGraw refused to take him out, and his confidence was fully justified in the four innings Matty was still to pitch.

The Giants tried too hard to come back in their third inning. Tenney began with a clean single, the first hit off Brown, and after Herzog had fouled to Kling, Bresnahan planted the ball into right field for another safety. But Donlin could only force Bresnahan at second, and Seymour sent a groan through the crowd with a fly to Sheckard.

Then it was a procession to and from the bat until the sixth inning, when both nines were active. Chance drove out his third hit—he was the only man on either side with more than one hit—but Bresnahan caught him stealing with a perfect throw to Herzog. Steinfeldt also singled, but Howard struck out again.

Agony was piled on agony when New York came up for the seventh time. With the crowd shrieking for the "lucky" seventh to work its spell, Devlin faced Brown and drove out as pretty a single as was ever made. McCormick followed with another safe drive, and when Bridwell walked, filling the bases, with none out, an explosion of dynamite would not have been heard.

Mathewson was the next man up, and the crowd groaned when

McGraw sent Doyle to bat for him. It was strange that he should do so, for Matty is a strong batter, and Doyle has not faced an opposing pitcher in a big game since he was hurt weeks ago. Doyle hit a high foul that fell into Kling's hands. Tenney sent a run home with a long sacrifice fly, but two men were left on base when Tinker threw Herzog out and New York's best chance was gone.

Wiltse finished the game, and only a great play by McCormick saved a run in the eighth. Evers had doubled with one out and gone to third when Tenney's error left Schulte safe at first base. Chance drove a fly to McCormick, and, after a great catch, McCormick made a superb throw to the plate that enabled Bresnahan to put Evers out.

New York could do nothing in the last two innings, and four pitched balls in the ninth disposed of Devlin, McCormick, and Bridwell. Chicago had won the game and the pennant.   —New York *Tribune*

NEW YORK, Oct. 8.—All honor will be given the Cubs as long as baseball is played, for what they did this afternoon in the shadow of Coogan's Bluff. They won not only decisively but cleanly and gamely, while their adversaries attempted to take cheap and tricky advantage of them in every way. The world's champions were compelled even to fight for the privilege of getting the meager practice allowed by the rules before the game.

Nor was defeat and loss of the pennant New York's only disgrace, for the crowd contained at least one man who will be remembered to Gotham's discredit as long as Merkle. That is the dastard who sneaked up behind Manager Chance as the Cubs were leaving the scene of victory and struck him a blow in the neck.

Before the Cub manager could wheel to defend himself the coward had been swallowed up in the tremendous throng. A hurried examination of the manager at the dressing room by a surgeon in attendance disclosed that the assailant probably had broken a cartilage in Chance's neck but it was not expected that the injury would keep him out of the world's series battles.

To Mordecai Brown will belong the lion's share of credit for Chicago's third pennant—to Mordecai and Joe Tinker. It was the mighty three-fingered star who pitched both of the crucial and "final" games of the year. It was the fleet-footed and scrappy shortstop who led the Cubs in that terrific unbeatable assault in the third inning which nailed the game to Chicago's flagpole and broke the back of the great Mathewson.

The game was preceded by a bit of petty trickery by the Giants which probably had much to do with prompting the cowardly slugging which was handed Manager Chance at the close.

The crowd was so great it compelled locking the gates long before time to start the game, and it was decided not to wait until 3 o'clock, as everybody who could get inside was there already.

But the 15 minutes gained in time was taken out of the Cubs' practice. The Giants took their full allotment of 20 minutes for batting practice, then when the Cubs started on their practice they were stopped at the end of five minutes. Chance objected to this after his club had traveled 1,000 miles and had no other opportunity to limber up. As McGinnity stepped to the plate under orders to begin knocking grounders to the Giants for fielding practice Chance tried to brush him away, and the "Iron Man" raised his bat threateningly.

For an instant it looked the beginning of a riot, which would forever have disgraced the game, but other players of both teams rushed in and surrounded the belligerents, smoothing out the incident quickly. When the thing was explained to Chance there was nothing for him to do but smile contemptuously at the trick and acquiesce. The Cubs proved later they didn't need the other 15 minutes of batting practice.

—I. E. Sanborn, Chicago *Tribune*

If we turn the clock back to about an hour or two before the game begins we note that some of the boxes still remain vacant. This is because the ticket holders are in the street trying vainly to get inside. But up there in her usual place leaning over the rail is little Mabel Hite, wife of Mike Donlin.

Everybody is happy and hopeful, for the game hasn't begun yet, and it is frequently stated and never disputed that this is the limit for baseball enthusiasm. It's also the greatest ever, outer sight or big casino, according to who is telling you. And if you listen to Clayton Hamilton, who writes books to which Brander Matthews, the greatest Simple Speller in captivity, writes introductions, you learn that the Polo Grounds are "really the thematic centre of the cosmic scheme," whatever that may be. {In 1908 Clayton Hamilton was the 27-year-old drama critic of the magazine *Forum*; he would become a highly regarded playwright and critic. In 1908 Matthews was professor of dramatic literature at Columbia University and was a distinguished writer of drama, fiction, and criticism.} All this time everybody and everything is getting cheered and pelted with wads of newspaper.

A fat man comes into the right-field bleachers carrying a baby who may yet grow up to be a pitcher like Matty. He is cheered frantically and he grabs the kid with one hand and waves at the crowd with the other. Pretty girls are cheered, homely girls are cheered, fat men, thin men, tall men, short men, the girl with a hat as big as three of Fred Tenney's mitts—anything and everything for a cheer.

Now a couple of players reserved from the minor leagues appear from the clubhouse and begin to throw the ball around the diamond that has only recently been uncovered. Uncovered from what? Why, from the huge canvas sheets that have been spread on it all night. They put the diamond to bed early the night before so that it would get a good night's rest for the game of all games.

Smiling Larry Doyle, who was the Giants' regular second baseman until he hurt his leg a month ago, is the first of the regulars to show. He gets many cheers.

And then from the clubhouse emerges a melancholy figure. Shall we say it is the figure of the man who lost the pennant? Well, anyhow, it's the figure of Fred Merkle, and everybody knows that if he'd run to second when Bridwell made that safe hit at the end of the now famous disputed game the pennant would be waving from the flagstaff in center field. Amid a silence that cuts, Merkle crosses the field and begins to toss a ball about. It's clear that he feels worse than anybody else about it. Nobody has the heart to jeer him. But all the same——

Suddenly several thousand persons are released from durance and allowed to scamper to standing room behind the ropes all about the field. It looks like the serpentine dance after a victory for the Blue on Yale Field. A moment ago the field was green; now it's black.

There aren't enough real cops to boss a lively Sunday school class, and how the deuce things are ever going to be straightened out doesn't appear, unless you've been there before and know that when the umpire is ready for play the field will clear itself like magic. Everybody begins to get happily restless, and one fan says to another, "Boy, you'll be able to tell your grandchildren about this day when the Cubs—or——" Fearful of the outcome he rubs his chin doubtfully and doesn't finish.

"Robber!" "Bandit!" "Quitter!" howls the crowd all at once. The row begins in the right-field bleachers and runs all over the field as Frank Chance appears from the clubhouse, loafing carelessly along on his bowed legs and looking as if he hadn't a care in the world. Roars, hoots, hisses, jeers are showered on him as he advances, but he smiles pleasantly as if the freedom of the city had been conferred on him. Just behind him comes Three-Fingered Brown. He is also called a number of things which he isn't. He doesn't seem to mind either.

But there's a greater uproar yet when John McGraw shows up, accompanied by the lean and haggard Tenney, and the New York manager has to doff his cap before the row lets up. One by one the rest of the Giants appear.

The New Yorks take batting practice methodically, one hit to each man. Then the Cubs go in for theirs. More roars, more hisses, more catcalls, howls of contempt, shrieks of "Oh, you robbers! You brigands!" And you think if you were a Cub you'd hunt the nearest cyclone cellar. But the Cubs wallop the horsehide as cheerfully as if the stands were empty. Meanwhile the jeers keep on. Somebody in the stand catches a foul tip from a Cub's bat. A hundred voices shout: "Keep it! Keep it! Don't give it back! Murphy will cry his eyes out if you keep it."

Meantime the twirlers are warming up, Pfiester, the left-hander, for the Cubs, and the only Matty for the Giants. This doesn't take long and at a quarter of three o'clock the real trouble begins. It is time.

—New York *Sun*

Never before has the capacity of Coogan's Bluff been strained beyond the limit as it was yesterday. Never before have veteran hillbillies, who have worn the grass out in their accustomed places, been rudely shoved aside by strangers and vandals occupying their favorite spots. Every hillbillie tradition was ruthlessly ripped to shreds by the pushing thousands, and Coogan's was no longer the Coogan's of other days.

By 2 o'clock Coogan's was loaded to the gunnels and the tens of thousands stretched along the entire semi-circle from the Jumel Mansion {the celebrated, still existent manor house built in 1765 at 160th Street and Edgecombe Avenue} to Eighth avenue. For nearly a mile there was a mass of people lining stairs, viaducts, streets, Speedway, bluffs, crags, rocks, peaks, grass, plots, trees, and any other available space not previously occupied.

The view from Coogan's was gorgeous and beggared description. It was one of those perfect October days which so seldom come when you want them, and the scene was like a Turner picture {a reference to the English landscape painter J. M. W. Turner (1775–1851)}. The broad bosom of the Harlem River palpitated in the Autumn glow, the hazy blue of the Bronx draped the towering palaces along the heights overlooking the silver stream, the city to the south stretched away into limitless azure, the bargains in real estate along Edgecombe avenue littered on their sacred sites, while at the foot of the bluff the eye rested on the gleaming billboards at the far end of the Polo Grounds.

If 35,000 were inside the fence, 35,000,000 were outside—the way they covered the ground and the roofs—but probably not so many as that. Never in the history of the game have there been so many to see a game who didn't see it. The standees had the call and no mistake. There were hundreds of women on the bluff, and one woman had brought her knitting along, and calmly sat on the grass and knitted while the pennant went to Chicago. She must have been a Chicago woman. Up on the lawn of the Jumel Mansion was a group of spectators. Somebody said George Washington, Aaron Burr, and Mme. Jumel were among those present. A society reporter (lady) from Brooklyn made a note of it. The enthusiasm was immense and intense, and soon soap boxes and other coigns of vantage began to appear at the back of the firing line along the bluff. Anything over two inches rented for 25 cents, and 10 cents an inch above that. Along the road, back of the bluff, delivery wagons, cabs, and automobiles lined the curb. Persons occupying them had a fine view of the backs of the front row. It was inspiring.

A little dumpy man, who couldn't see above the hip pocket of the men in front of him, said he was going home. Immediately there were cries of "Lynch him! He's a quitter!" and other personal remarks of a similar nature. He apologized and stayed till the game was over.

After a while—two hours after a while—somebody in front announced the game had begun. A hush fell on the throng on Coogan's Bluff. Every breath was baited. Never in the history of the game had there been such a moment. It sounded like a pork packer's cheer for Upton Sinclair {whose most famous novel, *The Jungle*, an exposé of the Chicago stockyards, had appeared in 1906}.

—W. J. Lampton, New York *Times*

Manager Frank Chance of the Cubs was assaulted twice yesterday. As if the blow Joe McGinnity handed him before the game was not sufficient, a frenzied fan had to inflict even more serious injury on the belligerent, hustling leader of the Chicago team.

Immediately after the failure of the Giants to score in the ninth, and it was all over but the shouting for the Cubs, Chance, with Pitcher Pfiester and Catcher Kling, started for the clubhouse. The trio kept their eyes on the crowd piling out of the east end of the big stand and out of the right-field bleachers. The policemen on duty were also apprehensive and closed around Chance and his teammates.

A fan who was scarlet from excitement and wrath bowled over two cops and let loose a right-hand swing to Chance's chin. Chance threw up his head quickly and the blow caught him flush in the neck. He went down to his knees and gasped for breath. While policemen were fighting the crowd back, someone landed a stinger on Pfiester's right jaw, staggering him. Johnny Kling fought like a Trojan for his teammates and his own skin.

A horde of policemen closed in around the three Chicago players and dragged them through the crowd like a football team rushing the men with the ball over the line. The uniformed officers found their clubs ineffective against the press of the howling mob, and revolvers were drawn. This seemed to stop the rush, for the mob stood back.

Chance and his two fellow-players were literally catapulted over and through the surging, howling mob of fans. An attendant in the clubhouse threw wide the door of the press entrance and the Chicago players were thrown inside. A little policeman defended the door in Thermopylae fashion {referring to a Grecian mountain pass, famed for its heroic, eventually suicidal defense in 480 B.C. by 300 Spartans against the Persian army of Xerxes}. With the mob about him and his brother policemen unable to reach him, he held that door with stones, pieces of boards and X water cans hurled at him.

Manager Chance was found to have been rather badly hurt. The blow had broken a cartilage in his neck. Together with President Murphy he was hustled to an automobile and hurried away before the crowd discovered the identity of the pair.

A conference resulted in the decision that it would be best for players to leave singly or in pairs and thus avoid attention. Pitcher Pfiester wasn't much hurt by the slam he got. Mordecai Brown was one of the last to leave. As he started to walk up the long chute toward the elevated railway station at 155th street, two policemen in uniform stepped up to accompany him. Brown looked at them.

"You fellows get away from me!" yelled Brown. "Those uniforms will surely tip me off." The policemen withdrew and the marvelous three-fingered one wandered unmolested in his ordinary street clothes. X

A physician was summoned to the Hotel Somerset, where the Cubs put up, to examine Chance's throat. It was found that while the crushed cartilage will give the captain some pain, he will probably be all right in a day or two. Hot towels were applied to his neck and Chance said he would continue this treatment on the train en route to Detroit. Chance was sick from the blow and unable to eat dinner.

"I have no ill feeling against anyone," said Chance to a reporter at his hotel, "but I don't see why I should be picked out as a mark for folks that wish to indulge in such calisthenics. Certainly my actions today did not warrant any such treatment as I received."   —New York *American*

Two stupid plays lost the championship to the Giants. Merkle's boyish desire to be the first man in the clubhouse on Sept. 23 was the first offense. Cy Seymour's wretched fielding yesterday was in a great measure responsible for the loss of the game.

In the third inning Tinker was the first batter to face Mathewson. Tinker is a bold, bad hitter against the Giants. Seymour was playing a short field, and he stubbornly refused to budge, though Matty and Donlin both signed him to go further back.

Tinker's fly to center should have been an easy out. It would have been had Seymour played the batter properly and it would have been

caught had Seymour not misjudged it so badly. Instead of sprinting back
and turning around, Seymour kept taking short backward steps. Finally
he lunged at the ball and missed it altogether. The fans in centerfield
moaned and after the game many of them said it was a play that any
schoolboy fielder would have made. Then Cyrus groped about in the
crowd and fielded the ball very slowly, allowing Tinker to get to third.
Had this fly been caught chances are there would have been no runs in
that inning, and the opportunity for a shut-out would have been splendid.

The scene yesterday was really the most disgraceful ever pulled off
around here and it is to be hoped that Mr. Brush will get proper protection for the Cubs when they come here again.

Baseball is baseball, and if the Giants couldn't win fairly there should
be no win otherwise.

No one who saw the game could say that the umpires were sore at
McGraw. Some decisions seemed to favor the local players and if with
that and the rowdyism they couldn't win, the game should go to the
better team. New York had everything in its favor.

They were playing on the home ground, they had the crowd and
umpires with them, the other team had spent the night on the cars coming here. Matty, the greatest pitcher we ever had, was in the box and the
whole team was right, except for a few scratched skins. What more could
a fellow ask for?

McGinnity started a row the very first thing by bumping Chance off
the plate while the latter was hitting out flies. That was only the first
incident. Once when Kling was chasing a foul from Doyle's bat, two beer
bottles, a drinking glass and a derby hat were thrown at him.

Is that baseball? Does that do New York any good?

Gee whiz! If we can't lose a pennant without dirty work let's quit
altogether.   —Tad, New York *Evening Journal*

The Cubs will be acknowledged as champions, but their title is
tainted, and New York lovers of baseball will never acknowledge them as
the true winners of the pennant.

Whenever I mention the Giants from now on I shall accord them
their rightful title, and I am firm in the opinion that I am right.

Yesterday they looked outclassed for the reason that they were far from being in the playing form the Cubs were. It cannot be denied that the Chicago players were far fresher and in better shape for such a crucial contest after their several days' rest than were the Giants, who were forced to play their very best up to the very day before the deciding game.

If those men on the Board of Directors had concocted a scheme to give the Giants the worst of it they couldn't have done it any more to the point. The Giants were not outgamed, but they were outplayed just from lack of condition.

The Giants did not play up-to-date baseball either. They should almost have cinched the victory in the first inning, for with men on first and second and none out, Bresnahan, instead of trying to advance the runners, tried to knock the cover off the ball and fanned. Herzog then made a play that possibly lost all chances the Giants had. When Kling dropped Bresnahan's third strike, possibly purposely, for Johnny Kling is a very foxy player, Herzog made a break for second although Bresnahan was already out whether Kling held the ball or not. Kling took advantage of Herzog's dumbness and threw to Chance and "Herzie" was pinched. As Donlin followed with a double, it can be seen how damaging Herzog's mistake was.

The minute that "Miner" Brown took Pfiester's place in the box, that strange fatality that has always followed Matty when against the great three-fingered boxman bobbed up and "Big Six" got his bumps.
                    —Sam Crane, New York *Evening Journal*

BUFFALO, Oct. 9—The world's champions Cubs are rushing to Detroit to meet the Tigers tomorrow and defend their title.

Frank Chance's Cubs have proven their title as the greatest aggregation ever gathered on a diamond, game, true and loyal to the core.

Chance was not seriously hurt when hit in the throat by a spectator on his way to the clubhouse. It broke a cartilage in his throat and pained him a good deal, but physicians assured him there was nothing serious about the injury, and he ate a hearty dinner last night. Steinfeldt was struck in the face at the same time Chance was hit, and Hofman was hit in the nose by a pop bottle hurled by an irate fan.

Telegrams of congratulations poured in on the club as it was rushing out of New York last night, including a message from Judge Keneshaw M. Landis {who in 1920 would become the first commissioner of professional baseball}. The one most appreciated was this message from Barney Dreyfuss: "Hearty congratulations. Clean baseball was bound to triumph over affidavits and rowdyism. Best wishes for success in world's series."

—Chicago *News*

Great are the Cubs and nearly as great are their fans.

Yesterday they massed themselves in Orchestra Hall, where the *Tribune* baseball board pictured the plays, a howling, shrieking, ball-mad crowd, wild in its enthusiasm, sometimes pleading, sometimes threatening, always "pulling."

Through it all sat a handsome young woman whose eyes shone and cheeks flushed as the cheering increased, and who, when the Giants retired at the close of the ninth, turned to the gray-haired woman by her side and said:

"This is our anniversary day, mother. He had to win. It's wonderful, isn't it?" and she laughed and cried at the same time.

If the crowd had known that the wife of the great Cub leader was in their midst, Mrs. Frank Le Roy Chance would have been given an ovation that seldom falls to the lot of a woman.

Another Cub wife was in the throng. With a party of friends Mrs. "Joe" Tinker sat only a few rows behind Mrs. Chance, madly waving a Cub banner.

Upon leaving the building she shouted over and over:

"Four to two, four to two." —Chicago *Tribune*

"We will beat Detroit easily," declared Mrs. Frank Chance last night, previous to boarding a train for the scene of tomorrow's battle. The wife of the Cubs' captain was excited and in a hurry to depart.

"I want to help Frank beard the Tigers in their lair," she said smiling. "I know we will win, but Frank says he always plays better ball when he can see me in the grandstand. Of course that is silly, but I want to be there just the same."

"You certainly have a chance," a friend suggested.

"Now, I think that's real mean of you," pouted the young woman. "You know everyone tells that, but as a pun I think it is awful.

"Just as soon as the season is over and we have demonstrated to Detroit that they are not in our class, Mr. Chance and I plan a fishing trip to Wisconsin. He is very fond of fishing, and so am I. Then we are going to California for the winter.

"Yes, we like Chicago, but those lake winds are fearfully chilly in the winter. California is the place for winter months. Besides, Mr. Chance has so many friends there. He formerly attended Washington College in that state and was offered a scholarship at Leland Stanford to play football. He played football but did not like it as much as baseball."

Mrs. Chance, young, pretty and with a large quantity of light brown hair, was recognized by a number of persons and several women stepped forward, introduced themselves and wished that her husband might have all sorts of luck in the championship games.   —Chicago *Journal*

Manager McGraw took things philosophically.

"I do not feel badly," McGraw said. "My team merely lost something it had honestly won three weeks ago. This cannot be put too strongly. Chicagoans always will remember the fight I gave them before they could gain their third pennant in succession."   —New York *Press*

Probably no member of the Giants took the defeat as keenly as did Christy Mathewson. Long after the other players had donned their street clothes and made for home Matty set down disconsolate in the dressing room.

Folks that lingered tried to cheer the peerless pitcher, but he could not speak. He seemed loath to go out and face the people. Some few of the faithful remained until toward dusk, when the great pitcher showed at the Eighth avenue gate. He got a cheer that must have gone a great way in uplifting his fallen spirits.

Matty tried to speak but couldn't. He waved at the crowd and hurried away with bowed head. "I did the best I could," he said as he left the clubhouse, "but I guess fate was against me."

—New York *American*

Bridwell was the only member of the New York team to offer the Cubs congratulations after their victory yesterday.

—Chicago *Journal*

A people who can become as excited about anything as the majority of New Yorkers can about the baseball pennant is far from being lost to hope.

Were we a wooden, lethargic populace, incapable of caring a rap whether the pennant of 1908 fluttered over the Polo Grounds or held horizontal in the breeze that sweeps over Lake Michigan, we might well account ourselves unworthy of the terrific work that must be done before the Augean stable of municipal rottenness has been cleaned. {A reference to the mythological King Augeas, whose stables contained 3,000 oxen and had not been cleaned in thirty years. One of the twelve "labors of Hercules" was the cleansing of the Augean stables.}

But we know now that we *can* become excited, energetically, masterfully excited, and as soon as we understand how properly to apply that tremendous dynamite force to the really important things of life, we will get what we ought to have, individually and collectively, and no thieving corporations, no swinish bosses, no bludgeon-bearing election thieves can stand a minute before us.

Today a multitude of men are bewailing the grewsome {sic} fact that Merkle did not run to second in that tie game. That omission cost New York the pennant. It was a common error, the slovenly heedlessness that keeps most of mankind in its rut, and exalts the men who play the game, be it business, or love, or war, to the bitter end.

Merkle's blunder cost New York the pennant. True. This does not lower the price of beef; it does not make travel on the Third avenue "L" any less hazardous; it does not save the old from toil or the poor from hunger. It affects not one jot the status of any of the hundreds of thousands who were wrought up over the victory that has been borne away to Chicago.

 But it evoked excitement. No human being in New York yesterday can deny that. And excitement makes the world go round; causes the pulse to beat higher, the thrill of battle to rouse the sluggish blood, the brain to do ten times the work it can do when plodding along in emotionless tranquility.

And in that possibility of enthusiasm lies the certainty of the future.

The day will come when the people of this city will be just as excited about the struggle over the rights of the masses, just as enthusiastic over the fight between public plunderers and their protesting prey; in brief, just as interested in the things that concern them, and concern them vitally, as in the settlement of a baseball championship, involving personally a handful of men.

When that day comes there will be trouble for public despoilers, long repentant years in jail for criminal bosses, and an epidemic of public welfare such as now seems too Utopian even to dream of.

This newspaper, being loyal to New York, chronicles its sorrow that the pennant has been rudely taken from us. But it rejoices in the patent fact that the people of New York are capable of tumultuous enthusiasm, for in that it sees the hope of every betterment that it has earnestly and honestly sought to bring about.

—Editorial page, New York *American*

—— FINAL NATIONAL LEAGUE STANDINGS ——

	W	L	PCT.	GB		W	L	PCT.	GB
Chicago	99	55	.643	—	Cincinnati	73	81	.474	26
New York	98	56	.636	1	Boston	63	91	.409	36
Pittsburgh	98	56	.636	1	Brooklyn	53	101	.344	46
Philadelphia	83	71	.539	16	St. Louis	49	105	.318	50

Postscript

In the world series of 1908, Chicago beat Detroit, four games to one. Chicago's winning pitchers: Brown (games one and four) and Overall (games two and five). The only home run in the series was hit by Joe Tinker in game two.

On July 19, 1909, in New York City, National League President Harry Pulliam committed suicide. Since the end of the 1908 season he had taken a leave of absence from his job, because of a severe state of depression, which, his doctors said, had been brought on by the turmoil that followed the Giant-Cub game of September 23.

On October 22, 1912, in New York City, Mabel Hite died of intestinal cancer at the age of 27.

Index

Entries of particular significance are marked with an asterisk (*). Parenthetical abbreviations identify the home base and position of those who were active in 1908. Thus, for example, Crandall, Otis (NY p), was a New York pitcher; Dryden, Charles (CH w), was a Chicago writer; and Cobb, Ty (AL), was an American League player. The following abbreviations have been used:

BO	Boston	AL	American League	of	outfielder
BR	Brooklyn	NL	National League	p	pitcher
CH	Chicago	c	catcher	pr	league president
CI	Cincinnati	co	coach	r	retired
NY	New York	d	doctor	s	secretary
PH	Philadelphia	g	groundkeeper	t	trainer
PI	Pittsburgh	if	infielder	u	umpire
SL	St. Louis	m	manager	w	writer
		ml	minor leaguer